TAROT PRED

TAROT PREDICTION

An Advanced Handbook of Images for Tomorrow

Emily Peach

The Aquarian Press
An Imprint of HarperCollins*Publishers*

The Aquarian Press
An Imprint of GraftonBooks
A Division of HarperCollins*Publishers*
77–85 Fulham Palace Road,
Hammersmith, London W6 8JB

First published as *Tarot for Tomorrow*
by The Aquarian Press 1988
This edition 1991
1 3 5 7 9 10 8 6 4 2

© Emily Peach 1988

Emily Peach asserts the moral right to
be identified as the author of this work

A CIP catalogue record for this book
is available from the British Library

ISBN 1-85538-097-8

Printed in Great Britain by Woolnough Bookbinding Limited,
Irthlingborough, Northamptonshire

Dedication

This book is dedicated to
the memory of the late
W. E. BUTLER
with love and gratitude.

Acknowledgements

Without help, encouragement, shoulders to cry on and ears to bend, an author's life is a miserable one. I would therefore like to thank Simon Franklin, Geoffrey Metliss, and Michael Ashcroft-Nowicki for their frequent loan of these invaluable items during the months that saw the birth of this book. Above all, I would like to thank D.A.N., whose resources of knowledge and patience are seemingly without end. Her price is above rubies. Thank you.

Contents

Chapter 1.

Images In Transition

Twenty-five years ago, ready-made Tarot decks were thoroughly standardized, and very, very basic. With the notable exception of Aleister Crowley's beautiful and innovative Thoth deck, differences in design between one deck and another were minimal, and the standard of production uniformly poor. Moreover, if you had to buy a deck over the counter (and most people did) then you took whatever was offered, warts, dog-ears and all, and thought yourself lucky, because getting a deck — any deck — was far from easy.

'Good' shops did not in those days stock Tarot decks. Neither did bookshops, toy-shops, newsagents, or any of the usual high-street emporiums. 'Speciality' or 'novelty' shops did; but such shops were hard to find, and there was, of course, no guarantee that they would have decks in stock if and when you did find them — or that they would be open on that day or even still in business at all. There was certainly no question of nipping out on the spur of the moment one Saturday afternoon to pick up a deck. This was a project — something that had to be researched and planned. There were, for instance, questions to be asked of 'people in the know', phone calls to be made, travel to be arranged, street maps to be looked at — and, above all, finances to be considered, because decks were as expensive to produce then as they are now, and were correspondingly dear to buy.

Today things are — to put it mildly — rather different. These days, Tarot decks of every conceivable size and description form neat little pyramids in the windows of extremely accessible — and highly respectable — shops. They lurk in odd corners at local newsagents, cheek-by-jowl with boxes of sweets and copies of women's magazines. Miniature silos of them trip people up in department stores, and over-sized hand-made versions (heavy with gold leaf and conspicuously lacking in price-tags) sit smug and sedate in little glass cases in luxury shops. Quite suddenly, in fact, we are up to our necks in decks —

all of them beautiful, glossy, and properly produced, and nearly all of them (like the one that illustrates this book) different and quite new.

This is, of course, all very nice. But it is also all very surprising and very, very odd. Twenty-five years is not, after all, such a long time; and while one wouldn't want to look a gift horse in the mouth, the sudden appearance of these incredibly available esoteric riches inevitably raises the odd question in the mind, such as 'Why has this happened?' and (more to the point) 'Where's the catch?'

The answers to both these questions are at once very simple and very complicated indeed. It has happened because we are presently living through a transitional period on the evolutionary spiral — a stretch of time when one Age is dying and a new one is beginning. The catch is that transitional periods are notoriously dangerous and uncomfortable for everyone concerned.

EVOLUTION

Evolution is one of those things that most people contrive to ignore as having absolutely nothing to do with them. Everybody knows about it in theory, and everybody plays their part in it (albeit usually unconsciously); but at the same time hardly anyone thinks about it very much, or worries about its practical application, until they absolutely have to. For the average person, in fact, the processes of evolution are rather like Musak: a ubiquitous background hum that goes unheard and unattended until it forces its way into consciousness — at which point, of course, it immediately induces a particularly nasty species of frenzy.

Unfortunately, one cannot solve the problem of intrusive Cosmic Musak as many of us are tempted to solve its irritating counterpart in daily life; i.e. by the simple expedient of threatening to throttle the Manager, or shouting 'Stop that noise!' When the processes of evolution force themselves into consciousness, action is certainly desirable — in fact it is actually required — but not that kind of action.

Evolution is growth, and it occurs as the result of a constant synergic interchange between all the forces of consciousness active within the cosmic whole.

The knowledge and experience gained as a result of that perpetual interaction of energy, and the very fact of the interaction itself, create new levels of energy, awareness, and response that spiral infinitely upwards.

Each new response/awareness level is really a plateau in evolutionary time that endures for approximately 2,000 years, and is the equivalent of what is called an 'Age'. Each level builds on the experiences of the previous one, and each brings change in its wake; for form — by which I mean the physical appearance *and* mental function of things in the cosmos — alters only in response to the dictates of the interaction of force; all form being only the manifestation of something that already exists on a less concrete level of being.

TRANSITION

Transitional periods occur when one response level or 'Age' is in the process of ushering in its successor, and while such periods last, the processes of evolution undergo a considerable alteration away from what might, for want of a better term, be called the 'norm'. Change, for instance, is vastly accelerated. The well-regulated synergic reaction between the forces involved becomes virtually a synergic collision instead. The elegant mechanics of evolution, usually so sedate and imperceptible, become intrusive, unpredictable and noisy — and in the process, of course, they become an unbearable irritant; an itch that must be scratched.

REVISION

The primary aim of the transitional process is revision — not the sort of evolutionary revision that goes on all the time as a matter of course, but a wholesale and drastic revision of all knowledge and all things, for literally everything must be updated if its validity is to be recognized and accepted by the form of consciousness enjoyed by the incoming response level.

Transitional revision, therefore, covers every area of life simultaneously and does so very, very thoroughly. Nothing is missed or overlooked. Everything — ideas, practices, symbols, forms of life, things esoteric and mundane — passes through the fine transitional sieve to undergo evaluation and alteration before being stamped 'acceptable', like so many fresh eggs, and passed onward into the new Age. Or not, of course, as the case may be.

Things that pass the acid test of future viability change and grow during the process of revision into something greater than the sum of their pre-transitional parts. Things that do not perish altogether.

TRANSITIONAL CONSCIOUSNESS

Every living thing responds as a matter of course to the cosmic call to transition. Given a synergic universe, in which all things are expressions or facets of a gigantic whole, it could not be otherwise. In human beings, this manifests as the birth of a whole generation of 'transitionalists'.

'Transitional consciousness' is itself naturally transitional in nature. It is a form of consciousness that stands Janus-like at a crossroads in time, forming a living bridge between two very different worlds, while having, really, a place in neither. It is essentially a single-minded form of consciousness, for its sole purpose is the revision of all the accumulated knowledge and experience of the preceding Age to ensure that it is either discarded, or altered sufficiently to be made fit for future consumption, and it is, in many ways, alien to that which has gone before it and to that which will come after it. On an individual level, it carries inherent within it the very real risk of personal 'alienation' in the current psychological sense of that word.

In human terms, the transitional process is therefore a very costly one, for it invariably inclines groups of individuals to polarize at opposite extremes of any given mean. Indeed it inclines human beings to extremes generally: some push too hard into the future, and are ready to discard useful and useless alike in the search for something better; others err on the side of preservation and fight for the retention of empty lifeless shells and outworn objects and customs, simply because they fear the onset of something unknown and consequently frightening. Usually — and as the history of the previous transitional periods shows only too clearly — the beliefs born of transition are very strongly held. Often, they result in ill-conceived or violent action. Nearly always it is very difficult — lacking hindsight — to decide who or what is right.

It is, of course, only too easy to see the process of revision going on around us at this very moment, and it is possible too to look back over the past eighty years and more and see plentiful signs of it there also; but we shall never in our lifetime have the benefit of the hindsight that would allow us to see the fullness of its pattern or judge of its progress and effects. New Ages occur very infrequently in human terms, and transitional periods are correspondingly long by the yardstick of the human lifespan.

TRANSITION, REVISION, AND THE OCCULT

In the main, esoteric revision consists of extracting new meaning for all the various means of transmittal of the Ancient Wisdom, so as to ensure that it is comprehensible to those who will need it in times to come. Much of the work that has been undertaken over the last fifty years and more by any section of the esoteric community has been revisionary in nature, and that work will go on for some considerable time yet on the same trial-and-error basis that applies to everything else in these circumstances. Hence, of course, the appearance of this book and the new deck that illustrates it, and all the other new decks and occult books and tools that have flooded onto the market over the past few years.

The esoteric community as a whole is now, and has always been, almost hypersensitive to the existence of transitional periods. It recognizes both the dangers and the advantages of the process, and is quite used to making a conscious response to them, rather than undertaking the process of selection and rejection unconsciously. Occultists in particular both forecast and prepare for these millennial landmarks in consciousness very carefully indeed, and consequently commence the revision of the material in their charge in a comparatively orderly and timely fashion. Indeed they must, for there are pitfalls inherent in all occult material that are peculiar to it and apply to nothing else.

Nobody is better aware than the average occultist that the past is always with us; no one is better equipped than he to bring forth by his own subjective methods the essence of the past into the light of the present day. Any well-trained occultist can salvage truths, practices, and above all knowledge, from the eternally-existing consciousness of the past as easily as an archaeologist can salvage ancient artifacts from the ground. An old pot, though, is a comparatively safe object. Old knowledge is not.

All the knowledge available to the occultist who is willing to spend time 'fishing' in the timeless waters of consciousness past has, of necessity, failed a 'revisionary examination' at some stage of its development. If it had not, it would be current knowledge and there would be no need to fish for it in the first place. It has therefore not been adapted for the use of what we might call 'present' consciousness or, in some cases, even the form of consciousness that preceded that. It has not, in fact, evolved at all since the date of its 'failure', but has remained instead frozen in time exactly as was. The form of consciousness attaching to it is naturally, therefore, considerably out of step — sometimes to the point of total incomprehensibility — with our own.

The need for a particular kind of knowledge — esoteric or otherwise — frequently recurs, for all sorts of unlikely and unforeseeable reasons, aeons after its original disappearance, and consequently there is much in the evolutionary scrap-heap that is worth fishing for. Quite a lot of the knowledge consigned to the garbage in pre-history, for instance, looks pretty good to us now and would be well worth retrieving. But while it is not impossible to retrieve and revise lost knowledge of this kind deliberately, this is not an exercise to be undertaken lightly.

Revision of 'lost' magical material in particular requires enormous strength, knowledge and inner resource on the part of the would-be reviser. It is a form of exorcism — a healing process of a very special kind — and not every occultist has the ability to pull it off. Most shouldn't even try — and none should be tempted to give revision the go by and work or use old material 'as found'.

Things that fail to evolve are by definition *involutionary* to all forms of consciousness that appear on the life spiral after their 'failure' and 'death'. Because of this, the use of unrevised material effectively qualifies as *black magic*, 'involutionary' being the true meaning of that over-used and much misunderstood term.

REVISING THE TAROT

The revision of Tarot design is already being very adequately dealt with, although further changes will inevitably take place before this settles again into comparative stability; but other aspects of the Tarot are still in desperate need of updating if the deck is to survive and play a meaningful role in the Aquarian Age. The meanings allotted to the cards in particular spring to mind here, because they have undergone no real change for very many years and are consequently not reflecting life (on any level) as efficiently as they should; but the meanings allotted to individual cards are not the only aspect of the deck that requires urgent attention. Some thought must also be given to sorting out the history of the Tarot, which must now be put into a more reasonable and realistic perspective — not least because some of the fairy-tales currently masquerading as 'Tarot history' are endangering the credibility of the deck as an entity, and that of the Western Tradition as a whole.

CONTROVERSY

To a very large degree, this unfortunate state of affairs is a direct result of the bitter controversy that has for so long surrounded the origins of the deck.

Based on the evidence of antique cards and contemporaneous paintings and literature, historians believe the Tarot to have originated in Europe sometime during the late Middle Ages as a wholly European development of ordinary playing cards, and thus, so far as they are concerned, the deck is nothing more than an interesting survival, an attractive and complex game that has endured to the present day practically unchanged.

Occultists very naturally do not agree with this theory. In their opinion, the deck is an important esoteric tool that originated in the thriving temples and mystery schools of Ancient Egypt, and was imported into Europe from that country — again, sometime during the Middle Ages — where it found exoteric expression as a game.

There can be little doubt that by their refusal to allow the Tarot any esoteric significance whatsoever, or to examine it at all save in an isolation that is in fact quite artificial, historians have effectively closed the door on any real understanding of the inception and role of the deck in Europe; but at the same time it must be said that they have unearthed facts that have destroyed the basis of the occult theory altogether.

Much digging in the Ancient World has produced many tombs, many temples, a great deal of treasure, and any number of holes in the ground, but it has not produced any Tarot cards — gold or otherwise. Furthermore, the translation of Egyptian texts makes it an absolute certainty that it will not produce any in the future.

These are facts, and they can no longer be ignored (as they have been conspicuously ignored for far too long now) in order to foster and perpetuate what is at best a romantic myth, and at worst an outright lie — particularly when there is much in the archaeological evidence that actually points to the genuine historical origins of the Tarot.

THE CONSTRUCTION OF THE DECK

The Tarot deck consists of a series of images that are universal and fundamental to the human psyche, instantly recognizable in any guise, however ancient, alien or strange; and there is no doubt that those same images are also symbolic initiatory ones of great antiquity, since similar — sometimes identical — images stare out from the shattered pavements and broken walls of temples throughout the Ancient World.

Thus it seems logical to assume that the Tarot is a 'modern' initiatory device, and also — more importantly — that it actually derives from and incorporates within itself the knowledge and beliefs of *more than one ancient Mystery System* which were once transmitted by way of other, and quite different, methods.

In addition, and in the light of a purely esoteric reading of recorded history — and particularly bearing in mind the immutable evolutionary pattern that underlies all events — it seems logical, too, to at least postulate that the original Mystery images evolved into the deck as we know it as a direct result of the period of transition immediately preceding this one.

If this theory as to the origin of the deck were to prove true, it would mean that the deck is merely a vehicle — albeit a very clever one —

for an eternally evolving idea that consistently develops such vehicles for its own use. Furthermore — and more importantly — it would mean that in seeking an origin in antiquity for the deck in its present form, i.e. as an entity consisting of seventy-eight pieces of pasteboard, occultists have made a fundamental error of judgement, and have consequently wholly missed the point.

NEW LAMPS FOR OLD

In order to demonstrate the validity of the idea that the modern deck is derived from images vital to the Mystery Traditions of the Ancient World, one need only examine ancient pictures and artefacts from an esoteric point of view. Figure 1 shows an example of an Ancient Egyptian initiatory image that has found modern expression in the Tarot deck. The diligent investigator will find many more for himself with very little trouble — and from many different ancient cultures, too — for the deck represents a synthesis of the gnosis of those eras preceding the Piscean Age.

Figure 1: Isis and Nepthys, from the Egyptian Book of the Dead.

Figure 1 is a modern line drawing from the Egyptian Book of the Dead. The copy of the text from which it is taken was written about 1080 BC. It is a representation of the same occult truths that are to be found depicted today in the sixth key of the Tarot — 'the Lovers'.

In this ancient picture, Isis and Nepthys kneel on each side of a large ankh. The ankh stands upon two uraeus serpents, which in turn support a solar disc. This design is flanked on either side by a row of three cynocephalus apes. The ankh and solar disc represent Osiris in his role of sun-god, while the serpents are symbols of initiation.

According to Egyptian mythology, the sisters Isis and Nepthys both bore sons to Osiris, though in vastly different circumstances. Thus both might be said to be the 'lovers' of Osiris.

The astrological rulership of the card 'the Lovers' is Gemini, the twins, and in the vignette, Isis and Nepthys are identical figures save for their head-dresses, which are in fact only cartouches showing the names of each.

The planetary force having dominion over this key is Mercury, ruler of Gemini, whose Egyptian equivalent was Thoth. Thoth had two totem animals — the ibis and the cynocephalus ape. Sure enough, on the Egyptian design, we find six of these dog-headed apes — six also being the face number allotted to the card 'the Lovers' in the modern Tarot deck.

The whole design therefore closely parallels one of the traditional ways of representing the card 'the Lovers' — a young man standing between two similarly-attired ladies who are differentiated only by their headgear (see Figure 2).

Naturally, and due to racial, ideological and mythological differences between the culture of Ancient Egypt and that of Western Europe, the symbolism of the two pictures differs considerably. The similarity

Figure 2: The card 'the Lovers' as it appears in one modern Tarot deck.

of intention, though, is obvious enough despite being filtered through the ethnic and other sensibilities peculiar to each race. It is, in fact, quite clear that Figures 1 and 2 show two representations of the same force, the later version being merely a revision of the earlier one.

WHY SYMBOLS CHANGE

The physical aspect of symbols alters in this way because it must. The old proverb says that 'every picture tells a story', and this is, of course, quite true; but the fact is that the picture must be topical if it is to tell the right story — and this remains the case whether the picture in question is intended to convey an esoteric truth or sell a packet of tea. The fact is that symbols are a language — a tool of thought — and any language that does not adapt to prevailing conditions, keep pace with consciousness, and reflect current perceptions of things, loses its impact and validity and eventually perishes altogether. Forces like the one represented by Figures 1 and 2 are immutable, but — as has been explained — human consciousness is not. Consequently, unrevised symbols of those forces, originally composed to serve one particular culture, inevitably show a style and a bias that is incomprehensible to other, or surviving, or modified, cultures.

Usually, symbols — like spoken languages — change very gradually. Words appear and disappear from current usage almost imperceptibly. Rapid change only ever occurs as a result of 'culture shock' or as a deliberate response to a pressing need.

Some 2,000 years ago, when the symbols of Figure 1 began their process of essential — and comparatively rapid — change, they did so as a response both to culture shock and to a pressing need. Humanity was then in the throes of a particularly aggressive period of evolutionary transition that changed the face of the Ancient World. Under its impact, the civilization of Egypt — the source of these particular symbols — fell under foreign domination. Within a mere 200 years or so, it had disappeared completely, and was forgotten, together with its language, its traditions, and its complicated and beautiful systems of writing.

Arcane knowledge, however, does not die as easily as the cultures that sustain it. It *either* goes underground and becomes a secret or 'alternative' religion, *or* attaches itself to a new culture and a new religion, wherein it 'finds its own level', *or* both. In any and every case, however, it survives — albeit often in a distorted and sometimes practically unrecognizable condition.

Thus (and as a result of exposure to a different environment, a different culture, and the then new religion of Christianity) the

Egyptian symbols shown in Figure 1 — and similar symbols sacred to other Mystery systems — took on the medieval, European, Christian veneer shown in Figure 2. They evolved, in fact — and it is only in consequence of that evolution that we are able to understand Figure 1 at all.

SYMBOL REVISION FOR THE AQUARIAN AGE

As it is the intention of the Prediction tarot to revise the deck and bring it in to line with modern culture and morality, it might legitimately be asked why the deck has once again been set, pictorially, in the Middle Ages.

The answer, paradoxically, is that it has not. The pictures on the cards place the deck not in a real place and time but in a 'Middle Ages of the Mind' — a time and landscape that never existed in reality, but which is part of the fundamental imaginative heritage of the peoples of Western Europe.

That time, that landscape and its inhabitants are legendary, immutable, and totally familiar. We know them, in fact, precisely as well as we know ourselves. They exist like a fixed star at the centre of our very being; free of the turmoil in which we live, clean of the wreckage of the past and the uncertainty of the future. They were, are, and will be the heart of the Matter of Britain. More importantly, they are what *we were*, *could be*, and *will be again*. I think it only right, therefore, that at least one of the many new Tarot decks this transitional period will produce should bear the ineradicable stamp of the Mystery Tradition of these islands, and shadow out for us again the Court of Arthur — *Past* and *Future* King.

Chapter 2.

Mirror Images

As was said in the previous chapter, the Tarot is a vehicle for an evolving idea, a method whereby one may realize or understand the truth that underlies the illusion of manifest reality. But the deck is not unique; it is not the *only* such vehicle. Simply, it is the most popular and the most successful, which is another thing altogether.

There are many, many 'vehicles of the Mysteries'. All share a common heritage and a common purpose. All are intimately related to the Tarot and to each other — tied together, as it were, by bloodlines of common origin and common function. A true study of the Tarot — or any other esoteric subject, for that matter — must therefore be a *holistic* study, and as such is best undertaken via the Qabalah, the precise and systematic body of esoteric knowledge that is the synthesizing agent of the Western Mystery Tradition.

THE QABALAH

The Qabalah as a system presupposes the existence of a Creator and an ordered plan of Creation. According to it, the universe was emanated from the Creator's self, and thereafter evolved sequentially and to a definite pattern. The Tree of Life (see Figure 3) is a symbolic picture of this process, and is intended to depict the entire *manifest* universe.

I stress the word 'manifest' here, because the symbol of the Tree of Life is primarily concerned with what *is*, and the complex interrelationship of things that *are*. The very tricky question of the genesis of the manifest universe (which obviously had to come from somewhere) is usually symbolized — as indeed it is in this diagram — only by three rather ambiguous lines, mysteriously labelled AIN, AIN SOPH, and AIN SOPH AUR, that hover at the top of the page, forming a kind of triple halo over the main body of the mandala proper.

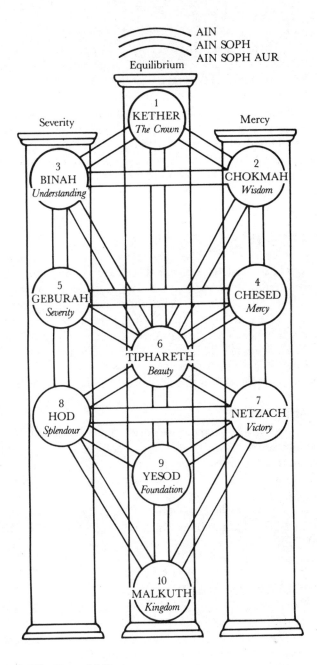

Figure 3: The Tree of Life

THE UNMANIFEST

AIN, AIN SOPH and AIN SOPH AUR mean 'nothingness', 'limitlessness' and 'limitless light' respectively, and are usually referred to as the Three Veils of Negative Existence. The Veils are the most abstract of all Qabalistic symbols, and they represent the Unmanifest, or ultimate source of things.

The Unmanifest — as one might expect from its name and title — is a concept that is totally incomprehensible to the human mind. It is a sort of pregnant pause — a nothing that is something in essence — and is perhaps best described as an androgenous fertile nothingness that holds within itself the potential for a manifest something. The Three Veils are therefore three distinct stages in the process of the birth of a 'something' out of a 'nothing'.

THE PRINCIPLE OF POLARITY

The Three Veils exemplify the very simple principle upon which the entire Qabalistic system is based: the idea that everything consists of three kinds of energy, a positive/masculine energy and a negative/feminine energy, which together produce a third, balancing, agent. This basic principle of two complementary forces reacting against each other to produce a third reconciliatory force is usually called the Principle of Polarity and — because it forms the background against which all Qabalistic ideas must be examined and tested — I shall be referring to it again and again throughout this book.

THE SEPHIROTH

The Tree that springs from the 'fertile nothingness' of the Unmanifest consists of ten spheres which are called Sephiroth or emanations, and which are in fact centres of energy. These appear in the diagram on page 27 as a series of circles marked one to ten. The Sephiroth are considered to represent stages in creation and manifestation which — according to Qabalistic thought — take place following the Path of the Lightning Flash, about which more will be said in Chapter 3. The Path of the Lightning Flash appears on Figure 6 (page 33) as a black zig-zag line.

THE PILLARS OF MANIFESTATION

The Tree can be further divided into three Pillars, the names, characteristics and situation of which also appear on Figure 3 (page 23). These are the Pillars of Manifestation, and naturally follow the basic 'triple energy' principle that lies behind all Qabalistic lore. The right-hand Pillar is called the Pillar of Mercy, is positive/masculine, and represents the principle of *force*. The left-hand Pillar is called the Pillar of Severity, is negative/feminine, and represents the principle of *form*. The central Pillar is called the Pillar of Equilibrium, and represents the reconciliatory and balancing agent required by the 'triple energy' principle.

The two outer Pillars are jointly referred to as The Pillars of Function, and are said to be complementary opposites — which means that one cannot exist without the other.

Although the Principle of Polarity might be said to exist most obviously as it is expressed by the Three Veils and the three Pillars, it in fact operates, as has been said above, throughout the Tree. It therefore naturally applies to the Sephiroth which form the Pillars, all of which contain within themselves the 'triple energies' basic to Qabalistic theory. Thus, individual Sephirah polarize *within themselves*, as well as with other Sephiroth; any given Sephirah being positive/masculine to the one below it, and negative/feminine to the one above it. Each complementary pair of Sephiroth polarize with each other and are equilibrated by a single Sephirah located somewhere on the Pillar of Equilibrium, i.e. the Chokmah/Binah pair equilibrate in Kether.

THE TRIADS

It is simple enough to discover which Sephirah on the Middle Pillar is acting as an equilibrator to a complementary pair of Sephiroth on the Pillars of Function by dividing the Tree into a series of triangles like those marked with a thick black line on Figure 4.

These triangles — or Triads — are individually referred to as the Supernal Triangle, the Ethical (or Moral) Triangle, and the Astral (or Magical) Triangle respectively, and they also reflect the 'triple energy' principle. Thus the Supernal Triangle as a whole takes on the positive/masculine role, and is usually referred to as being activating; the Ethical Triangle becomes negative/feminine (formative), and the Astral Triangle provides the necessary balancing agent. The Triads, their function, and their relevance to the Tarot deck are discussed at some length in Chapters 3 and 4.

THE FOUR WORLDS

The Tree can further be divided into four Worlds, a division intended to show the process of manifestation from first beginnings to end result. These Worlds are, of course, levels of existence or being, and as such they form the background of all four-fold esoteric symbolism, including that which is found in the Tarot.

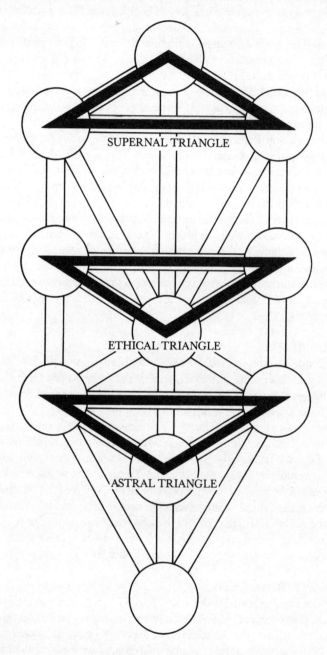

Figure 4: The Triads on the Tree of Life.

The four Worlds are called Atziluth, Briah, Yetzirah and Assiah, and to each one of them is allotted a single letter of the Divine Name, or Tetragrammaton, and one of the four elements — Fire, Water, Air and Earth respectively.

'Atziluth' is the Archetypal World or World of Pure Spirit. It is represented by the letter YOD or Primal Fire. 'Briah' is the Creative World, and is represented by the letter HEH, Primal Water. 'Yetzirah' is the Formative World, to which is allotted the letter VAU, Primal Air. 'Assiah' is the Material World, and is represented by the letter HEH final, or Primal Earth.

Each of the four Worlds is considered to contain a complete Tree of Life, and of each evolves the World below it. Thus manifestation appears first in Kether of Atziluth as an Archetypal blueprint, and, following the Path of the Lightning Flash, ends in Malkuth of Assiah as the concrete and tangible expression of that blueprint.

Figure 5 illustrates two ways of symbolizing the complex concept of the four Worlds. The first is the 'Tree in every world' idea referred to in the last paragraph; the second shows how the Sephiroth of a single

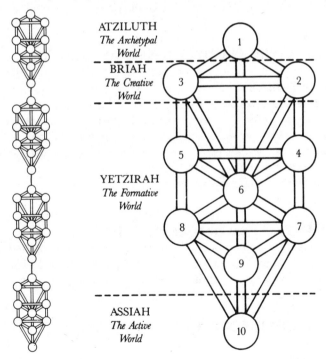

ATZILUTH
The Archetypal World

BRIAH
The Creative World

YETZIRAH
The Formative World

ASSIAH
The Active World

Figure 5: The Four Worlds.

Tree may be divided to symbolize the four separate stages of manifestation.

The Worlds grow progressively denser as spirit falls into matter, and thus each one is more material than that which preceded and evolved it. Atziluth is therefore often referred to as the World of Pure Spirit, while Assiah is thought of as the physical world. Naturally, of course, it must be understood that this 'fall' into matter does not involve a lessening or degradation of spirit. The process is an alchemical change of state: it does not involve a fundamental change of nature. Matter is 'solidified' spirit. Malkuth of Assiah is as holy as Kether of Atziluth — indeed it actually *is* Kether of Atziluth, after another fashion.

MICROCOSM AND MACROCOSM
The Tree of Life as a whole may be considered on two levels. It represents the Microcosm, or man as a miniature of the Creator, and the Macrocosm, which is the image in which the microcosmic man is created. Thus the understanding of the self which may be gained through the use of the Tarot as it is applied to the Tree of Life will naturally lead to an understanding of the whole of creation, for one is *like* the other, and reflects this likeness.

SEPHIROTHIC ATTRIBUTIONS AND THEIR MEANING
The Sephiroth are, of course, symbols, as are the various attributions traditionally made to each of them. Lists of these attributions, which mirror the complex nature and interrelationship of cosmic forces, and mark the effects of those forces upon each other and upon the cosmic whole in a way that we can realize and understand, appear under the appropriate headings in Chapter 4 and are labelled **(a)** to **(f)**. These attributions appear in nearly all Qabalistic literature, but unfortunately their presence and purpose is rarely explained. Their basic meanings are as follows:

(a) THE TITLE OF THE SEPHIRAH.
The Title of the Sephirah is a single word intended to encompass and express all that the Sephirah stands for. It appears in the list in Hebrew letters with an English transliteration and translation following it, e.g. כתר — KETHER — The Crown.

(b) THE DIVINE NAME (*World of Atziluth*).
The Divine Name is literally *a* name of the Creator, which expresses *a* facet of the Creator's being. It is therefore *one single aspect* of *the single deity*, expressed by the Sephirah at its most spiritual level. I would

stress the fact that the Sephiroth of the Tree express *individual aspects of the one God*, because it is easy, when studying the Qabalah, to obtain the impression that the system is a pantheonistic rather than a monotheistic one.

(c) THE ARCHANGELIC FORCE. (*World of Briah*).
Archangelic forces are organizing principles — beings of superhuman condition that hold presidency over the Briatic world and which may be contacted subjectively in meditation.

(d) THE CHOIR OF ANGELS (*World of Yetzirah*).
The Choir of Angels allotted to each Sephirah are termed the 'builders' or 'servants' of the Creator and of the Archangelic forces that hold presidency over the Briatic World. They are complexes of mind stuff that act as intermediary links between centres of individualized consciousness in Assiah and Briah.

(e) THE MUNDANE SYMBOL (*World of Assiah*).
The Mundane Symbol represents cosmic and stellar forces like those represented by the zodiac; but care must be taken not to interpret them as meaning the actual planetary bodies involved. The Mundane Symbol is the force behind the *being* of those bodies, rather than the physical bodies themselves. The science of astrology is based upon the effect these forces have upon human beings.

(f) THE YETZIRATIC TEXT
This is taken from the 'Sepher Yetzirah' or 'Book of Formation' which describes the emanation of the universe in terms of the letters of the Hebrew alphabet and therefore, of course, in terms of number, since the letters of the Hebrew alphabet *are* numbers.

(g) COLOUR
You will see that beside each of the four items marked (b), (c), (d) and (e) on each of the lists there is a hyphen, followed by a colour, e.g. 'Eheieh — Brilliance' and so on.

These colours are attributed to the four Worlds and are called *King* scale, *Queen* scale, *Emperor* scale and *Empress* scale respectively. They are used along with the relevant Divine or Archangelic name to contact the force of a Sephirah at a particular level. Most meditation work is done at the Briatic level, using the name of the Archangel, and the appropriate Queen scale colour.

Queen scale, as it is given in this and other books, is the Qabalistic

colour scale which has direct relation to colour — or rather
pigmentation — in the material world. The remaining three colour
scales refer to different aspects of the One Reality, and are more
symbolic in their use of colour than is the functional Queen scale.

Chapter 3.

Ancient Images

The Tarot is divided into two sections: the Major and Minor Arcanas. For the next two chapters, we shall be concentrating strictly on the latter of these two 'decks within a deck' — the Minor Arcana.

THE FOUR SUITS

The Minor Arcana is made up of fifty-six cards which are divided into four suits — *Staves, Cups, Swords* and *Coins*. Each suit is associated with one of the four Worlds mentioned in the previous chapter, and with all the four-fold symbolism attributed to that World. Thus it is possible to begin to make up an easy reference chart of Tarot/Tree symbolism, as follows:

ATZILUTH	— YOD	— *Fire*	— Staves
BRIAH	— HEH	— *Water*	— Cups
YETZIRAH	— VAU	— *Air*	— Swords
ASSIAH	— HEH	— *Earth*	— Coins

The four suits as a whole are allocated to the Sephiroth of the Tree of Life according to the elemental attributions shown above — Staves to *Chokmah* (Fire); Cups to *Binah* (Water); Swords to *Tiphareth* (Air); Coins to *Malkuth* (Earth).

These so-called elements are, of course, essentially symbolic. They represent the four basic states that matter can assume in the physical world — solid, liquid, gaseous and electrical — and should not be associated in a literal way with their purely physical counterparts. All four conditions are capable of passing from one state to another in some circumstances and modern occultists use them *analogously* to explain a wide variety of phenomena, most of which are concerned with changes in consciousness.

So far as divination is concerned, the four suits are considered to

cover every area of our lives; but usually (and so as to simplify matters
somewhat) life's complexities are broken down into four main areas,
each one of which is allotted to a single suit — *career or work* to Staves;
emotion to Cups; *mentation* to Swords, and *money and material matters* to
Coins. Thus it is possible to make further additions to the reference
chart — and it is worthwhile taking the time to do so, since all
Tarot/Tree attributions are interrelated, and each throws light upon
the others.

THE SMALL CARDS

The fourteen cards that make up each suit are divided into Small cards
and Court (or Picture) cards. Small cards represent *trends* or *events*,
while Court cards represent (in the main, in any event) *people*. There
are ten Small cards and four Court cards per suit.

Like the suit entities of which they form parts the Small cards are
attributed individually to the Sephiroth of the Tree of Life — and
their placement on the Tree is particularly easy to remember, because
each card is simply allocated by its face number and according to the
Path of the Lightning Flash. Thus Small card placement begins with
the Aces in Kether and ends with the Tens in Malkuth, as per Figure 6.

Accordingly, and if reference is made to the chart opposite, it can
immediately be seen that there are *four* Small cards allocated to each
Sephirah, and that each one of those four cards represents the action
of that particular Sephirah in one of the four Worlds.

For example: Staves as a suit are attributed to Atziluth, and all four
Aces are attributed to Kether. Thus the Ace of Staves represents the
action of the Sephirah Kether in the World of Atziluth — and is
frequently referred to as Kether of Atziluth. In the same way, the Ace
of Cups is Kether of Briah, The Ace of Swords is Kether of Yetzirah,
and the Ace of Coins is Kether of Assiah.

Naturally, much can be learned from a consideration of the Sephiroth
and their associated groups of Small cards, *but only if it is appreciated
that Small cards represent manifestations of the powers of the ten Sephiroth in Malkuth
and that the Sephiroth themselves form specific patterns within the Tree system.*

Qabalists believe that a complete Tree of Life exists in every Sephirah,
and that human beings appreciate and experience everything from
the vantage point of Malkuth of Malkuth; the last sphere of the Tree
that exists in the last Sephirah — the very bottom of the Ladder of
Being, in other words. Small cards are therefore considered to function
in the material universe only, and to stand for the four levels upon which
the Sephiroth may function *in Assiah.* The application of the Small
cards to the Tree of Life makes clear their attribution and application

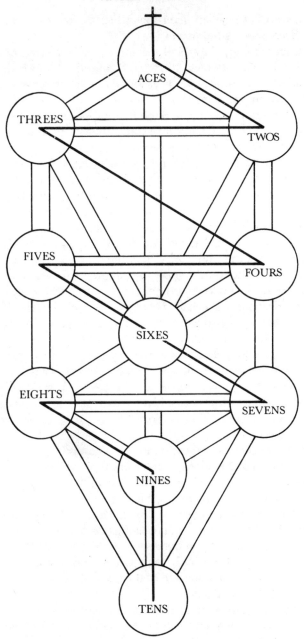

Figure 6: The Small Cards and The Tree of Life — The Path of the
Lightning Flash.

to the material plane — the level upon which the four-fold symbolism of the Tree finds its full expression.

The alternating polarities of the three Triads referred to in the previous chapter naturally affect the Sephiroth of which they are constructed — each one of which, as you will recall, conforms *individually* to the 'triple energy' theory of polarity — on every level of function.

According to the principle of alternating polarity, the Supernal Triangle is positive/masculine, the Ethical Triangle negative/feminine, the Astral Triangle positive/masculine, and Malkuth — the only Sephirah not to form part of a Triad — negative/feminine. Thus Sephiroth can be categorized as being *negatively negative, positively negative*, and so on, according to their function in a particular Triad and the over-all polarity of the Triad itself. Geburah, for instance, is a *negatively negative* sphere because it performs a negatively polarizing function within a negatively polarizing Triad. Figure 7 (whereon *positive* Triadic areas are shaded, and the word 'force' indicates a *positive* Sephirah while the word 'form' indicates a *negative* one) illustrates the working of this scheme, which is a particularly important one, because, of course, the categorizations of alternating polarity automatically refer not only to the individual Sephiroth themselves but also to the Small cards with which they are associated.

The question of polarities and the way in which they operate on the Tree is a very complex one, and an understanding of it is not assisted by the use of the terms 'positive' and 'negative' or 'masculine' and 'feminine', for these words are ambiguous and imprecise in this context, and have connotations within the English language that are inapplicable to this subject.

In order to overcome these difficulties and understand 'positive' and 'negative' manifestations of power, one must consider the implications of the fact that the two lowest Sephiroth are expressions of potencies drawn from the *negative* Pillar and *brought on to* the middle Pillar; for it will thus become quite clear that the word 'negative' cannot be taken as a synonym for 'evil', nor 'positive' as a synonym for 'good'.

Positive forces are not brought over onto the Middle Pillar in the same way as negative forces because a *force* must first be given *form* — or, in the technical language of the Qabalah, made negative — before it can be equilibrated.

All the Small cards are entitled 'Lords' because they represent *dynamic forces*. Thus, according to Qabalistic terminology, all Small cards are *masculine* potencies — and logically so, for their sphere of operation is Assiah, and were the forces signified by these cards *passive* in relation to Malkuth they would be utterly incapable of effect, and it would

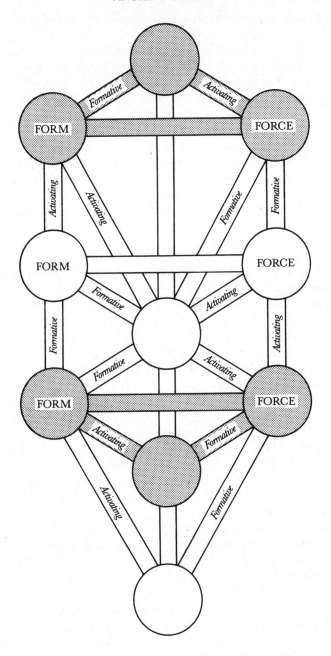

Figure 7: The Polarities of the Triads and Sephiroth on the Tree of Life.

be redundant for us to take them into account when reading or using the Tarot.

The titles of the Small cards sometimes throw light on the meaning of individual cards, but this is not always the case, and it is unwise nowadays to attempt to actually *build* meanings from one's own interpretation of card titles. The meaning of certain words in the English language has changed so considerably since these titles were first constructed that many of them are now highly ambiguous. The late Aleister Crowley attempted to revise and modernize them in his *Book of Thoth* — indeed, his revised titles are actually printed on the deck he designed — but unfortunately, the attempt proved unsuccessful. Crowley was a superb Qabalist, but his Tarot nomenclature is at once too idiosyncratic and too precise for general use.

THE COURT CARDS

Court cards are much harder to deal with from the point of view of the Qabalah than are Small cards, because their allocation to the Tree is not so straightforward. However, if you look again at the chart on page 23, and relate it to the positions of the Court cards on the Tree of Life as shown by Figure 8, the process will become much clearer.

Court cards, like the suits, have elemental attributions. They represent, in fact, the elemental powers of the Tetragrammaton in the four Worlds. Thus: all Knights are *Fire*, all Queens are *Water*, all Kings are *Air*, and all Pages are *Earth*.

Court cards are attributed to the Sephiroth according to these elemental attributions, which are the source of their elemental names and titles.

For example: Knights are attributed to Chokmah with the suit of Staves (Fire); Queens to Binah with the suit of Cups (Water); Kings to Tiphareth with the suit of Swords (Air), and Pages to Malkuth with the suit of Coins (Earth). Thus the elemental name of the Knight of Staves automatically becomes *Fire of Fire* because he is a Knight (Chokmah — Fire) of the suit of Staves (Chokmah — Fire). The titles of the card — 'Lord of the Flame and the Lightning', 'King of the Spirits of Fire' and 'King of the Salamanders' — emphasize its fiery nature.

I have said that the Small cards are considered to function *in the material universe only*. This stricture also applies to the Court cards, and has great relevance to understanding their nature and function.

Court cards fall under the presidency of HEH final and are thus fixed irrevocably in the world of Assiah. They are referred to as existing *beside* the Sephiroth, rather than on or as a part of them — and consequently they almost invariably represent *people*.

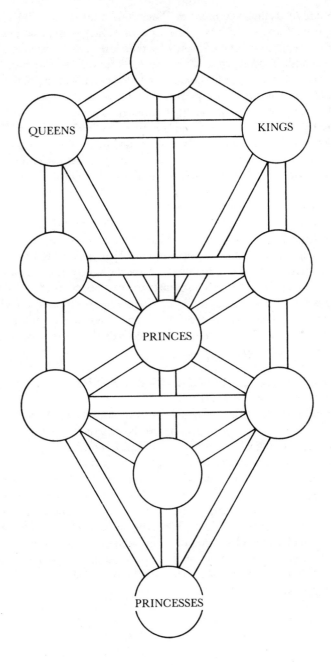

Figure 8: The Court Cards and The Tree of Life

Small cards illustrate *causation*. They symbolize the specific action of specific force — which is why, of course, it is possible to predict accurately the outcome of events by their use. Court cards, on the other hand, illustrate *effect*. They are — *in the main* — illustrative of the effects of cosmic conditions upon, and their action through, a single type of microcosmic consciousness: man.

The scheme of Qabalistic attributions of Court cards is rendered more complex than it really needs to be by the design of most Tarot decks — or rather by the titles that are allotted to the figures of the Kings and Knights and which result in the Queens apparently being 'paired' with the Knights and not the Kings. Obviously it would be more logical were the Kings to sit opposite the Queens in Chokmah and Binah respectively, as indeed they do.

In most Tarot decks the cards called Kings depict *seated* figures, while the cards called Knights depict *mounted* figures. This is in effect quite wrong, for the rule for the attribution of Knights and Kings to the Sephiroth of the Tree of Life is that the *mounted* figures go to Chokmah, while the *seated* figures go to Tiphareth. This is because *seated* figures always represent *consolidation*, while *mounted* figures represent *forces in movement* in the Qabalistic symbol scheme. A glance at some of the attributions of the Sephiroth concerned will show the logic of this method of allocation.

THE RELATIVE IMPORTANCE OF THE DIFFERENT SECTIONS OF THE DECK

The cards of the Minor Arcana are commonly thought to be less important in some way than those of the Major Arcana. The very application of the words 'major' and 'minor' to the separate parts of the deck seems to imply a marked difference in status between them. This apparent division of the deck into 'greater' and 'lesser' parts is, of course, quite illusory — and provides a graphic illustration of the sort of semantic man-trap that can gobble up the unwary student. As implied already many times in this book, the deck is a *multi-purpose* esoteric tool: different sections of it may lend themselves more readily to certain purposes than do other sections, but in essence all its parts are of equal importance, and demand equal attention and understanding.

Chapter 4.

Images

Small cards have two levels of meaning, *General* and *Particular*, and because at the end of the present transitional phase, particular meanings may no longer have much (or, indeed, any) relevance to the way human beings live their lives, the meanings given in this book are divided into these two categories. In this way, the reader will be able to see clearly the relationship between the two, and — in time to come — should not have too much difficulty working out how particular meanings apply to the general conditions then prevailing. The meanings given in this section are *General* and closely reflect the nature of the Sephiroth and Worlds to which they are attributed — and from which, indeed, all meanings are extracted in the first instance. *Particular* meanings can be found in Appendix I on page 242.

THE ACES

a) בתר — KETHER — The Crown.
b) **Eheieh** — Brilliance.
c) **Metatron** — White Brilliance.
d) **Chayoth a-Qadesh** — White Brilliance.
e) **Primum Mobile** — First Swirlings — White flecked Gold.
f) The First Path is called the *Admirable* or *Hidden Intelligence* because it is the Light giving the power of comprehension of the First Principle, which hath no beginning. And it is the Primal Glory, because no created being can attain to its essence.

Kether is the source of all things, a directive and pure energy that is complete unto itself. It is not possible to experience Kether, nor to truly understand it, because it is beyond the reach of our consciousness and is therefore incomprehensible. It is, indeed, the *Hidden* Intelligence of the Yetsiratic Text. We can, however, establish some facts about the sphere by way of its symbols.

The primary symbol of Kether is the Crown. A crown is something that is *above* and yet *part of* a unified whole. In an absolute Monarchy, for instance, the Crown is the Head of the State — a symbol of the unity of the people — and it rules, directs, and is the source of all honour. In the same way, Kether is the Crown of Creation. It is the source of Creation and is above and yet a part of it. It determines the nature of everything that is through its own nature, because it *is* Creation in essence, complete and entire.

The second of the symbols associated with this sphere emphasizes its quality of completeness, for it is the Point, and a point represents total unity; something that is wholly defined, and complete unto itself.

The Point and the Crown are *static* symbols expressive of unity, permanence, and stability; but it must be remembered that Kether is not static *per se*, but is perpetually in motion, perpetually pouring out the essence of itself into Creation. This eternal motion is expressed by the Mundane Chakra associated with the sphere, which is *Primum Mobile*, or First Swirlings. This latter attribution introduces the important idea of *motion around a point*, which is essentially *parametrized* motion, or motion which is perpetual within a fixed area, and which follows a fixed mode of expression.

Kether is called the *Root of the Elements*. The Roots of the four individual elements are symbolized by the four Aces of the Tarot deck, which cards thus represent pure energy, the nature and density of which is determined by their position in the four Worlds. These elements are unified in Kether as they are unified — albeit after a different fashion — in Malkuth, for Malkuth *is* Kether on a lower arc.

Because the four Aces are associated with the four elements — which naturally symbolize four aspects of consciousness or four forms of expression — they are also associated with the four seasons which represent the four forms of expression of the planetary body, Earth. Fire and Staves therefore represent Spring; Water and Cups, Summer; Air and Swords, Autumn; and Earth and Coins, Winter.

The Ace of Staves
The Root of the Powers of Fire

Because of their association with Kether — First Swirlings — all the Aces signify new beginnings of some kind. The Ace of Staves is the Root of the Powers of Fire, and rules that portion of our daily lives that is concerned with career. Thus, the dignified Ace of Staves

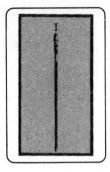

represents new enterprises, new ideas, new projects, and changes in career direction.

However, because of its fiery nature, this particular Ace also symbolizes creativity and can consequently indicate fertility of mind and/or body.

An ill-dignified Ace of Staves therefore frequently signifies false starts, or disappointing career changes and blocked creativity. It might also (in a man's spread) denote impotence, or (in a woman's spread) barrenness contingent upon her partner's impotence — this latter because Staves, being Fiery, symbolize *inceptive*, rather than *conceptive* creativity.

However, it must be remembered in this regard that impotence is not always *physical*, but may be *symbolic*, and further that a low sperm count does not indicate a condition of impotence as that term is usually understood. Most importantly, it must be appreciated that quite mundane things must first be taken into account before any such high-flown interpretations of this card are ventured into. Much, in any event, depends on the kind of spread in which this Ace is found.

A man suffering financial difficulties, for example, or a man long unemployed and unable to find work, suffers feelings of impotence. So does a man incapable of influencing a much loved child, his wife, or the Inland Revenue. The stress created by any of these situations might or might not find physical expression, but all would nevertheless and in either event be reflected by an ill-dignified Ace of Staves.

At the same time, any given man may not be capable of inceptive creativity in the realm of ideas, and this, too, might well induce the appearance of the ill-dignified Ace of Staves in his or in his wife's spread. This appearance would not, of course, indicate any purely physical disability at all, but would simply be a statement as to his mental capabilities.

Care must therefore be taken in the interpretation of this card, and no hasty or facile decisions taken as to its import. Its most memorable meaning is rarely the correct one!

The Ace of Cups
The Root of the Powers of Water
The Ace of Cups is the Root of the Powers of Water, which element represents the emotions. Thus the appearance of this card, when dignified, usually indicates love, joy, happiness, the beginning of a new love affair, or the commencement of a creative work of some kind.

Like the Ace of Staves, this Ace is concerned with fertility and can therefore signify a birth — particularly if it is associated with other cards that point in the same direction. The difference between the fertility associated with the Ace of Staves and that symbolized by this card is determined by the Sephirah to which each card belongs *according to its suit*. Staves as a suit are attributed to Chokmah, the Father, which is situated on the *force* side of the Tree. They therefore represent *in*ception. Cups, on the other hand, are attributed as a suit to Binah, the Mother, which is situated on the *form* side of the Tree, and consequently signify *con*ception.

An ill-dignified Ace of Cups is much more difficult to interpret than a dignified one. It can signify lack of trust or a failed affair, but basically it covers emotional upsets of every kind, and its accurate interpretation therefore depends on the cards that surround it.

In addition, the Ace of Cups — like the Ace of Staves — can signify blocked creativity of some kind, and — because it is *con*ceptual creativity that is at issue — this can take the form of physical sterility (and the emotional distress associated with such a condition) in women. In men, however, it usually signifies the existence of something like a 'writer's block', or even the simple stress that is contiguous on the consistent repression of emotion in order to comply with social mores.

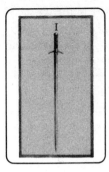

The Ace of Swords
The Root of the Powers of Air
The Ace of Swords is the Root of the Powers of Air, which element rules mental activity and the thought processes. The appearance of the dignified Ace of Swords therefore symbolizes a *change of mind* — a period during which the Querent re-assesses some or all of the aspects of his life. Correct interpretation of the card is consequently dependent upon the nature and dignity of the surrounding cards, for it is these cards that determine the *area* of re-assessment or change.

A change of mind about or a personal re-assessment of anything is never a painless process, and an ill-dignified Ace of Swords is therefore never going to signify a jolly time; but in reality the time is usually much less gloomy than it is usually made out to be.

Swords in general have a bad reputation, and the Ace of Swords in particular — because it traditionally represents death — has always been viewed with some trepidation by Querent and reader alike; but it must be remembered that basically this card simply represents the forces of *change*.

Any kind of change is a little death. Because of change something inevitably stops. However, this 'something' is not always life and breath, and although change is uncomfortable, it is frequently beneficial in the long run. Therefore, although the dignified Ace of Swords regularly indicates that some area of the Querent's life will come to a sudden halt, it rarely means that he will shortly fall under a passing bus or meet a violent — or any other — end. Surrounding cards will obviously indicate what sort of change is coming — and if it is that final change that marks the transition between one form of life and another, the reader will be left in no doubt that this is so, because the line-up of cards for such an event is unmistakable.

The Ace of Swords represents *invoked* force, and it is a fact that misused force frequently rebounds with devastating effect on the wielder of it. Indeed, this card more than any other in the whole of the Minor Arcana shows the working of the laws of cause and effect.

Thus, one of the ill-dignified meanings of this Ace is that some of the Querent's past sins will come home to roost; but really whether the card appears dignified or ill-dignified, the primary thing to remember about it is that it represents a power for good or evil that the Querent has called down upon himself. Neither the benefits nor the troubles signified by the appearance of the Ace of Swords are unearned.

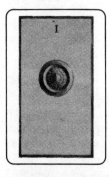

The Ace of Coins
The Root of the Powers of Earth
The Ace of Coins is the Root of the Powers of Earth. It indicates material gain and material power achieved through work. The element of Earth rules over the material aspect of our daily lives: money, how money is earned, and what money can buy.

In a spread, therefore, the dignified Ace of Coins often means a change for the better financially — and because all Aces signify new beginnings, such a change is usually due to a new job or a promotion that involves increased responsibility or power rather than just a simple rise in salary.

Sometimes — and particularly when the card is ill-dignified — the improvement in finances and enhanced job responsibilities represented by the Ace of Coins may prove to be short-lived. Thus bonuses — 'financial improvements' that are usually spent in the imagination long before they fall into the purse — are often symbolized by the Ace of Coins, as are winnings, financial gains that are smaller than anticipated, or monies which fail to materialize at all.

In addition, and depending on surrounding cards, this ill-dignified Ace can often signify failure pure and simple for the Querent. It is, after all, easier to earn responsibility than to exercise it, which is why many a promotion has been swiftly followed by a job loss.

When accompanied by a majority of Coins *and* ill-dignified Major Arcana cards, the ill-dignified Ace of Coins often symbolizes an over-acquisitive nature, and/or a very unscrupulous approach to finance and personal power. In such an event, of course, the primary determining factor is the nature of the Significator — the Court card that represents the Querent — for the seriousness of this particular failing and its potential for damage to the life of the Querent and his associates is very much determined by the fundamental character of the individual involved.

THE TWOS

a) תבמה — CHOKMAH — Wisdom.
b) **Yah** — Blue.
c) **Raziel** — Grey.
d) **Auphanim** — Mother of Pearl.
e) **The Zodiac** — White flecked Red, Blue and Yellow.
f) The Second Path is called the *Illuminating Intelligence*. It is the Crown of Creation, the Splendour of Unity, equalling it. It is exalted above every head, and is named by Qabalists the Second Glory.

Chokmah is the Second Sephirah on the Tree of Life, and the male component of the Supernal Triangle. It is called the Supernal Father, and its most important symbols are the phallus, the line, the number 2, the element of Fire and the belt of the Zodiac. Thus, it is a dynamic, positive, expansive and masculine sphere.

When I say 'masculine', however, it must be appreciated that I do not use that term as it is commonly understood. The actions and reactions of the cosmos are sexual, and that fundamental sexuality is reflected in manifestation by the sexual differentiation of living creatures and by the sexual act, but it is important to see this in a proper perspective. Dion Fortune writes, in her book *The Mystical Qabalah*, that: 'Manifestation, then, is sexual insomuch as it takes place always in terms of opposites; and sex is cosmic and spiritual because it has its roots in the Three Supernals.' It is hardly possible to put the matter more clearly or more concisely than that.

The Yetsiratic Text terms Chokmah the 'Crown of Creation', and thus implies that it, like Kether, is *above* the manifest universe, a part of it and yet separate from it. Consequently, this sphere is the masculine principle at its most abstract. It is the impulse to manifestation — an outpouring of energy or force that will be organized by Binah into form. It is therefore termed 'masculine' simply because of the nature of its action within the whole of the Tree, which is *in*ceptive and fertilizing, rather than because it is 'masculine' or in any way 'sexual' as we normally understand those terms.

The number 2 with which Chokmah is associated symbolizes the initial balance of the duality that is inherent in all Creation, a balance that will stabilize with the appearance of Binah, The Supernal Mother. This, too, is the basic meaning of the symbol of the line; for a line is an extension of a point into, effectively, two points that are linked and balanced.

As stated above, Chokmah is a dynamic and expansive sphere, but it is nevertheless subject to the Principle of Polarity. Thus, while it is positive on its own Supernal level, it is negative on the next adjoining level.

The words 'positive' and 'negative' in this context can be misleading. The fact that Chokmah becomes negative on the level adjoining its own does not mean that it changes its basic nature, but rather that its impact upon that level is rather different. This is best understood by reference to the laws of physics and chemistry, which state that where positive and negative forces meet, both are neutralized — or at least they are if both components are roughly equal in strength. Thus — since all levels of manifestation are equal to one another in strength — it becomes obvious that when a positive or dynamic force like Chokmah enters a negative or receptive phase, the result will be its neutralization. Basically, a reconciliation of opposites is what takes place, not a switch-over into a diametrically opposed state.

This property of neutralization is demonstrated by the colour assigned to Chokmah — grey — and by the very name of the sphere itself, for Chokmah means 'wisdom'.

Grey is produced by mixing black and white, the colours assigned to Kether and Binah respectively; and wisdom is a quality that can only arise from the reconciliation of opposites, which is really a state of dynamic equilibrium where no one thing is in excess of any other.

The attribution of the Zodiac to this sphere naturally expresses a similar idea, and additionally introduces the important concept of synthesis; for it must be appreciated that this particular attribution demands that one make a balanced synthesis of many disparate ideas rather than — as is often the case when one is dealing with the cards of the Major Arcana — a synthesis of many symbols all of which express the same idea.

The process of synthesis in Tarot work — indeed, in the occult generally — is a vital one, for although analysis of a single symbol enables one to see the truths behind that symbol very clearly, it fails signally to produce any understanding of the whole that is inevitably the background of that symbol, which is itself only an aspect of the whole in any event. True understanding of the Tree, or of the situation revealed by a particular spread, or indeed of anything at all, is therefore only achieved by the process of synthesis that is part of the experience of the sphere of Chokmah.

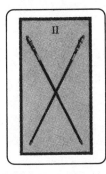

The Two of Staves
Lord of Dominion
All of the Twos signify some form of harmony. The Two of Staves is the 'harmony of rule' and — in the first instance, in any event — the 'rule' referred to is the rule over self. The card itself signifies 'dominion' — influence over others, ambition and success — but its title, the Lord of Dominion, nevertheless infers traits like self-discipline and self-control simply because the degree of 'dominion' achieved over the outer environment is wholly dependent upon the degree of 'dominion' we exercise over ourselves.

Because this is so, the card tends to signify the presence of those childish and unattractive human qualities that are born of lack of self-discipline and self-control — like obstinacy, and a tendency to brood over wrongs (sometimes imagined) or plot revenge on 'wrongdoers' — when it is ill-dignified.

However, and because Chokmah of Assiah manifests primarily as harmony, these negative traits rarely achieve expression in real life, and essentially damage only their author, who wastes much time and energy in such unproductive pursuits.

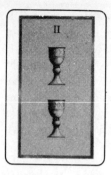

The Two of Cups
Lord of Love
The title of the Two of Cups is the Lord of Love, and the card represents the harmony of man and woman, or positive and negative. Thus, when dignified, it usually signifies love, partnerships, friendships, and unity of action.

When it is ill-dignified, it obviously indicates the reverse of all the pleasant things outlined above, and presages emotional difficulties in one relationship in particular, or just relationships in general.

Such difficulties are usually minor, but more importantly they generally stem from the Querent's own behaviour, and hence can usually be solved very readily if only the Querent can bring himself to act in a more reasonable manner. Unfortunately — and as outlined below with reference to the Two of Coins — ill-dignified Twos frequently signify habitual or stubborn behaviour, and the little difficulties usually symbolized by this card are therefore rarely as simple of resolution as they ought to be.

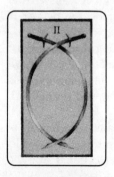

The Two of Swords
Lord of Peace Restored

The Two of Swords is called the Lord of Peace Restored — a title which infers the commencement of a peaceful and harmonious period following a stressful and unbalanced one. The dignified Two of Swords therefore usually signifies *relief* pure and simple — the sort of peace of mind that comes when any problem is resolved.

When it is ill-dignified, the Two of Swords is a card of illusions shattered, but it nevertheless retains its basic meaning of 'relief', because it represents the discovery by the Querent of what is true and what is not — in himself, in his life, and in the people around him.

Thus, the very appearance of this card will naturally almost certainly reveal the existence of lies and misrepresentation of some sort — the nature and source of which will be shown by the surrounding cards — for the ill-dignified Two of Swords represents not the relief that comes when a problem is resolved, but that which is felt when the ramifications of a complex situation sort themselves out into a simple and obvious pattern.

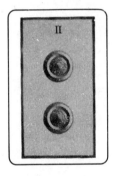

The Two of Coins
Lord of Harmonious Change

Coins as a suit basically represent stability because the element to which they are attributed is Earth, the densest of all the elements. Thus, although the Two of Coins — the Lord of Harmonious Change — is attributed to a Fire Sephirah, it nevertheless does signify exactly what its title suggests: change that occurs slowly and in a balanced and orderly fashion. Thus the appearance of a dignified Two of Coins usually signifies *planned* change — an alteration that is self-regulated and self-determined, rather than unexpected or sudden.

Because this is so, the appearance of an ill-dignified Two of Coins usually indicates a minor problem, the cause of which can be traced to the Querent's own silly behaviour. Minor arguments, misplaced and baseless suspicions, and talking out of turn are the sort of 'silly behaviour' that is usually associated with this two; and because such behaviour rarely causes really serious difficulties, any problems highlighted by the card can usually be put right fairly quickly if only the Querent will bring himself to do so.

And there, alas, lies the rub; for ill-dignified Twos in general usually signify, as has already been stated above, habitual behaviour and stubbornness. Thus, if the 'talker out of turn' does not queer his own pitch in the first instance by refusing to recognize his error and apologize, he will almost certainly compound his sin sooner or later by repeating it. Therefore, although ill-dignified Twos usually indicate problems that are very minor, they also indicate problems that are likely to recur unless the Querent makes a strong effort to regulate his habits, or curb his temper — unless, in other words, he once chooses to deal with the *cause* of the problem, rather than consistently struggle with its *effects*.

THE THREES

> a) בינה — BINAH — Understanding.
> b) **Yhvh Elohim** — Crimson.
> c) **Tzaphqiel** — Black.
> d) **Aralim** — Dark Brown.
> e) **Saturn** — Grey flecked Pink.
> f) The Third Path is called the *Sanctifying Intelligence*, the Foundation of Primordial Wisdom; it is also called the Creator of Faith, and its roots are in Amen. It is the parent of faith, whence faith emanates.

Binah is the last of the three Sephiroth that form the Supernal Triangle, and is the formative, or feminine, principle of that Triad. Its primary symbols are the Yoni, the Triangle, and the planet Saturn.

The Sephirah Binah is the will to form. It is the principle that shapes, inhibits or disciplines the outpouring energy of Chokmah. Binah is therefore a womb, the most abstract aspect of the feminine principle, and the Great Mother in both her Bright and Dark aspects — Bright because the Great Mother is the giver of all life, the shaper of form as a vehicle for life, Dark because all such vehicles are finite and transitory, and the gift of life carries implicit within it the idea of inevitable eventual death.

One of the titles most frequently allotted to Binah is the *Great Sea*. In Qabalistic — and Tarot — symbolism, water always represents consciousness; and this title therefore implies that Binah is the root of the Primordial Unconscious, the 'water' from which all things are born and to which all things return, and which contains the experiential record of all life.

The allocation of Saturn to this sphere is one of the most important and revealing of all its attributions, for the planet Saturn is the ruler of time — a restrictive and disciplinary principle that measures the passage of life and determines its extent in any given form.

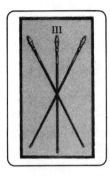

The Three of Staves
Lord of Established Strength
The Three of Staves signifies endurance, determination and persistence, and consequently — when dignified — indicates completion after struggle, or the ultimate realization of the Querent's career ambitions.

When ill-dignified, however, the excellent qualities referred to above degenerate into false pride and obstinacy pure and simple, which — more often than not — takes the form of a stubborn refusal of offers of much needed assistance, and too great a reliance upon the inadequate resources of the self.

The Three of Cups
Lord of Abundance
The Three of Cups represents abundance, fecundity, great happiness and joy. It can indicate a birth, an engagement, or a marriage, or simply hopes fulfilled. Often, the success signified by the dignified appearance of this card is all the more pleasant for being so unexpected.

When ill-dignified, however — and because of the nature of its suit and its position on the Tree — the Three of Cups almost always signifies self-indulgence, sensuality and selfishness to some degree; it is, however, important to retain a proper perspective in this respect.

Everybody is self-indulgent, sensual and selfish sometimes and in

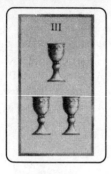

some situations. Consequently, it is only when this card makes its appearance in very bad company indeed that it will signify *real* self-indulgence, *damaging* sensuality, *gross* selfishness, and so on. Usually it is merely an indication of a tendency to play or lie in the sun when one really should be working, to rifle chocolate boxes to the detriment of one's teeth or one's figure, or to secrete one's favourite snacks behind the bread box to save them from marauding children!

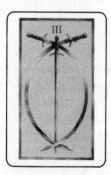

The Three of Swords
Lord of Sorrow
The Three of Swords shows the negative side of its associated sphere and planet, for — even when dignified — it generally signifies hatred, strife, disunion and unhappiness.

When the card is ill-dignified, it is an indication that these feelings might well crystallize into actions in the material world, and thus the card usually signifies incipient separation or divorce, and all the feelings of disillusionment, hurt and confusion that usually accompany such events.

Again, however, the reader must strive to retain perspective when it comes to interpreting an ill-dignified Three of Swords, for although the card often appears relative to family difficulties, unless it is accompanied by the Major Arcana card 'Justice' it is less likely to indicate disagreement between partners *per se* than difficulties between partners caused by a third party — usually a troubled or troublesome adolescent. Surrounding cards must therefore be scanned carefully if a correct interpretation is to be made.

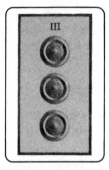

The Three of Coins
Lord of Material Works

The Three of Coins signifies the mundane work that will eventually result in the abundance promised by the Three of Cups, for it generally indicates the commencement of matters which will bear fruit at a later date. Thus, it frequently signifies future gain through present employment or commercial transactions.

When ill-dignified, the card represents an extremely materialistic approach to life. Naturally, this does not in any way defer the arrival of those financial benefits promised by the dignified card, but it certainly affects the quality of the Querent's life — inner and outer — and the lives of the people around him.

This latter occurs simply because there is a certain degree of fanaticism — misplaced single-mindedness — associated with this card, the tendency indicated by its presence being the formulation of plans that might — albeit rarely — result in loss, but which (and much more importantly) rarely take into account the feelings or needs of other people, and tend to absorb much more of the Querent's time than is healthy.

THE FOURS

a) חסד — CHESED — Mercy.
b) **El** — Deep Violet.
c) **Tzadqiel** — Blue.
d) **Chasmalim** — Deep Purple.
e) **Jupiter** — Azure flecked Yellow.
f) The Fourth Path is called the *Cohesive* or *Receptive Intelligence* because it contains all the Holy Powers, and from it emanates all the spiritual virtues with the most exalted essences. They emanate one from another by virtue of the Primordial Emanation, the Highest Crown, Kether.

Chesed is the first Sephirah and the masculine principle of the Ethical Triangle, and it is therefore a positive sphere in a negative Triad, for — following the Principle of Polarity — as the first and Supernal Triangle is *positive*, the second and Ethical Triangle is *negative*. Chesed is thus a *negatively positive* sphere — a *positive* Sephirah functioning on a *negative* plane.

This means that, when functioning on the plane of Assiah — which is also negative — the action of Chesed manifests primarily as a condition of stability. The Magical Image of Chesed in any event reflects the fundamental stability of the sphere, for it is that of a mighty enthroned King — and, as I have said, enthroned (or seated) figures in the Qabalistic system invariably represent consolidation.

The Yetsiratic Text says that Chesed 'contains all the Holy Powers'. This reference to 'Holy Powers' occurs because Chesed is the first of the six Sephiroth that make up Microposopos or Adam Kadmon, a primary channel of the original creative energy, and the source of the impetus toward actual physical manifestation, which — as will be explained later in this book — only becomes inevitable with the emergence of this sphere.

Because this is so, all the symbols of Chesed — the pyramid, the square, and the planet Jupiter — refer to conditions that are receptive, cohesive, stable and organizing.

The Four of Staves
Lord of Perfected Work
The presence of the Four of Staves in a spread always indicates the successful completion of something — a state of affairs where matters are 'definitely settled and arranged to the enquirer's satisfaction', and

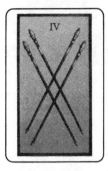

this holds good even when the card is ill-dignified, for the reversal of dignity in this instance merely indicates a short delay. Usually, such a completion represents the fulfilment of an ambition that has been worked towards, or the success of a project begun some time previously.

Even when surrounded by unhelpful cards, the ill-dignified Four remains comparatively stable. At worst, it will indicate a quiet period before completion, and therefore — although such periods can appear to be rather ominous omens — its appearance even in difficult circumstances will never be anything to worry about.

The Four of Cups
Lord of Blended Pleasure

The Four of Cups represents a condition of boredom or discontent that has little foundation in reality, and this holds true whether the card is dignified or not.

As its title, the Lord of Blended Pleasure, indicates, this card represents a situation that is basically stable, secure, and to some degree happy or pleasurable, but which is marred or overshadowed by something irritating or depressing. Consequently, the card often foreshadows an 'explosion' of some kind as the Querent draws nearer to that point at which the bad things about any given area of his life begin to outweigh the good ones *in his own mind* .

This last phrase is very important to a true appreciation of the meaning of this card, for it must be understood that the action it represents takes place only in the mind and the emotions. A good example is the woman who has a secure part-time job that pays almost as much as she would get from full-time employment elsewhere. In theory, the job is perfect. In practice it is so dull that the short time she spends there stretches into an eternity, and she ends every day in a frenzy of irritation. Eventually, mental and emotional pressure will force her out of this job — but the job itself will not have changed: it will remain exactly as it was on the day she was so thrilled to get it, and was considering only the amount of money she would get and the amount of free time she would retain.

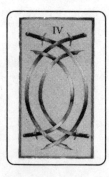

The Four of Swords
Lord of Rest From Strife

The Four of Swords can signify the sort of material stability that allows of long, relaxing holidays; release from tension or anxiety, or the cessation of stressful conditions; but its primary meaning is physical convalescence — which can as easily signify recovery from adverse emotional or financial conditions as recovery from actual illness.

Sometimes, this particular card (when ill-dignified) can mean enforced seclusion — isolation, ostracism, imprisonment or institutionalization — but this holds good only when it is surrounded by very badly aspected cards indicative of conditions that would demand such seclusion. It is worth remembering, too, in this regard, that some individuals deliberately seclude themselves, being stand-offish or natural loners. Care should therefore be taken in the interpretation of this card even when surrounding cards are badly aspected, and particular attention paid to the nature of the Significator.

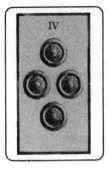

The Four of Coins
Lord of Earthly Power
The Four of Coins signifies a gain of money and/or influence that
is usually traceable to a promotion involving a considerable increase
in salary. Again, however, I would point out that a promotion is
not an end in itself, and also that money and/or power does not buy
happiness.

A promotion can precede disgrace, demotion, or dismissal if the
individual concerned does not prove worthy of his new responsibilities;
and there are many grass widows who can testify to the disastrous
effect of a successful career on a personal relationship.

Relationships are the achilles heel of this particular four. Dismissal
if it comes is less likely to be due to incompetence than an impossibly
abrasive personality that directs all its attention to work and none to
the individual.

The presence of this card in a spread therefore — whether ill-
dignified or not — always demands that the reader look to its long-
term effects before reporting its presence in simple terms.

THE FIVES

> a) גבורה — GEBURAH — Justice.
> b) **Elohim Gebor** — Orange.
> c) **Kamael** — Scarlet.
> d) **Seraphim** — Bright Scarlet.
> e) **Mars** — Red flecked Black.
> f) The Fifth Path is called the *Radical Intelligence* because it
>   resembles Unity, uniting itself to Binah, Understanding,
>   which emanates from the primordial depths of Chokmah,
>   Wisdom.

Geburah is the fifth sphere of the Tree, and is the negative or feminine principle of the Ethical Triangle. Its symbols are the pentagon, the sword, the spear, and the scourge.

Dion Fortune calls Geburah a 'negatively negative' Sephirah (the *negative* factor in a *negative* Triad), and states that the prime attribute of such a sphere is destruction — and certainly the four cards associated with this sphere are all extremely negative and *seemingly* destructive.

However, it must be remembered that Geburah has two further titles, *Din* which means 'justice' and *Pachad* which means 'fear' or 'awe', if the sphere and its associated Tarot cards are to be correctly understood.

Geburah, like Binah, is an inhibitor. In fact, it is a necessary corrective, a disciplinary force which is essentially positive in that it restores balance and harmony. Surgery, for instance — the drastic cutting away of disease — falls under the rule of Sephirah Geburah, while (despite the martial symbols of Geburah) militarism falls under its complementary opposite, Chesed.

The symbols of the sphere show that its energy acts in two ways. The first is represented by the scourge which infers continuing discipline or preventative action. The second is represented by the spear and the sword, both of which imply a sharp but short-lived discipline and curative action. Thus the sphere represents both continual and long-term control (and thereby implies self-control) and the swift and essential destruction of outdated or diseased elements.

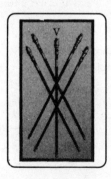

The Five of Staves
Lord of Strife
The Five of Staves signifies power, will, and ambition — the Querent's own, and that which is in opposition to his own. The result of this is, inevitably, a conflict that can neither be avoided nor won. Indeed, the dignity of this card records only the terms of a declared truce or

the exact dimensions of a complete defeat.

Whatever the nature of the surrounding cards or the Majority, this simple fact holds true. Sadly, therefore, the reader is forced to simply retail a fact — and assess from surrounding cards the ramifications of that fact. These will not be pleasant. This particular Five signifies the existence of not just a fight, but a dirty fight that will leave neither side with much satisfaction or self-respect, and which will have long-term and far-reaching effects.

The Five of Cups
Lord of Loss in Pleasure

The Five of Cups signifies loss of pleasure, and can therefore indicate anything from acute and apparently baseless depression to a death in the family. Crowley calls it the 'Lord of Disappointment', and that — in all its varying degress and shades of meaning — is exactly what this card generally means.

When ill-dignified, the card is more inclined to mean present loss or disappointment that is due to the Querent's own expectations — which are themselves the result of past negative experiences. Quite often, therefore, the appearance of the ill-dignified Five of Cups will signify disasters that could have been avoided, being literally self-created by the Querent's own negative thought patterns.

The Five of Swords
Lord of Defeat

The Five of Swords is the most difficult of all the Fives to interpret. It can show the ultimate and disastrous failure of a treasured project or relationship, or purely temporary worries of a fleeting and unimportant nature. It can signify real poverty and loss, or emotional poverty, or that money, fame or prestige has brought the Querent little happiness. In short, correct interpretation of the Five of Swords

— whether dignified or not — depends very heavily on accurate interpretation of the cards that surround it.

The Five of Coins
Lord of Material Trouble

The Five of Coins signifies all material difficulties — lack or loss of employment, for instance, or an inability to find affordable accommodation, and so on; but primarily it will always show a shortage of sufficient money to put things right.

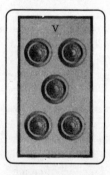

Because the card itself is a Five, it will always represent ills for which there is a solution — and this holds true however hopeless the situation looks at first glance. However, the remedy will equally always involve fairly drastic action on the part of the Querent, and might therefore prove unacceptable for a multitude of reasons. Such solutions are naturally nearly always to be found in a spread where this ill-dignified Five appears. The most the reader can do is to relay them to the Querent in the best and most optimistic light.

Despite what we have said above with reference to these four cards, it is worth bearing in mind that the effects of an act of destruction are different in the *long term* to its effects in the *short term*. The connotations of the Biblical phrase 'If thine right eye offend thee, pluck it out', for instance, are drastically changed by the addition of the phrase 'before it infects the entire physical system, causing death'. Long term vision, in effect, is the secret of Geburah, which is the sphere of *destruction in the now*, so as to ensure *construction in the future*.

THE SIXES

a) תפארה — TIPHARETH — Beauty.
b) **Yhvh Eloah Ve D'aath** — Rose Pink.
c) **Raphael** — Golden Yellow.
d) **Melechim** — Salmon.
e) **The Sun** — Amber.
f) The Sixth Path is called the *Mediating Intelligence* because in it are multiplied the influxes of the Emanations; for it causes that influence to flow into all the reservoirs of the blessings with which they themselves are united.

Tiphareth is the sixth sphere of the Tree of Life, the central Sephiroth of the Tree, and the equilibrizing principle of the Ethical Triangle. The Yetsiratic Text calls it the 'Mediating Intelligence' because it is the balance wheel of the Tree — the sphere where all the energies of the Tree are equilibrized. Thus it is primarily a sphere of *harmony*.

It must be remembered, of course, that equilibrium does not equate with a state of inertia, but is the result of tension: harmony is unlikely to exist where there is no inherent tension — an equal 'pull', as it were, from forces in opposition.

The primary symbols of Tiphareth are the Rose Cross and the cube, and — because Tiphareth is the sphere of all Sacrificed Gods — the Calvary Cross. From this latter symbol it can be rightly inferred that neither equilibrium nor harmony can be achieved without sacrifice of some kind.

The Six of Staves
Lord of Victory
The Six of Staves signifies victory after strife; gain and success through effort; or tactfulness and diplomacy — which is really the deliberate *avoidance* of strife.

All these meanings obviously infer that the result gained is equal to the effort expended, and consequently the appearance of the ill-

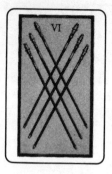

dignified Six of Wands — the primary meanings of which are delay or disappointment due to the success of a rival over oneself — naturally infers that insufficient effort was expended to gain the desired result in the first place.

The Six of Cups
Lord of Pleasure

The Six of Cups signifies the beginnings of happiness and emotional fulfilment or the commencement of steady material gains.

The emphasis here is on the words 'beginning' and 'commencement', for it must be noted that nothing is said of 'continuance'.

Thus the meanings of this card also infer that only if effort is expended — tension applied, in other words — will these good things continue rather than just begin. Hence, the ill-dignified meanings of this particular card all refer to problems arising from selfishness — self-assertion, for instance, or vanity, self-love, and contentious behaviour — which is a state of being that arises when the delicate tension lines that exist in relationships begin to sag on one side because no deliberate effort is being made to keep them taut.

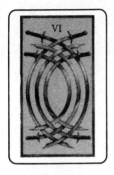

The Six of Swords
Lord of Earned Success
The Six of Swords signifies the possession of accurate information, and consequently decisions that are based on full or correct knowledge, plans that are well-formulated, and final success and achievement. Hence, of course, the title of the card, the Lord of Earned Success.

The card can signify journeys — and particularly journeys across water — but more usually the 'journeys' referred to are *mental* ones. These mental journeys can be the formulation of the well-laid plans referred to above, but if the card is ill-dignified they can equally be 'escapist' journeys — travels into a never-never land where everything always goes right.

Because of its connection with such journeys, this Six can signify actual physical journeys too; but their nature differs according to the dignity of the card. A dignified Six is more likely to signify a business-oriented journey or travel to another place to take up a fresh appointment than a carefree holiday; while the ill-dignified Six — which you will recall has connotations of 'escapism' — rarely means anything but a carefree holiday during the length of which all problems and difficulties are laid aside and forgotten.

The Six of Coins
Lord of Material Success
The Six of Coins signifies power, rank and authority over others responsibly exercised, prosperity in business, gain from commercial ventures, and success in material undertakings — all of which depend upon the harmonious interaction of many disparate factors. When it is ill-dignified, the Six of Coins merely shows the results of an inability to blend such factors into such a rounded whole.

The ill-dignified Six of Coins often represents a person who has been spoiled by success — who has begun to let his ends of the 'tension

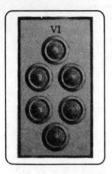

lines' of his relationships slacken, and has consequently become impossibly selfish and arrogant.

From these meanings, it can be seen that *all* the Sixes, when ill-dignified, signify the existence of problems that are self-created because they are the result of pure selfishness. However, this rarely means that the success promised by these cards will not be forthcoming. Rather, it will simply mean that it will arrive at the *wrong price*. All success must naturally be paid for — it demands that sacrifices be made. The extent of those sacrifices, however, depends wholly upon the individual, who determines their extent and nature by his own actions.

THE SEVENS

a) נצח — NETSACH — Victory.
b) **Yhvh Tzaboath** — Amber.
c) **Haniel** — Emerald.
d) **Elohim** — Greenish Yellow.
e) **Venus** — Olive flecked Gold.
f) The Seventh Path is called the *Occult Intelligence* because it is the refulgent splendour of the intellectual virtues which are perceived by the eyes of the intellect and the contemplations of faith.

Netsach is the seventh Sephirah of the Tree of Life, and the first sphere of the Astral Triangle. It represents the feminine principle in that Triad, and its primary symbols are the girdle, the rose, the lamp, and the planet Venus.

The sphere of Netsach is ruled by Venus, the Goddess of Love, and is the Sephirah of 'right relationships'. It represents the creative instincts, the emotions, and the forces of Nature.

However, all these things prove to be 'red in tooth and claw', as the saying goes, when they are examined realistically; and this feminine sphere on a masculine pillar is indeed closely associated with Geburah and the planet Mars. Thus, it has a negative and destructive aspect that is revealed by all the cards associated with it, and some of its symbolism is apparently uncharacteristically masculine and positive.

Three of the four symbols of this Sephirah given above — the rose, the girdle, and the astrological attribution — all refer to Venus, and hence to beauty; but it is worth considering that there are two kinds of symbol allocated to this sphere: those that represent the concept of beauty, as these do, and those that represent the masculine concept of power. Of these latter symbols, the lamp is one, and the very title of the Sephirah is the other.

Netsach means both 'victory' and 'firmness', and thus infers the sort of dynamic energy usually associated with the masculine, positive 'force' side of the Tree upon which this Sephirah appears. This dynamic aspect of the sphere is also symbolized by the lamp, which is allocated to Netsach simply because, when the four elements are attributed to the four lower spheres of the Tree, it is the element of Fire that is allotted to this Sephirah.

Thus it can be seen that it is the forces of Mars and Venus that are at work in this sphere, one representing the powerful forces of Nature, the other the power to direct and channel them.

The Seven of Staves
Lord of Valour
The Seven of Staves usually signifies the existence of various hindrances and obstacles that must be faced and overcome in order to succeed. It is, as its title suggests, the card of courage in the face of adversity, and its presence in a spread usually infers that if the Querent is firm enough and tenacious enough, he will finally succeed in his efforts.

Naturally, when it is ill-dignified, this Seven means that there is a danger of allowing oneself to be worn down by persistent opposition; but it is also a warning that the Querent should neither make nor accept any concessions either in the heat of the moment, or because he is being pressed to do so (or even because he is tired of the struggle), since any concession, however minor, might endanger his future prospects of the success that is assured to him if only he will persist in his efforts.

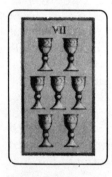

The Seven of Cups
Lord of Illusory Success
This card has two meanings, one of which is of vital importance to the Querent, and one of which is not; for the Seven of Cups means possible victory or success, or — as its title infers — illusory success.

In the first instance, the accent is on the word 'possible', for the appearance of this card often signifies that the success that is within the Querent's grasp is not that which he either expected or wanted. Thus in this context, success or the lack of it in any given area is something that is wholly in the Querent's own hands. Frequently, and because it is not what he wants, it is something which he is quite happy to see go by.

In the second instance, however, the key word is 'illusory', for which read 'ephemeral'. This aspect of the card has much graver consequences for the Querent simply because it infers the loss of something that he needed, or at least very much desired.

The 'illusory success' referred to by this card when ill-dignified is usually due to a misrepresentation of facts by another person. Thus it covers situations like that of a man who gives up one job on the understanding that he has another, only to find that such verbal assurances as he has received are worthless, and that the new job has gone to someone else.

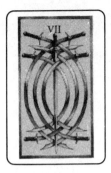

The Seven of Swords
Lord of Unstable Effort
The dignified Seven of Swords primarily signifies fear of success. This fear can manifest as fear of *handling* success or as fear of being *limited to one sphere of activity* by a single success, but in either event the result will be the same. The individual involved will begin to avoid success, or to sabotage it deliberately. Often, such sabotage is quite unconscious — indeed, the individual concerned may even express acute disappointment at his frequent failures.

Like the Six of Swords, this Seven can also mean journeys, but these are always journeys by land, and they are always quite short. The card has a tendency, too, to turn up presaging a simultaneous change of job and residence, or — when ill-dignified — the sort of persistent changes of job and residence that are the sign of a very irregular life.

With reference to this latter point, the title of the card is the Lord of Unstable Effort, and quite often the instability referred to manifests as an inability or unwillingness to keep a job; or as a simple (and usually incurable) wanderlust that renders an individual wholly incapable of sitting still in one place.

Here, too, of course, is the person who works in fits and starts — either very hard, or not at all — and the child whose homework is either very good indeed or simply dreadful, depending on the level of his interest in the subject concerned.

From these latter examples in particular it becomes obvious that many of the traits symbolized by this card stem from a simple lack of self-discipline, which manifests as a lack of desire to complete *specific* tasks, but not *all* tasks.

The Seven of Coins
Lord of Success Unfulfilled
The Seven of Coins always signifies little reward for much labour,

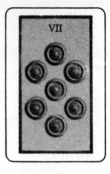

but this is not always as disastrous as it may seem, since not everyone works solely for monetary reward. Charitable work, hobbies, pastimes, and housework are all things that people do, if not for love, then at least without any thought or desire for financial reward. It must be remembered, too, that job satisfaction is becoming more and more important to the average person, who is no longer willing to do a boring or dirty job simply because it pays very well indeed.

Despite all this, however, the title of the card is the Lord of Success Unfulfilled, and often this is exactly what the card means — great disappointment, because despite much hard work and effort some plan or project has failed. Usually, this meaning will only apply either if the project is a business project that has *recently* failed, or when the failure of some ambition has cast an almost permanent blight over the life.

This latter phrase would seem to be an exaggeration, but it is not.

Often, hobbies reflect things that people would like to have done, but could never have made a living at simply because they were physically incapable of doing so, or just not talented enough. Sometimes, too, they are 'next bests' — things that are 'like' professions that there simply wasn't enough money to train for.

These — given a certain kind of person — can be permanent and lasting disappointments that rankle and fester and infect the entire life; and it must be remembered that even easy-going and well-balanced people can be stirred to fresh disappointment and grief when a son or daughter, with better opportunities or a bigger talent, shows no interest in fulfilling a parent's vicarious ambition, but persists in pursuing his or her own.

THE EIGHTS

a) הוד — HOD — Splendour.
b) **Elohim Tzaboath** — Violet.
c) **Michael** — Orange.
d) **Beni Elohim** — Russet.
e) **Mercury** — Yellowish Brown flecked White.
f) The Eighth Path is called the *Absolute* or *Perfect Intelligence* because it is the mean of the primordial, which has no root by which it can cleave or rest, save in the hidden place of Gedulah [Chesed], from which emanates its proper essence.

Hod is the masculine element in the Astral Triangle, and is, like Netsach, a Hermaphroditical sphere — a masculine Sephirah positioned at the base of a feminine Pillar. It is the sphere of Mercury and therefore represents the rational mind and — again like Netsach — it tends to swing to and fro between a positive and negative manifestation of power.

Hod is a coagulating principle that — as the Yetsiratic Text reveals — receives its impetus from Chesed, the organizing Sephirah that builds the individual units produced by Binah into more complex group structures. Consequently Hod operates in much the same way as Chesed, but on another level. Hod, indeed, is the shaper of the raw force of Netsach, and provides forms for ensoulment by that force. Thus its primary effect is that of necessary inhibition, the formulation of form.

The symbols of Hod are the names and versicles, and the apron. The names are the Words of Power, and relate to the power of the spoken word when it is projected or vibrated. The versicles are mantras — phrases that prove auto-suggestive when they are repeated or intoned over and over again. The apron is a Masonic symbol that relates to the grade of that Order that is deemed to be the grade of the craftsman or builder — the creator of form. It relates also to the Moon, and so to Thoth, God of Magic and Writing, Teacher of the Mysteries.

The Eight of Staves
The Lord of Swiftness
The Eight of Staves signifies things done swiftly, hasty communications, or the need to do things quickly. However, in this latter context it must be remembered that the Golden Dawn states that the card means 'too much force applied too suddenly, very rapid rush but too quickly passed

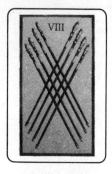

and expended, violent, but not lasting', and the appearance of the card is therefore often a warning that there is a need to act with speed *and* forethought — a difficult combination to achieve successfully.

When this card is ill-dignified, it is sometimes a warning of possible theft or robbery — which certainly is a 'hasty communication' of a sort, if one reads the word 'communication' after its old and original meaning — but more frequently it is a warning, not against haste *per se*, but against *ill-considered* hasty action.

The Eight of Cups
Lord of Abandoned Success
The presence of the Eight of Cups in a spread often indicates a tendency to rest on one's laurels when one would be better employed consolidating one's gains. Thus it usually signifies temporary rather than permanent success, or even success abandoned — the 'when you get what you want you don't want it anymore' syndrome.

Occasionally, this card means renunciation — the act of deliberately giving up something important or pleasurable for something more meaningful — but (and particularly when it is ill-dignified) it is more likely to mean laziness pure and simple.

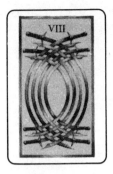

The Eight of Swords
Lord of Shortened Force

The Eight of Swords indicates the presence of restrictive situations
— the imprisonment of an individual by circumstance or by his own
actions or outlook or upbringing. This latter meaning in particular
is referred to in the Golden Dawn meaning of the card: 'too much
force applied to small things; too much attention to detail at the expense
of the principal and more important points'. Thus — and particularly
when the card is ill-dignified — it can signify narrow-mindedness,
small-mindedness, fanatical religious (or other) beliefs, and so on.
However, it must be remembered the true meaning of any given card
is determined by those cards that surround it — and it is these cards
that will reveal the area of operation and the nature of the restriction
represented by the Eight of Swords.

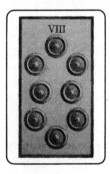

The Eight of Coins
Lord of Prudence

The Eight of Coins signifies carefulness, prudence and circumspection
in financial or material matters, a willingness to work hard, and the
prospect of prosperity for those who are prepared to work for it.

Like the Eight of Swords, this card also signifies care in small things at the expense of more important ones, but is inclined to refer to money or material goods rather than other areas of life.

THE NINES

a) יְסוֹד — YESOD — Foundation.
b) **Shaddai El Chai** — Indigo.
c) **Gabriel** — Violet.
d) **Kerubim** — Dark Purple.
e) **Moon** — Citrine flecked Azure.
f) The Ninth Path is called the *Pure Intelligence* because it purifies the Emanations. It proves and corrects the designing of their representations and disposes the unity with which they are designed without diminution or division.

Yesod is the Ninth Sephirah, and the equilibrating factor in the Astral Triangle. Like Binah, with which it has much in common, Yesod is a *positively negative* Sephirah. It is the sphere of the Moon — a fluid and fluctuating force — and the Astral Aether, which is the magnetic, electrical and highly plastic substance that stands behind manifestation, and which is neither mind nor matter, but partakes of the nature of both.

The Yetziractic Text says of Yesod that it 'purifies the Emanations and proves and corrects the designing of their representations'. Thus, it can be seen that Yesod, which is the sphere which acts as the receptacle for the outpourings of the Sephiroth that precede it, collects the myriad ensouled forms that stem from Hod and arranges them in a unified whole without in any way interfering with their essential uniqueness. Yesod provides the material of which the Etheric Body — the system of electrical stresses that stands behind every living thing — is constructed, and is thus called the 'Foundation'.

The symbols of Yesod are the perfume and the sandals. Perfume represents the Etheric, for it reacts upon the subtle nature of man. The sandals affirm contact with the Earth. Thus these symbols signify the dual nature and function of Yesod by presenting two images representative of mind and matter respectively.

The Nine of Staves
Lord of Great Strength
The dignified Nine of Staves — the Lord of Great Strength — signifies

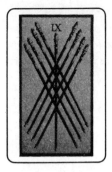

good health, great power, and success. Often, however, all the benefits outlined above are subject to doubt in the mind of the Querent; and this card consequently frequently appears in the spread of the robustly healthy hypochondriac, or the highly successful, but secretly very insecure, individual.

When it is ill-dignified, this Nine still represents substantial achievements in the material world or recovery from illness, but its appearance nevertheless nearly always signifies the need to make a determined effort, or the presence of disagreements and strife. Thus, and where the requisite effort has not been made in a timely fashion, it can signify the loss of an apparently secure position or a job — or such a simple thing as a tooth, the condition of which has been ignored for much too long!

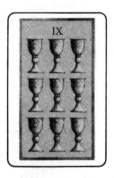

The Nine of Cups
Lord of Material Happiness
The Nine of Cups signifies contentment, physical well-being, material success and an assured future. It is the card of wishes come true, and often signifies the fulfilment of a lifetime's ambition.

When ill-dignified, however, the appearance of this card is often a warning against complacency — and particularly against complacent or ill-placed trust in partners or business associates. Success and contentment all too often result in a careless lack of attention when it comes to the unromantic 'nuts and bolts' aspects of living that can lead to disaster.

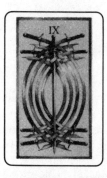

The Nine of Swords
Lord of Despair and Cruelty

The Nine of Swords signifies sickness, misery, persecution, loss, want, oppression, and hard and unedifying labour — but it must be remembered that all these things are relative.

Morning sickness is sickness — and it is misery, too, as many of us can testify from personal experience — but it is not terminal cancer or sickness unto death. A neighbour who consistently plays a radio much too loudly may be guilty of persecution and oppression, but he is not a Mengele. Office or factory work may be hard, unedifying labour, but it is not the Gulag. Want is always determined in relation to the possessions and status of others: certainly 'want' in the West at the end of the twentieth century bears no relationship to the truly hideous conditions that the word described a hundred years ago.

Consequently, this card is by no means as black as it is often painted, although it does demand that the reader interpret it carefully and retain a sense of proportion, while relating it to the feelings of the Querent.

When ill-dignified, this card often signifies that it is the Querent himself that is the author of the misery of other people — that it is he who is acting as a persecutor, oppressor and so on; that it is he who is burdening others with intolerable work-loads, or rendering their lives hideous with noise. Indeed, the ill-dignified Nine of Swords puts the meaning of the whole card into a more reasonable perspective. It is, after all, quite unlikely to say the least that the average Querent is really guilty of torturing people in his garage, or acting out the part of 'Jack the Ripper' on his evenings off — or that he is at all likely to meet someone else who is.

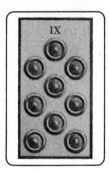

The Nine of Coins
Lord of Material Gain

The Nine of Coins always represents 'easy money', but it must be remembered that everything has to come from somewhere. Thus retirement is one of the inferred meanings of this card, as are redundancy and other lump sum payments, together with inheritances, or substantial incomes from stocks and shares or alimony.

When ill-dignified, the card still shows 'easy money', but this is the sort of 'easy money' that comes 'under the table', as it were. Thus the card often appears ill-dignified in spreads belonging to people who work in the 'black market' or in those trades where cash changes hands as a matter of course and therefore need not necessarily be reported to the Inland Revenue.

Naturally, it also appears where individuals are working for cash and collecting Social Security — in which case the card takes on its meaning of illegally-earned or 'tainted' money — or where they are stealing money by even more reprehensible means, like breaking into houses or thumping people over the head in the park.

There are, of course, more sophisticated and more commonplace ways than these of 'making a few bob' — and all of them fall under the aegis of this ill-dignified Nine and are practised by a wide variety of otherwise law-abiding citizens. The usual interpretation of the ill-dignified Nine of Coins is therefore 'technical illegality' rather than anything more serious.

THE TENS

---

a) תלכות — MALKUTH — The Kingdom.
b) **Adonai a-Aretz** — Yellow.
c) **Sandalphon** — Citrine, Olive, Russet and Black.
d) **Ashim** — Citrine, Olive, Russet and Black flecked Gold.
e) **Sphere of the Elements** — Black, rayed Yellow.
f) The Tenth Path is called the *Resplendent Intelligence* because it is exalted above every head and sits upon the Throne of Binah. It illuminates the splendours of all the Lights, and causes an influence to flow from the Prince of Countenances, the Angel of Kether.

Malkuth is completion — the last of the Sephiroth, and the culmination of all that went before it. It is the only Sephiroth that does not form part of a Triad, and is the most complex of all the spheres.

Malkuth is the manifest expression of the process that began in the Unmanifest, and is therefore the manifest expression of the Creator also. Indeed, the Qabalah teaches that Malkuth *is* Kether after another fashion, and that these spheres are complementary opposites. Certainly both Sephiroth express a state of unity, albeit in rather different ways.

Malkuth is the Sephirah where the elements that are rooted in Kether blend to produce the matter and stability that 'ground' the interactive forces of the cosmos. It is entitled the Inferior Mother and is therefore also an expression of the energies of Binah (a sphere with which it has much in common and which is called the Superior Mother) on a lower arc.

The primary symbols of Malkuth are the equal armed cross, or Cross of the Elements, and the mystic circle. This latter obviously represents an enclosure, or defined area of operation, that is sacred or blessed.

The Ten of Staves
Lord of Oppression
The dignified Ten of Staves always signifies energy directed toward material ends. Its failing is that such energy is somewhat one-pointed, and can therefore lead to a rather blinkered — and consequently very selfish — approach to life.

It is this one-pointedness that creates the situation signified by the ill-dignified card, which is a failure of ambitions, in whole or in part, due to the words or actions of another person. Often, those actions

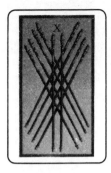

are the actions of somebody who is 'getting their own back' for past slights. Consequently, the appearance of this card, whether dignified or not, is always a warning against trampling on the feelings or ambitions of others in pursuit of ones own ambitions.

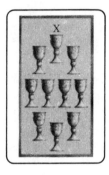

The Ten of Cups
Lord of Perfected Success
The Ten of Cups signifies good fortune and lasting success and happiness, but it must be remembered that these things can be negative as well as positive. There is, after all, a condition of happiness that exists simply because nothing has gone wrong rather than because something has gone right! In addition, the Ten of Cups can show that the Querent is stuck in a rut — a pleasant rut, but a rut nevertheless. He may be blissfully unaware of this fact, but is more frequently subject to the nagging question: 'Is this all there is?' — which is why this card frequently appears in a series of apparently incongruous ill-dignified Sword cards. It is prone to appear, in the spreads of quite happily married middle-aged men — and for obvious reasons — in which case the reader should look carefully at the opportunities life may offer such men, and utter the appropriate words of warning!

When this card is itself ill-dignified, it tends to represent domestic disruption. This is frequently caused by the arrival of a new baby or by older children going through puberty, or by the unfaithfulness of one member of a family partnership to the other. In any case, the disruption is temporary rather than permanent, and the card therefore does not signify any lasting family difficulties.

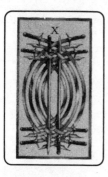

The Ten of Swords
Lord of Ruin
The Ten of Swords — whether dignified or not — has a bad reputation. It signifies sudden misfortune, accidents, muggings and so on. However, it must be remembered that the suit of Swords is the suit that represents *mental action* — thought, speech, and communication — and it is therefore to these aspects of life that one must look to understand the causes of the misfortunes that the card represents.

The eloquence associated with the suit of Swords is often used to talk the individuals in possession of it out of trouble, but there are times when a facility with the spoken or written word can actually *cause* trouble. If a kind word turneth away wrath, for instance, then a 'smart remark' will often occasion a punch on the nose or a swift clip round the ear. When dignified, this card therefore often signifies difficulties encountered — either physical or otherwise — because of a tendency to speak or write maliciously or without thinking.

When it is ill-dignified, the card retains its association with unfortunate communication, but in a way that is rather more difficult to understand, because the communication referred to is in this instance unspoken.

Body language (as its name implies) *is* a language, a valid form of communication that is at least as expressive as the spoken word. Because it is rarely wholly under our control, this 'language' is often a good deal less guarded than speech. Consequently, and because of the nature of the Ten of Swords, the body language signified when the card is ill-dignified is of a particularly negative kind, and this can cause many problems, some of which are very serious indeed.

Victims — both those of real crime and those for whom nothing ever goes right (and who might therefore be thought of simply as 'victims of life') — express their availability as victims by way of body language.

Obviously they do not do this deliberately, but they do do it nevertheless, and quite consistently too. All body language is the result of, and an expression of, mental attitude — negative body language is the result of and the expression of a *fearful* mental attitude.

It is therefore simple fear that is at the bottom of the stories one hears of the woman who has had her handbag stolen two or three times, or the man who has been consistently attacked, or the woman who is persistently sexually harrassed, or even the family who has been two or three times burgled; and it is the overcoming of fear that will make these unpleasant things stop.

The average person has no conception of the power of the mind, or of the nature of its link with the body. Many, indeed, think of their fear or defensiveness as a weapon rather than as a weakness, and consequently fail to understand that it is the causal factor of misfortune rather than a defence against it. It is very difficult to convince such people of the dangerous nature of fear, or to make them see it as a fifth column that is betraying them from within; the appearance of this card ill-dignified in a spread nevertheless makes it essential that the reader make some effort to put this point across, since it is above all indicative of the presence of a damaging fear of some kind.

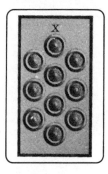

The Ten of Coins
Lord of Wealth
The Ten of Coins signifies completion, material gain, prosperity,

financial acumen, and the manifest results of all these things. Above all, therefore, it is indicative of material security.

When ill-dignified, it can signify either the complete reverse of all these things, or the presence of factors that create a sense of insecurity. Thus, the ill-dignified Ten of Coins can represent matters pending or uncompleted, litigation (over wills or trusts for example), loss, bad investments, and the like.

Chapter 5.

Images of the Almighty

In Chapter 3, it was stated that the Court cards are considered to represent man, and to exist *beside*, rather than *on* or *as a part of* the Sephiroth. This statement would seem to set the Court cards irrevocably apart from the rest of the deck and, by logical inference, man apart from his environment; but to accept this inference as true would be to place a manifestly false interpretation upon the word 'beside' as it is used in this context.

As must be obvious from the preceding chapters, the Sephiroth of the Tree of Life are interconnected both with each other and with the Unmanifest — the single primal source which both permeates and transcends them. All therefore form a totality, and enjoy qualities in common. Indeed, it is only the predominance of a particular quality that differentiates one Sephirah from another, and the fact of manifestation that differentiates the Sephiroth from the Unmanifest. Thus it can be seen that the spheres of the Tree and the source from which they spring share a fundamental underlying *unity* — as do the four Worlds, the Triads, the Pillars, and all the other components of the Tree — and this wholeness of being means that the entire Tree system, from 'first swirlings' into final manifestation, experiences influences in common. What affects a part affects all.

Qabalists consider the undivided unity of the Sephiroth to form a Great Man (see Figure 9).

This figure is variously called *Zaur Anpin, Adam Kadmon, Heavenly Man, Microposopos,* or *The Lesser Countenance,* and can be imagined standing with Kether (the Crown) above and resting upon its head, and Malkuth (the Kingdom) beneath its feet. A line of force representing the Middle Pillar stretches between these two Sephiroth, while D'aath (the unnumbered and 'invisible' Sephirah that is placed astride the Abyss between the Sephiroth Kether and Tiphareth) is positioned at the throat; Tiphareth at the breast, and Yesod at the

Figure 9: Hildegard's Vision of the Godhead, Nature, and Man; from *Liber Divinorum Operum Simplicis Hominis*.

genitals. Thus it can be seen that the descending Triangle of Spirit meets and merges with the ascending Triangle of Matter within the figure of Adam Kadmon, which is so arranged upon the Sephiroth as to encompass within itself their inherent qualities of *will, intellect* and *emotion*.

Zaur Anpin is the *archetype* upon which man himself is patterned; and because man's body is considered to be a copy of that of Heavenly Man, the upper and lower Worlds are thought to meet in him also, exactly as they do in his heavenly 'prototype' — Kether, D'aath, Tiphareth, Yesod and Malkuth forming his spiritual, intellectual, emotional, magnetic, and functional centres respectively.

In man, however, the *potential of action* in the material world that is applicable to Adam Kadmon becomes the *capability of action*, so that *Neschamah* (the Spiritual Self — spheres 1, 2 and 3), *Ruach* (the Higher Self — spheres 4, 5 and 6), and *Nephesch*, (the Personality — spheres 7, 8 and 9) have the potential to reflect into each other and react upon the World of Assiah.

Thus man, like his archetype Adam Kadmon, is thought to contain within himself a Triad of elements, each one of which has its source in one of the Sephiroth of the three Triads of the Tree, and all of which are pre-existent in the world of Atziluth; for — so far as Qabalists are concerned in any event — man existed in the Atziluthic body of Adam Kadmon before Creation began, and he alone constitutes the only *complete* image of the Divine, all other creatures being *based* upon the Adam of Atziluth but left in some way *incomplete*.

The idea that man, and man alone, is the image of the Divine is based upon the fact that Zaur Anpin — Heavenly Man — is itself patterned upon *Arik Anpin* the *Great Countenance* or *Macroposopos*.

The Great Countenance is in essence a reflection of the Unmanifest — a manifestation, in other words, of negative existence. Because this is so, man is directly linked through the Sephiroth to the ultimate source of Creation and is effectively patterned directly upon the Creator. Hence, of course, the verse in Genesis which says: 'So God created man in His own image, in the image of God created He him; male and female created He them'.

The manner in which the archetypal link between man and the Creator is formed through the Sephiroth means that the powers of the Sephiroth are active in man; and that he has the power to influence them — and through them all Creation — for better or worse. In short, man is considered to exist *beside* the Sephiroth rather than *on* or *as a part of* them, simply because he has inherent within him the capability of *transcending* them.

Arik Anpin — the Greater Countenance — has its roots in Kether and is formed of those Sephiroth which go to make up the Supernal Triangle. Arik Zaur, on the other hand, has its roots in Tiphareth and is made up of Sephiroth 4 to 9. Thus the Sephirah Malkuth is excluded from the construction of either 'Countenance'; and from this fact it may be correctly surmised that this particular sphere occupies a singular position within the scheme of things.

As the last of the Sephiroth, Malkuth is the most complicated of all the spheres. It represents the culmination of the essential unity of creation mentioned above. It is the 'point of completion' — the final expression of the harmonious force first emanated from the

Unmanifest — and because it is the 'point of completion', it enjoys a special relationship with the Unmanifest, which is the 'point of inception'. Indeed, these two 'ends of the spectrum of creation' form a polarity and are, effectively, complementary opposites.

This latter polarity is based upon the fact that the Unmanifest *is* the Creator, emanating all creation *of* itself, while the sphere of Malkuth *is* Creation, or *the Creator's self made manifest*. Thus Malkuth (which implies and actually means 'the presence of the Creator in Creation') not only contains within itself the presence of the Creator, ubiquitous and divine, but actually *is* the Creator, or — more properly — *is* a facet thereof.

The Qabalistic title of Malkuth is 'the Bride of Microposopos' or 'the Inferior Mother' — just as Binah, the sphere with which, as I said in Chapter 4, Malkuth is closely associated, is said to be 'the Bride of Macroposopos' or 'the Great Mother'. This fresh title for Malkuth reveals what would at first glance appear to be a fresh and autonomous polarity between that sphere as *Kallah*, the Queen, and Microposopos, the King; but the title is in reality only expressing the original and fundamental polarity mentioned above upon another, and more material level.

The Microposopos/Kallah polarity is therefore essentially a reflection of the Creator/Creation pairing (a fact which is best appreciated by reference to those spheres which are said to be the 'roots' of Arik and Zaur Anpin and the relationship between the respective 'Brides' of the two 'Countenances'), and its function and existence provide important clues as to the nature of a third coupling — that which exists between man and Malkuth.

In this latter pairing, Malkuth becomes *the Shechinah* (which means 'the manifestation of the divine in the lives of men') and the nature of the relationship that exists between man and the Shechinah is best expressed by yet another verse from Genesis: 'And God blessed them, and God said unto them, Be fruitful, and multiply, and replenish the earth, and subdue it: and have dominion over the fish of the sea, and over the fowl of the air, and over every living thing that moveth upon the earth.'

It is very important, however, when evaluating this piece of prose and attempting to come to terms with this particular relationship, to bear in mind all that has gone before.

We have said, for instance, that Malkuth (under whatever name) *is* Creation, and that Creation *is*, in effect, the Creator, or a facet thereof.

We have also said that man is patterned upon Zaur Anpin, which is patterned upon Arik Anpin, which is in turn a reflection of the Creator.

Given a little thought, it therefore becomes obvious that everything that *is*, is infused with the Divine nature of the Creator, and further that man's function within the scheme of things is to act as the essential third force in a Triad of forces that is made up of Creator, Creation and Created, *all of which* forces *are* the Creator, or facets thereof, the differences between each being a matter of level, nature and degree.

In the beginning, the unity of Creator and Creation was complete; but due to what is usually called 'the Fall of Man', the perfection of the cosmic scheme was upset and perverted.

So far as man was concerned, this latter failure of perfection meant that the Shechinah — instead of being present in *all* men — 'went into exile' and thus came to exist only in a *few* special men. From the point of view of Creation as a whole, however, it meant that the will of the Creator — and so Creation itself — was imperfectly expressed.

In order to understand the reality behind these concepts, it is necessary to first come to an understanding of what is really meant by 'the Fall of Man'.

In general, the Fall is considered to be a descent into evil, caused by the sin of Adam, who ate from the Tree of Knowledge at the instigation of Eve.

In reality, however, the Fall is a descent into manifestation, one of the by-products of which is 'evil'.

The fact that 'evil' is a by-product of manifestation does not, of course, mean that manifestation itself is 'evil' — and it is very important to understand that this is so, and hold onto the fact firmly, for many erroneous ideas have stemmed from this misinterpretation of the relationship that exists between dense matter and 'sin'.

According to Qabalistic thought, evil is unbalanced force and unbalanced force is a side effect of *duality*.

True duality — as opposed to that which is merely inherent — appears only when true differentiation appears; and it is important in this context to observe that unbalanced force makes it first appearance on the Tree *below the Abyss* (the Veil that divides the Superiors from the Inferiors) in the World of Formation, where the 'Fall of Man' also occurs.

Above the Abyss, in the higher Worlds, manifestation itself is fully potential, but it is not actual — and in effect it is not inevitable either. Thus, above the Abyss all remains essentially and *consciously* one, despite the duality that is inherent within it.

Below the Abyss, however, in the World of Formation, the dual and related aspects of male and female take up active and passive roles, bringing about true duality and differentiation. Thereafter, manifestation becomes actual — and inevitable. At this point, all still remains, of course, *essentially* one; but it is no longer *consciously* one. It is differentiated, and consequently suffers from the illusion of separateness. Thus within the arena of actual — as opposed to potential — manifestation, all the spheres of the Tree reflect actual duality; and each has a positive and a negative polarity, a vice and a virtue, a balanced and an unbalanced aspect.

The deviation from the plan caused by the appearance of duality and its side-product, unbalanced force, forced the Creator to undertake a work of salvation (which means 'safe return home', incidentally) in order to restore the unity of the Worlds. Because man is patterned upon Adam Kadmon, and is thus the only complete image of the Creator, he is also the Creator's most direct link with Creation. Logically, therefore, this work of restoration, or *Yichud*, takes place *through* man, whose primary function in manifestation is the complete and perfect realization of the Divine intention.

Yichud occurs through a gradual process of realization *within* man, who alone is capable of perceiving all the Worlds and who, looking inward and outward, increases unity above and below.

Man refines the fabric of the elements and thus 'initiates' them; raising the consciousness of the planetary body and all life upon it — pulling it with him Age after Age along the great spiral of evolution. He has already passed through the levels of consciousness that correspond to the vegetable period of mere survival, and has mastered those which correspond to the animal period of striving for dominance. His next step — already visible — is the greater awareness and spirituality by means of which he may unify all three of the lower Worlds within himself and thus inevitably within the cosmic whole.

Man's place in the scheme of things as described by Qabalists is obviously a very important one. Indeed, as 'Lord of the Earth', man occupies a pre-eminent place in Creation. But — at first glance, in any event — this 'pride of place' is not accorded him in the Tarot deck, where the cards representing him sometimes appear to be (and are frequently treated as) nothing more than a rather uninteresting appendage to the Minor Arcana. But this apparent relegation of man to a 'poor third' within the deck is deceiving.

In Chapter 3 — following tradition — I stated that the Minor Arcana consisted of four suits, each one of which could be divided as to Small cards and Court cards. In reality, however, apart from suit symbolism and a mutual association with the four elements, Court cards have little in common with Small cards and, in fact, there is nothing save common usage to suggest that Court cards were ever intended to form part of what is now called 'the Minor Arcana' at all. Indeed, the fundamental differences that exist between Court cards and Small cards are manifold — and all become particularly obvious when the Small cards are examined in the light of their relationship to the Tree of Life, and their basic function is contrasted with that of the Major Arcana cards.

Placed as they are on the Sephiroth, Small cards follow a clear and consecutive route from Kether to Malkuth, encompassing all four elements and all four Worlds. In this, they achieve a universality of expression and an essential wholeness of being within the deck that is quite foreign to the Court cards which, you will recall, are confined absolutely in both expression and action to HEH final — the area in which the Small cards merely achieve their final function.

In fact, it is only when the Court cards are viewed as an entity in their own right — virtually as a third Arcana, and free of the arbitrary alliance with the Small cards created by their implied inclusion in the Minor Arcana — that any hint of their true nature can be grasped at all; for it is only then that their function as a link between, and a focus for, the Major Arcana and the Small cards becomes apparent.

Small cards, as I have said, represent dynamic forces which, in essence, mirror an intricate web of trends. Those trends eventually manifest as a circumstantial environment which varies in response to the reaction of human consciousness, thus giving birth to events.

Major Arcana cards are placed on the *Netibuth* of the Tree — the twenty-two pathways which link the Sephiroth into the coherent pattern you see on Figure 12 on page 125 — and *underlie* the concepts symbolized by the Sephiroth.

Netibuth conduct the forces of *cosmic consciousness* — the complex web of mind-stuff upon which the entire structure of reality on every level is built — and therefore function (as do the Major Arcana cards that are associated with them) in the *world of mind*, Yetzirah of Assiah, the formative world that stands behind manifestation. Netibuth are therefore essentially excluded from direct or immediate function in Assiah of Assiah, and Major Arcana cards are not considered to have any reference to the element of Earth at all, as the attributions given in Chapters 7 and 8 reveal.

When all these facts regarding the function and areas of influence of the Small and Major Arcana cards are considered together with the apparently limited area of function permitted the Court cards, it immediately becomes apparent that Court cards offer a *means of expression* for the forces represented by the Major Arcana cards, and *interact* with the forces represented by the Small cards. Indeed, Court cards might almost be said to be *focuses for the former upon the latter* — a scheme which precisely accords with the Qabalistic assessment of man's function and purpose as outlined in this chapter.

Chapter 6.

Images in Miniature

As stated in Chapter 3, there are sixteen Court cards altogether. These are divided by suit into four 'families' or related groups, and between them they represent sixteen permutations of the four elements with which the four suits are identified.

The four elements have always been associated with *the four humours*, which divide humanity into four basic personality types — the *choleric*, *sanguine*, *bilious* and *melancholic* temperaments of Classical and Medieval literature.

These four 'temperaments' correspond to the elements of Fire, Water, Air and Earth respectively and — obviously — they are less 'personality profiles' than caricatures pure and simple, for they are over-stated, over-drawn, and a good deal less than lifelike. Despite this, however, it is unwise to dismiss the four humours out of hand as being useless or merely quaint. The humours do not, after all, pretend to indicate what *is* the case when the elements manifest in man in a *blended* and *interdependent* condition — as of course they do in reality — but only what *would be* the case were the elements to manifest in him in a *pure* condition. In this latter task they succeed very well, so that although the 'portraits' they provide are fundamentally unrealistic, they nevertheless offer very broad but essentially quite accurate guidelines to the fundamentals of human psychology.

It is therefore well worth our while looking at the characteristics associated with each of the four humours here, if only because they offer a ready-made, tried-and-true basis from which to begin to draw narrower, more realistic and more precise conclusions about the role of the four elements in the human constitution.

THE FOUR HUMOURS

The Choleric Temperament

The first of the temperaments, the *choleric*, is attributed to the element of Fire and hence to the suit of Staves, and the three Fiery signs of the Zodiac — Aries, Leo and Sagittarius.

Fire is *radiant* energy. It is associated with heat, light, will, and speed. When energy like this is expressed in human terms, it produces strong, outgoing and sometimes overpowering personalities in which all experience is centred in self and personal identity. There is an intense desire for self-expression; for activity, for direct intervention, for speed of action and reaction.

Because these latter qualities are invariably uppermost in the temperament, overshadowing the more pleasing and less abrasive attributes of the nature, Fiery individuals can appear to be self-centred, impersonal, tactless, over-hasty and destructive to both physical things and the feelings of other people; but it must be borne in mind that such destructive behaviour — although there is no doubt that it frequently occurs — is not deliberate. Indeed, as individuals, people of choleric temperament have a very strong sense of justice and fair play; and an excellent and well-deserved reputation — particularly when it comes to friendship — for courage, loyalty, and honesty.

It must be remembered also that negative qualities of any kind are often merely an overplus or excess of positive characteristics — and this fact is particularly germane to the Fiery temperament, which finds moderation in anything difficult due to its abundance of energy.

Thus pride, arrogance, jealousy, intolerance, vindictiveness, self-interest and violence are all qualities that are potential in the Fiery nature, and all inevitably find outward expression at some time or another. Fortunately, however, these latter unpleasant tendencies are both mitigated and limited by the very factors that cause their appearance in the first place. Fire is too volatile to sustain any emotion for very long, and thus expression of the negative aspects of the nature, however regularly they occur, are in general as fleeting as they are violent. The choleric temperament is basically generous, good-humoured and expansive: its frequent quarrels are soon over and genuinely forgotten simply because the nature itself is constitutionally incapable of brooding or bearing a grudge.

The only real flaw in the nature, therefore, lies in its lack of self-control and its insensitivity to the feelings of others — either of which qualities can, if given free reign, lead to self-indulgence and a destructive, theatrical, and superficial approach to life.

The Sanguine Temperament

The second of the four humours is the sanguine temperament, which is associated with the element of Water, the suit of Cups, and the three Watery signs of the Zodiac — Pisces, Cancer and Scorpio.

Individuals of sanguine temperament are optimistic, happy-go-lucky people who generally possess great personal grace and the indefinable gifts of charm and magnetism. Unfortunately, however, they are rarely either constant or very reliable.

To a very large degree, these latter failings are due to the fact that Watery individuals are inclined to be very much — sometimes too much — in touch with *feelings*, both their own and those of other people; and are in addition uncommonly susceptible to the subtle levels of life. Thus, they are often unconscious of much that motivates their actions and reactions — or even that they have been so motivated at all — because while they are naturally in touch with the intangible factors and subtle forces that lie immediately behind the facade of reality (and frequently draw on the information gained from that source to their own advantage) they remain unaware on a conscious level that this is so.

The strong natural link with the subconscious realms and subtle levels of being that is possessed by all individuals of Watery temperament enhances their latent sensuality, psychism and artistic potential. In addition, the innate sensitivity of the temperament makes them deeply emotional and poetic people who, because the heart rules the head in natures of this kind, are in general kindly, compassionate, tolerant, and also fervent.

However, the same unconscious contact with the subtle realms that provides the essentially attractive qualities outlined above is equally inclined, in its negative aspect, to produce shallow, manipulative and emotionally unstable individuals who lack consistent personal shape and identity. Thus the face individuals of sanguine temperament present to the world can shift chameleon-like to please — or placate, or fool — the onlooker; their vivid imagination leads them to lie on a consistent basis, and the willingness that their apparent fragility and great charm inspires in others to nurture and protect can in turn inspire them to extraordinary selfishness and enormous laziness.

All Watery signs are easily swayed by people, 'atmospshere', and other of the subtle nuances of life, and it is therefore only too easy to conclude that they are fundamentally weak and vacillating. In this context, however, it is important to bear in mind that the fluid element of Water is immensely strong — the strongest, indeed, of all the elements. The sanguine temperament is not *weak*, it is *lazy*. Moreover, although it is a temperament that rarely attacks, and is also one that gives ground very easily when threatened; by its very nature it invariably wins the all-important last round of any battle.

The Bilious Temperament

The bilious temperament corresponds to the element of Air, the suit of Swords, and the three Airy signs of the Zodiac — Gemini, Libra and Aquarius.

Just as individuals of sanguine temperament are oriented towards feeling, so individuals of bilious temperament are oriented towards *thinking*, the whole emphasis of their being lying in the realms of the theoretical and the abstract.

Individuals of Airy temperament are intellectual, clever, and logical. They have a great desire to give and receive knowledge and the capacity to do either with ease. They are highly articulate, communicative and well-informed, and consequently make brilliant and interesting conversationalists. *But* — they are very inquisitive. It is difficult to prevent persons of bilious temperament finding out something — whatever it may be — that they *really* want to know.

Individuals of bilious temperament possess a marked degree of manual and mental dexterity, and are very careful, diligent and persevering in everything they undertake. Their natural detachment enables them to gain perspective and utilize an objective and rational approach to all things.

This latter quality in particular can sometimes make those of bilious temperament appear cold and unfeeling; but in fact they make very good and firm friends — and equally bad enemies.

The negative side of the temperament stems to a large degree from simple pride in its gifts. Individuals of Airy temperament are proud of their intellectual attainments and capacity. They dislike having their opinions or the quality of their intellect disparaged, and have a particular dislike of being ignored. They are inclined, in addition, to project their own failings onto others, and are consequently frequently extremely mistrustful and suspicious.

The leaning toward the theoretical side of life which enables individuals of this temperament to cope so well with abstractions can, in its negative aspect, incline them towards mental imbalance, eccentricity, and fanaticism — and may, if taken to extremes, end in their becoming totally out of touch with reality. On the negative side, also, the prudence and carefulness inherent in the nature can err on the side of parsimony, for there is a tendency in any event to value small issues in all things at the expense of larger and more important ones.

In general, however, the truly negative side of the Airy temperament simply produces 'care-for-nobody's' — cynical, vacillating, shallow, posturing and deceitful individuals who consider nobody's opinion and feelings but their own.

The Melancholic Temperament

The melancholic temperament corresponds to the element of Earth, the suit of Coins, and the three Earthy signs of the Zodiac — Virgo, Taurus, and Capricorn.

Individuals of this temperament respond best to *manifest reality*; the world of the physical senses, the here-and-now. They are inclined to rely on practical reason and the witness of their own senses to the total exclusion of everything else; and have a very great understanding of exactly how the physical world works. Consequently, these people have more patience with the material in all its many aspects than individuals of any other temperament. They are, in addition, generally thrifty, practical, industrious, stable, conscientious, reliable, punctual, conservative and prudent — and in consequence are often considered to be rather dull by others of less staid turn of mind.

Because Earthy individuals have a practical grasp of the mechanics of life on the physical plane, they are clever in financial matters, and make very good organizers. Additionally, under a slow-thinking — and sometimes very blunt — exterior, they are often very soft-hearted, obliging, and tolerant of the weaknesses of others.

However, where lies the greatest strength of the melancholic temperament also lies its greatest weakness. With the best will in the world, people of this temperament cannot free themselves of their concern with the material. The subtle is to them a closed book, and their lack of ability to deal with the abstract in any form is total. The same preoccupation with the practical and material side of life also limits the imagination, and can lead to an increasing narrowness of outlook and an addiction to neatness, routine and order.

At its most negative, the Earthy temperament produces mean, dull, and rather stupid individuals. Negative melancholics are materialistic and avaricious — despite a tendency to be both wasteful and prodigal when it comes to themselves and their own comfort — capricious, foolish, and self-pitying. Frequently beset by self-doubt and suspicion of their fellows, they can also be both fussy and hypercritical.

In addition, it should be remembered that because this temperament is essentially goal-oriented in nature, it is inclined — in either its positive or its negative aspect — to produce a single-minded and utterly ruthless pursuit of success and power for its own sake.

THE COURT CARDS

As we have previously explained, the four elements that are associated with the four humours are considered to be the basic components of existence which, when blended together, produce manifestation.

Each of these elements has two properties — e.g. Fire has the properties of dryness and heat; Water those of fluidity and coldness; Air those of heat and fluidity, and Earth those of coldness and dryness. Thus the elements blend by means of their shared properties — Fire into Air by heat, and so on, as per Figure 10.

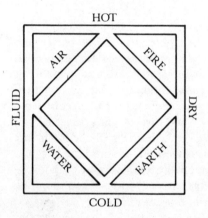

Figure 10: The Qualities of the Four Elements.

The various combinations of the four elements illustrated by this figure are the source of the 'personality profiles' offered by the Court cards; the elements associated with each individual card being specified by the 'elemental name' allotted to it. Thus the four basic personality types described by the four humours are expanded four-fold in the Tarot to number sixteen by means of combining the elements according to the rules governing their qualities and the progression of force symbolized by the four Worlds.

In this way, *twelve* of the Court cards are associated with *two* elements each — a 'predominant' one, which is determined by suit, and a 'subservient' one, which is determined by the name or face pattern of the card and its position on the Tree of Life — while *four* of the Court cards are governed by only *one* element, and are thus considered to be the 'essence' of their suit (see Figure 8, page 37).

THE SUIT OF STAVES

> **Predominant element:** Fire.
> **Predominant qualities:** urge for action, self assertion, recognition. Pride. Sense of drama. Vitality. Energy. Temper. Idealism. Generosity.

The King of Staves

*Prince of the Chariot of Fire**
Prince and Emperor of the Salamanders

Air of Fire
When Fire is the predominant element in an elemental equation composed of Air and Fire, the resulting individual will be both creative and idealistic. In addition, he will possess the ability and drive to put his plentiful ideas into action — but only in the short term, for inherent in the same equation there is a distinct lack of any appetite for prolonged hard work or the physical and mental stamina to undertake it. There is therefore an acute need for these individuals to complete any project quickly, before the original impetus dissipates or is rechannelled into other areas.

The combination usually produces clever, skilful, active people who

* The titles allotted to the cards were conceived by those members of the Golden Dawn who were responsible for the production of the Order deck. In that deck, Pages are entitled 'Princesses' — a title that obviously well befits cards associated with the sphere that is called 'the Bride of Microposopos' — thus balancing the Court cards evenly between masculine and feminine forces. For more information about the card titles, see Chapter 7, page 124, 'The Esoteric Title'.

can, however, be rather domineering. In addition, while the presence of subtle and diplomatic Air certainly modifies the outspoken, rather tactless qualities of the Fiery personality, it cannot negate them altogether and, indeed, often serves only to exacerbate Fire's tendency to talk out of turn by lending it a fluency that it would not otherwise possess. Thus, this particular combination is only too given to making barbed remarks and cutting speeches that it afterwards lives to regret.

The really negative qualities of the equation, however, are a tendency to hide Airy craftiness and deceit under the wholly open and guileless countenance common to the Fiery personality — which can lead to Fiery displays of temper that are literally 'produced to order', stage managed in order to cow or impress others — and a disposition to erratic and tyrannical behaviour, particularly in a domestic environment.

The Queen of Staves

Queen of the Thrones of Flame
Queen of the Salamanders

Water of Fire
This combination produces excitable, impressionable individuals with a marked lack of self-discipline and self-control; for the hysterical tendency of the Watery temperament and the rashness of the Fiery one cannot help but exacerbate each other.

Such individuals are impulsive, emotional, explosively unpredictable: temper can give way to tears, or caresses to blows, with bewildering speed and regularity. In addition, and although the combination itself is intensely creative, Water of Fire individuals lack logic and the capability of building or adhering to a system, so that the creative projects they are so good at formulating rarely reach an altogether successful conclusion on the material plane.

On the other hand, however, individuals of this nature work very well under the sort of intense pressure that would destroy people of more even temperament, and they are in addition generally warm, supportive and protective towards people they like or those weaker than themselves.

Their most negative quality is a Watery tendency towards emotional blackmail, which is inclined to manifest in Water of Fire as frighteningly hysterical behaviour or extravagant threats. They also suffer from the purely Fiery attribute of an enduring and irritating egotism and selfishness.

All in all, therefore, Water of Fire needs to be handled very carefully and firmly by its relatives and friends, for the temperament is such that it will rule the lives of those around it if not curbed — a state of affairs that suits it very well, since it is essentially manipulative in type.

The Knight of Staves

Lord of the Flame and the Lightning
King of the Spirits of Fire
King of the Salamanders

Fire of Fire
Individuals ruled by a single element in this way generally suffer from that overplus that results in positive qualities becoming negative ones — and this is particularly true of Fire of Fire, for there is a very great danger that individuals of this type will use their abundance of energy unwisely and 'burn themselves out'.

The overruling quality of the temperament is hyper-activity. Fire of Fire people are over-concerned with doing things — making things happen — and this can cause problems for them both physically and in their relationships with other people. Certainly their impulsiveness, self-centredness and desire to act directly and immediately are not endearing qualities — particularly when they result as they often do, in an insensitive and crude approach.

At best, Fire of Fire individuals are self-motivated go-getters who consistently and successfully start new enterprises. They are extremely idealistic, have tremendous courage and energy, and can be passionately interested in the welfare of those less fortunate than themselves. Indeed, if the nature can be steered towards enterprises in this latter area in particular, all will go very well for it.

The negative qualities of the temperament naturally all show the disastrous results of the over-plus factor to a very marked degree. Negatively oriented Fire of Fire individuals are over-confident, self-indulgent and given to exaggeration. They are in addition generally vain, self-important and fond of pomp, grandeur and personal display. Most dangerously of all, they are attracted to both drugs and alcohol, for these things are *like* the Fiery temperament, and this — obviously — can lead them into grave difficulties.

The Page of Staves

Princess of the Shining Flame
The Rose of the Palace of Fire
Princess and Empress of the Salamanders
Throne of the Ace of Staves

Earth of Fire
This is one of the most creative and productive of all the elemental combinations illustrated by the Court cards, for the addition of subservient Earth to predominant Fire lends the latter the stability and stamina it needs.

Individuals of this temperament have both the will and the power to succeed in the material world. They love to work, gaining their greatest satisfaction from seeing the results of their energies manifested in the world. They prefer to work in large organizations that give sufficient scope for their expansive personalities and suitable channels for their competitive instincts rather than in small one-man businesses — and thus it is large enterprises and huge and powerful corporate structures with far-flung interests that attract Earth of Fire.

Earth of Fire people are not generally given to reflection about themselves or others, and this is their worst shortcoming, for it makes them steamrollers — blunt, outspoken, and overbearing to a degree. The mixture of confidence, egotism and humility that is typical of Earth of Fire leads them to do their best for others — to arrange lives and outings with equal impartiality and genuine thoughtfulness — for they are, on the whole, kindly disposed and often astonishingly generous towards their fellow men. Sadly, however, the qualities mentioned above also leads Earth of Fire to concern itself in the affairs of others — albeit with the best intentions — when others would really prefer them not to do so; and this gains them not the recognition and liking they seek, but a reputation for meddling and interfering.

Earth of Fire people are inclined to expect much too much of others, too, simply because their own standards and capabilities are so high, and their constitution so strong. Thus, if you want this individual to notice that you are not feeling well, and are therefore not able to undertake the extremely fatiguing and activity-full schedule they have planned for you, then you will have to tell them so, for they would never notice this fact for themselves.

Earth of Fire individuals are on the whole very likeable, genuine and well-meaning people; but they are nevertheless nearly always extremely ambitious and frequently unbearably irritating and abrasive to others of more sensitive make-up. They are not, however, generally inclined to misuse the power they seek if perchance they find it in their hands, being more inclined to philanthropy than they would appear to be on the surface.

THE SUIT OF CUPS

Predominant element: Water
Predominant qualities:
Emotional. Moody. Sensitive. Self-protective. Deep. Secretive. Idealistic. Vulnerable. Passionate. Poetic.

The King of Cups

Prince of the Chariot of the Waters
Prince and Emperor
of the Nymphs and Undines

Air of Water
This is the most sensitive of the combinations, and is therefore the one which produces the poet, the mystic, the artist and the dreamer — and, of course, the escapist, the liar and the fantasy-prone malcontent.

Air of Water individuals are very attractive to others generally, and super attractive to the opposite sex. They have great wit and charm, and an unfailing talent for making the right gesture, saying the right thing. They have genuine creative ability in both the Arts and the Sciences; very fertile imaginations, and a great capacity for verbalizing the unconscious. They are sensual, entertaining, thoughtful, and very kind.

Air of Water unites conscious and subconscious, and the child of this union has an intense awareness — of itself, of others, and of life itself. In private life, this quality makes Air of Water a voyeur of life — a confirmed people-watcher. In a commercial world, it makes him a negotiator, an arbitrator, a barrister, and an actor.

The same quality enables Air of Water to fulfil its greatest need. Individuals of this particular temperament are essentially unreliable in any area unless they are happy — and they are happiest where they can exploit their own best asset, which is themselves. Clever, gregarious and witty, Air of Water is always to be found 'up-front' — but they do not enjoy this public exposure so much as actually *need* it. Consequently they make very bad 'back room boys' — tied to a desk and some inconspicuous corner — and rarely stay in such an environment for very long.

Because Air of Water is so sensitive and so aware itself, it is hyper-sensitive to the feelings of others and will go to extraordinary lengths to avoid hurting another person. Sadly, this often backfires — either on the other person involved or on themselves. Air of Water finds it impossible to say goodbye — and is thus content either to remain in a uncomfortable situation, present in body but noticeably absent in spirit, or to disappear suddenly and completely without any warning at all. In either state, they are almost impossible to pin down, because their dislike of 'upsetting others' causes them to avoid confrontation either by backing down or by lying — which is one of their greatest faults, and something they do very well. Frequently, this behaviour deprives their partners of any ability to 'clear the air' and bring things out in the open, so that both parties exist in an increasingly fluid and tenuous atmosphere that only one of them is able to exploit, or even tolerate, with any equanimity.

It is, therefore, the quality of fluidity that causes all the problems in this combination — the very quality that gives it its greatest gifts, and makes it such an attractive personality in the first place.

Air of Water people can be extremely selfish, compulsive 'Walter Mitty'-like individuals. Indeed, in their negative aspect they are given to extremes of behaviour generally, and can prove in the last analysis to be aware only of their own emotional needs and comfort, and totally — indeed, wilfully — blind to those of others.

The Queen of Cups

Queen of the Thrones of the Waters
Queen of Nymphs and Undines

Water of Water
Water of Water is another 'single element' temperament, and all that we have said above about such temperaments naturally applies to this one too.

Water of Water people are receptive, understanding, compassionate, modest, abstemious, tranquil, graceful, artistic, imaginative, loving, sensual, *and* extremely manipulative. They are also much too easily influenced by others, being overly impressionable. They lack emotional self-control, and their ease of access to the subtle side of life can lead them to be eternally apprehensive, insecure, fearful, and self-protective; and these qualities in turn can make them compulsively demanding and, as has been said, frighteningly manipulative. They are inclined, too, to suffer from hypochondria, and to develop negative reaction patterns which cause relationships of any kind consistently to founder on the rock of one single bad experience.

In addition, Water of Water has a tendency to withdraw from life's challenges into some secret fantasy world which can become much more real to them than reality itself — and this is particularly so, of course, if there happens to be someone else conveniently to hand to take up those challenges for them.

Individuals of this temperament literally must be involved in active concern for others if their inherently negative qualities are not to get the better of them; for, once dedicated to an ideal, Water of Water forgets itself completely and is satisfied to pour out its talents in service to others.

There is usually a natural attunement to spiritual and occult realities and a very marked psychic ability inherent in this combination — and once again, all will go well if only the nature can find its level and stabilize itself. If it does not, however, disaster will swiftly follow in the form of increasing hysteria, mental instability and nervous breakdown, for this aspect of the temperament is particularly prone to fall victim to its own negative potential.

The Knight of Cups

Lord of the Waves and of the Waters
King of the Hosts of the Sea
King of Nymphs and Undines

Fire of Water
Fire of Water people make great entertainers. They love display, and they love to display themselves — particularly to an admiring audience,

the larger the better. They have the ability to project their feelings convincingly, and — more importantly — to genuinely produce those feelings for an audience. In other words, they have real histrionic talent.

Unfortunately, this remains the case whether a Fire of Water individual takes to the boards or not; and in private life the very gifts that make these people such wonderful entertainers can become very wearing — for themselves as much as for other people.

Fire of Water is very intense — given to emotional extremes and severe swings of mood. As individuals they are extremely sensitive to what other people say and think, and can become very suddenly elated or depressed accordingly. There is a tendency, too, to 'take on a character' and wear it to suit the occasion. Unfortunately, it is obviously impossible to sustain any given character for ever if it is not very close indeed to the genuine one; and thus while Fire of Water is very good at getting jobs and making friends, it is often not terribly good at keeping either.

The combination is basically a dissonant one anyway. There is a very great conflict in the nature between the Fiery love of freedom and the Watery need of attachment: between aspiration and a need for security. This conflict is rarely resolved unless the Fire of Water individual can find an environment that allows him to enjoy the best of both worlds. It is therefore particularly important that this combination finds a job to suit it, and people that are understanding and supportive of its needs.

The Page of Cups

Princess of the Waters
Lotus of the Palace of the Floods
Princess and Empress of Nymphs and Undines
Throne of the Ace of Cups

Earth of Water

Because Water is the predominant element in this equation, the Earth of Water individual is motivated by feelings. Unfortunately, the admixture of the element of Earth turns all those feelings in a single direction — towards the material.

Earth of Water people seek security above all else. They lack the faith in the subtle that is the birthright of all other Water-oriented souls, and this dearth of faith and solid ideals causes them to revere the past and all traditional values, and to fear the future and all innovation.

Often too, they are conditioned by the past — as Watery individuals are inclined to be — and thus live their lives by rote, depending on habit to see them through.

At their best, these individuals are intellectual, artistic, responsible and practical; but frequently these talents and abilities lack development or direction. Earth of Water does not have the self-confidence in its own ability to take much trouble with self-improvement, and positive thinking is not its forté.

Like all Watery people, too, Earth of Water individuals tend to be manipulative — particularly, of course, when it comes to matters of the home, that great symbol of security.

THE SUIT OF SWORDS

Predominant element: Air
Predominant qualities: Balance. Impartiality. Individualism. Tactfulness. Curiosity. Friendliness. Talkativeness. Extremism. Love of Freedom. Changeability.

The King of Swords

Prince of the Chariot of the Winds
Prince and Emperor of Sylphs and Sylphides

Air of Air
Air of Air is the third of the four 'single element' temperaments. These individuals are intellectual, clever, logical, detached and self-possessed. Unfortunately, because they are over-active mentally, all these talents frequently go to waste.

Air of Air people are worriers, prey to endless second thoughts. They are invariably full of plans, but these rarely come to anything because the execution of plans demands decisiveness, and real decisiveness is something that these individuals lack.

Above all, Air of Air *dabbles*. The mental and manual dexterity and inquisitiveness of Air is obviously present in Air of Air as it is in all individuals of Airy temperament; but the over-plus of the element usually results in dissatisfaction with any conclusions reached, and with the fruits of any labour undertaken.

Thus projects and interests — and jobs and people — are regularly taken up by individuals of this type, and just as regularly dropped. Air of Air people always have a new interest — or hobby, job or friend — that is always more interesting than anything or anyone they have seen, or thought about, or met with before; but none ever last long, and all are quickly replaced with something or someone else.

Air of Air also tends to be over-cautious, wasteful of its energy and resources, and extremely deceitful and crafty. The tendency to project their own failings onto others that is always present in the element of Air is very marked indeed in Air of Air — as are distrust and suspicion.

Thus, Air of Air's failings are all directly attributable to those qualities that are its best attributes — and this is particularly noticeable when it comes to the extremes of the negative aspects of the temperament.

Individuals who can't do anything without thinking about it incessantly and at great length not only rarely achieve anything worthwhile, but frequently fall victim to paralysis of will as well. In addition, they can suffer severe psychological disorders stemming from the same basic cause. To make matters worse, there is a pronounced tendency to ignore the body that houses and feeds the organ of thought, and this results in the sort of physical exhaustion that is very detrimental to the already over-sensitive nervous system.

The Queen of Swords

Queen of the Thrones of the Air
Queen of the Sylphs and Sylphides

Water of Air
Here is a dichotomy, and it is a very difficult one, for it is that of the intellect and the emotions.

The positive side of Water of Air brings this temperament the capability of using both abstract and intuitive thought with ease. It gives depth to their ideas and allows them to view their feelings with detachment and perspective. At the same time, however, the combination can be disconcerting to others, for sometimes the actions of a Water of Air do not match their words — or vice versa.

Water of Air combinations make good counsellors, welfare officers and the like, because their natural qualities are admirably suited to such employment; but these very qualities are also those that produce the very worst aspect of the combination.

The most markedly negative quality of Water of Air is a tendency towards gossip, speculation and 'instant analysis'. Water of Air always knows what anyone should do in any given situation, and does not hesitate to say so — to anyone and everyone who will listen. It cannot keep a secret, and frequently cannot differentiate between what it thinks, assumes or supposes to be true, and what is in fact the case. Indeed, so far as this particular combination is concerned, the pronounced faculty of communication which is Air's greatest asset can be grossly and mischievously misused for, sadly, Water of Air can be exceedingly and deliberately malicious and spiteful.

In addition, the combination produces individuals who frequently find it difficult to stop talking; for the Airy desire to 'air its opinions' is particularly marked in this combination — and this can prove unbearably irritating to others in the long term.

It is particularly important that of all the combinations Water of Air should try to channel its qualities in a natural direction because if home and children, an absorbing job, or some other worthwhile outlet for its best gifts does not present itself, the negative qualities of the equation invariably come to the fore — often with disastrous results.

The Knight of Swords

Lord of the Winds and Breezes
King of the Spirit of Air
King of Sylphs and Sylphides

Fire of Air
This is an idealistic, aspiring and positive combination, but it is not a particularly realistic one. Fire of Air individuals are optimistic and creative, but their aspirations and expectations are frequently unrealistically high — with the natural consequence that they

frequently fall victim to disappointment and disillusionment.

It is these unrealistically high expectations, of course, that so frequently cause such pain to their partners and friends. No one can live up to someone else's mental image of perfection indefinitely, because every human being without exception is born with a very good pair of nice serviceable clay feet — and Fire of Air is particularly good at building truly magnificent and unreal images for itself and does not hesitate to superimpose those unwieldly mental structures upon its nearest and dearest.

The combination has marked verbal ability and a keen sense of humour, but unfortunately this latter is all too often cruel, because Fire of Air lacks real emotional depth and so lacks the ability to stand in another's shoes or appreciate another's feelings also. In addition, this type suffers, too, from the Fiery tendency to lash out — but not, as is usual with Fiery temperaments, without thinking first, which is obviously inclined to make matters worse rather than otherwise.

Often, too, this is a combination that can't be bothered with mundane necessities or responsibilities, and lacks the ability to cope with projects that demand persistent effort. It can, in fact, be unacceptably personally scruffy, and is likely to prove a nightmare adolescent.

At best, therefore, the combination produces innovators, scientists, cartoonists, journalists and comedians; at worst, it produces cynical and scruffy 'care-for-nobody's who lack emotional depth and live, as they say, 'in their heads and out of other people's pockets', giving life, and the world — and themselves — the go-by; feeding their own appetites, their own desires, with a total disregard for the feelings, welfare and comfort of others.

The Page of Swords

Princess of the Rushing Winds
Lotus of the Palace of Air
Princess and Empress of the Sylphs and
Sylphides
Throne of the Ace of Swords

Earth of Air
Earth of Air individuals are remarkable for their forethought and practicality. These people have an ability to plan in the abstract those things that must function on a material level, and this makes them excellent architects and very good designers of practical functional

goods. Because Earth of Air distrusts all emotion, however — his own and that of other people — his inherent and quite genuine artistic qualities never blossom as they should. Earth of Air is not a painter — his art is functional after another fashion, and can be rather lifeless and drab.

Like all Airy individuals, Earth of Air is able to detach himself from his immediate environment, and make rational decisions on the basis of logic alone; but in this particular temperament, these latter qualities are marred by the mistrust of emotion that is characteristic of the Earthy temperament.

Earth of Air is essentially a loner, and does nothing without thinking about it first. Consequently, his relationships with other people are frequently rather shallow. This is a combination that has acquaintances rather than friends — and affairs rather than marriages. Indeed, even when the emotions are engaged, the nature is frequently incapable of expressing them well, if at all.

THE SUIT OF COINS

Predominant element: Earth
Predominant qualities: Caution. Self-control. Reserve. Ambition. Possessiveness. Retentiveness. Steadiness. Perfectionism. Discrimination. Analysis.

The King of Coins

Prince of the Chariot of Earth
Prince and Emperor of the Gnomes

Air of Earth
Air of Earth unites the abstract and conceptual faculties of Air with

KING OF COINS

the practicality and efficiency of Earth. There is thus an excellent grounding for its ideas that admirably befits this combination to get things done in the material world.

The temperament is highly work-oriented. Air of Earth enjoys intellectually demanding work — and suffers if this is not available to him. He is extremely ambitious in all things, but his organizational and communicative skills usually take him into local government, because the temperament is essentially analytical and bureaucratic in nature — well-fitted for such a conservative and comparatively rigid environment by its predominant element, from whence comes its neatness, its conservatism, its reliability and its prudence.

Air of Earth is a perfectionist in all things — and expects perfection of others. In addition, individuals of this nature have extraordinary self-control — and expect it of others also. There is an inherent tendency to extend this control over other people, which is sometimes taken to extremes.

These latter tendencies exacerbate the greatest failing of this particular nature, which is an unwillingness to adapt or change — and it *is* unwillingness, for flexibility of mind is certainly inherent in the combination.

Air of Earth's ideas, however, once formulated, are likely to remain unalterably fixed, and may in the course of time become almost fanatically rigid and inflexible. This can make things difficult for its relatives, friends and workmates — and for wives and children in particular — for Air of Earth, always tending to be old-fashioned and inflexible, is less likely than anyone to either tolerate or understand the mental and emotional needs of others, let alone the fads and passions of adolescence.

All in all, indeed, although hardworking, utterly reliable and far from stupid, Air of Earth is dull, mistrustful of emotion, resentful of change and rigid in outlook and attitude.

The Queen of Coins

Queen of the Thrones of the Earth
Queen of the Gnomes

Water of Earth

This combination produces serious, tenacious, and very self-protective people. They are extremely security conscious, and there is therefore a strong adherence to family, home and community, and an equally strong attachment to money, possessions, jobs and children.

Because of these latter factors, and because they are basically both hard-working and conscientious people, Water of Earth individuals dislike holidays away from home (which are inclined to make them feel uncomfortable) or, indeed, holidays of any kind; and will often fill their lives with tasks in and out of the home that are designed to keep them near the home and in a safe, comfortingly familiar environment.

Water of Earth has enormous endurance, and can survive any calamity. Often, indeed, it appears to its best advantage when it is called upon to face, or organize resistance to, catastrophe. In daily life, these estimable qualities usually find their way into jobs that demand loyal, conscientious, 'unflappable' people who are prepared to beaver away in the background while less perfect — and certainly less deserving — mortals take all of the credit and most of the cash.

Individuals of this type are often the linchpin of their family, and will strive to hold it together against all odds — and this holds true whether the 'family' in question is a real one that involves husbands and children, or an 'adopted family' that is really a place of work and the people in it. This trait is obviously a good one in moderation; but it is nevertheless true that the very tenacity of Water of Earth can prove its undoing.

In its negative aspect, Water of Earth often believes itself to be indispensable to everyone around it. It undertakes any and every task, and refuses to delegate any of its workload — although it will have no hesitation in complaining of the weight of that load to anyone who will listen. In addition, the need for security that is so very pronounced in the nature can make these people greedy — both for money and affection — but paradoxically it will never make them mean, for Water of Earth is invariably extremely open-handed to those it loves, and very protective of those weaker than itself. In a domestic situation, individuals of this type can, in addition, at once both spoil their children and repress them — refusing to let their 'babies' grow into real adulthood by preventing them from obtaining true self-expression in the outside world.

The Knight of Coins

Lord of the Wild and Fertile Land
King of the Spirits of Earth
King of the Gnomes

KNIGHT OF COINS

Fire of Earth
This is a highly productive combination. Predominant Earth conserves and directs the vitality, energy and enthusiasm of Fire into practical channels, and thus produces self-motivating entrepreneurs; the wheeler-dealers of this world.

Fire of Earth can bring its talents to both small businesses and large enterprises; but is always happier dealing with the former rather than the latter. Large enterprises eventually grow too large for individuals of this temperament to keep their fingers on the rock-bottom pulse of things — the 'Earth' that they need to touch to preserve their own vitality.

Fire of Earth is thus essentially a manufacturer rather than — as

is the case when the predominance of the elements is reversed —
someone happy to deal in intangibles like money or stocks.

This urge to produce tangible goods, things that he can see, touch,
and count, and to be surrounded by them, makes Fire of Earth a
collector in his private life of things such as houses, boats and cars,
and indeed, all the trappings of a successful life, including, sometimes,
people — and it is an *ostentatious* collection. Fire of Earth is not given
to leaving the fruits of his labours in the bank. He likes to see it and,
above all, he likes other people to see it.

In its negative aspect, the insensitivity inherent in both Fire and
Earth come to the fore in this combination. Fire of Earth can be grossly
insensitive — quite happy to crush others in order to get where it
is going or serve its own ends. In addition, the tendency to collect
becomes the tendency to hoard, while the tendency to deal all too easily
becomes the tendency to steal. Indeed, Earth of Fire is an expert at
remaining legally guiltless and morally liable in every area of its
life, and can at worst be quite ruthless and utterly without
conscience.

The combination is in any event likely to produce 'driven' people,
for success — visible, ostentatious success — is very important to it,
often overriding all other considerations, including personal happiness.

The Page of Coins

Princess of the Echoing Hills
Rose of the Palace of Earth
Princess and Empress of the Gnomes
Throne of the Ace of Coins

Earth of Earth
Earth of Earth represents an over-plus of a single element, and Earth

of Earth individuals therefore exhibit many of the negative aspects
of that element. They are, for example, cynical, sceptical, and lacking
in imagination, ideals, and inspiration, but very practical, efficient,
and strong. Naturally, their concern with the material frequently
operates to the detriment of theoretical and ethical — and indeed moral
— principles.

Primarily, Earth of Earth is a worker. Work — and the money
gained from work and the things that money can buy — dominate
its life. Indeed, because the Earthy temperament generally suffers from
self-doubt in its negative aspect, Earth of Earth can suffer a considerable
blow to its self-esteem if threatened with an unforeseen change in job,
or if it cannot find a job in the first place, or if it has no money in
its pockets, or if it cannot have the things it sees in shop windows and
other people's houses.

To make matters worse, Earth of Earth is a brooder, and on the
whole inhabits a narrow world. Its vision of life, indeed, is very narrow
and frequently it sees, so to speak, no further than the end of its own
nose. Thus, if large-scale redundancy affects an individual of this
temperament, the fact of redundancy will become a personal matter
— a personal slight even — rather than a social tragedy. The wider
issues involved, and the impact of those issues on others, will not be
examined at all. And, naturally, if matters are reversed, the same rules
will apply. It is not Earth of Earth who will strike on a principle, and
nor is it that combination that will consider the fate of others less
fortunate than itself.

Indeed, Earth of Earth is only too inclined to put anything that
goes wrong for it down to someone else. All its misfortunes are someone
else's fault, and all its successes are due to its own acumen and hard
work. The roots of this rather unpleasant philosophy lie in the concern
of the Earthy temperament with the material.

Earth of Earth's world is inclined to be peopled with faceless,
nameless 'theys', whose problems and points of view it can neither
see, nor appreciate. When individuals of this nature are in a fortunate
phase, then they have, in their own words, 'got the better of *them*'. When
the situation is reversed, 'they' are being vindictive or 'getting their
own back' — usually for reasons which, although forthcoming, are
wholly unrealistic, and often based in some unimportant incident which
anyone else would have instantly forgotten or hardly noticed in the
first place.

The temperament suffers from a sense of acute helplessness in this
regard, for although it has an excellent grasp of the material plane
and the functioning units thereof, it has no faith in anything beyond

that, and therefore rarely feels that it is truly in charge of its own destiny. Further, it can never be brought to an appreciation that its destiny does not lie in the hands of other incarnate beings. Thus, things that people of more sensitive temperament would shrug off as being 'just one of those things', cause acute suffering and an enormous fruitless anger in Earth of Earth.

The temperament at its worst is dull, stupid, and easily led — indeed it is the mob mentality incarnate — and will wreck, with appalling ferocity and efficiency, what it cannot have and spoil what it cannot appreciate.

COURT CARDS AS SIGNIFICATORS

It is from the Court cards of the deck, and by reference to the astrological attributions shown at the beginning of each of the sections on the four humours, that *Significators* (the cards that represent the Querent in a spread) should now *always* be chosen; and I would particularly stress this point because although there are various methods of choosing Significators currently in use, none are as efficient as this one, and some are fundamentally incorrect.

The old system of choice by physical colouring, for instance (i.e. 'very fair-haired and red-haired persons with fair complexion = Staves generally') is obviously no longer functional, since it effectively excludes that three-quarters of the world's population whose colouring is predominantly black or brown, and is therefore not only manifestly obsolete, but unpleasantly discriminatory as well.

Choosing Significators from the Major Arcana (by astrological rulership), is more acceptable; but it is still basically incorrect — firstly because Major Arcana cards are not intended to function in this way, and secondly because the removal of a Major Arcana card from the main body of the deck during a reading may disturb its integrity, thus rendering the reading inacurrate or incomplete.

The practice of using Spot cards as Significators *is* correct, but it is rarely used because it not only demands a considerable knowledge of astrology — which, to be blunt, most people do not possess — but is also so unwieldy a process as to be impractical for normal daily use.

The system of 'choice by astrological attribution' advocated here has none of these drawbacks. It is simple to learn, simple to use and, moreover, utilizes that portion of the deck that was actually designed, and is intended, to represent man. It leaves four Significator options open to the reader (two for women, two for men), and demands only that the reader be aware of which suit represents which sign of the Zodiac and, of course, the relevant dates that correspond to each

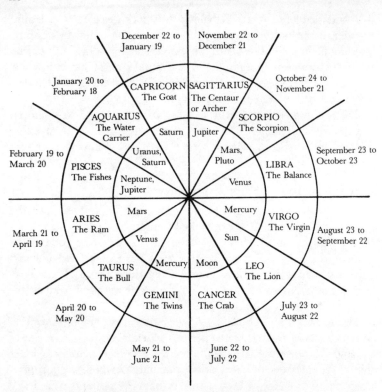

Figure 11: The Astrological Signs and their Revelant Dates.

of those signs — this latter because many people do not know their astrological sign. Figure 11 shows these dates, together with other relevant information.

Thus, according to this system, all men over the age of thirty and all women over the age of twenty-five take the Kings and Queens respectively as their Significators; while the Pages take on a double role, representing either young women or very young children of either sex.

All sixteen of the Court cards are, therefore, attributed to the twelve signs of the Zodiac by suit under the system; but it is as well to be aware that only twelve of them can realistically be so attributed.

The remaining four cards are the Pages which, since they are attributed to HEH final of the Tetragrammaton, the world of Assiah, and the sphere of Malkuth, represent the *highest manifestation* of the four elements — which, although they have their source in Kether, reach their apogee in Malkuth.

We have said that Court cards represent people; but in fact matters are not quite as simple as they might appear to be from that rather bald statement; since all Court cards are essentially *multi-representational*. Indeed, depending upon their placement within the spread, and upon surrounding cards, they can signify any one or more of the following factors:

★   The Querent.
★   An aspect of the Querent's personality.
★   An individual other than the Querent.
★   Gender and sexuality.
★   An event, thing, or commercial entity.

Primary Significators

Court cards that have been deliberately chosen by the reader to represent the Querent should present no difficulty in interpretation; but sadly even these cards are frequently misused and under-utilized. To a very large extent, this failure is due to a fundamental misunderstanding as to the nature and meaning of 'solo' Court cards — those single Court cards that appear alone in a spread to represent the Querent, and are called 'Primary Significators'.

'Solo' Court cards could not — and do not — purport to express all the complexities of character that go to make up a living human being. The wooden, restricted 'personality profiles' given for the Court cards in this book, for instance (or any other Tarot book that I know of, for that matter), are based upon qualities that are drawn from a maximum of *two* elements. They do not illustrate combinations of all *four* elements and are therefore not intended to provide full or complete descriptions of the individuals they represent *by themselves*. Indeed, they *could not* do so — a fact that would become obvious from even a moment's meditation on the cards in question. Rather, they express (as do the humours, for that matter) those *extremes* of character which are in effect *facets of personality* — and this remains the case whether such cards are deliberately chosen, Primary, Significators or not.

The presence of a 'solo' Court card in a spread indicates only how the Querent is *feeling* or *reacting* to a certain set of circumstances: it does not indicate *what he is like*; and it is very important in practice to realize that this is so. Indeed, if the tendency (and it is a very *marked* tendency) of 'Solo' Court cards to reflect attitude rather than basic character is overlooked or ignored, it is only too easy for the reader to come to some very peculiar (and very erroneous!) conclusions about his Querent.

Because 'solo' Court cards are indicative of attitude, they make available to the reader information that cannot be gained from the rest of the spread. It is therefore obviously not enough to choose a Significator by some unspecified method known only to yourself (or by a method quite manifestly out-of-date) and thereafter approach it simply as a focus for concentration. Significators must be chosen logically and methodically, and evaluated in the light of the rest of the spread, just like any other card.

The specifically chosen Primary Significator is certainly in the spread to act as a focus for the reader's concentration; but work on the card should not automatically cease there — as it all too often does. Interpretation is the name of the game in Tarot reading, and the Primary Significator *must be interpreted*. After all, it is part of the spread, and reacts to and influences its surrounding cards just as it would were it a randomly appearing Court card totally unrelated to the Querent.

Randomly Appearing Primary Significators

When a Querent's Significator appears randomly within a spread where no Significator is chosen beforehand, it behaves and should be treated in the same way as an ordinary Primary Significator. It is therefore not enough to recognize the appearance of such a card, and then pass over it once its identification with the Querent has been made. Indeed, because most spreads are deliberately divided into sections of some sort, the very position of a randomly appearing Significator can be very revealing.

A Querent who consistently appears in his own past, for example (particularly if the past as revealed by the spread is considerably more interesting and lively than the present or the future), obviously has a severe problem that is self-explanatory and needs no further comment from me — and the same can be said for a Querent who consistently appears in a rosy Cups-and-Swords future.

Unless the Significator cards are actually *interpreted*, however, rather than just *looked at*, these subtle inferences will be lost, and the reading rendered comparatively incomplete in consequence.

Serial or Secondary Significators

Court Cards as Indicators of Character and Personality
The rounded complexities of human character and personality are revealed in Tarot spreads by the presence of *multiple* Court cards — by which I mean a series of two or more such cards — *all* of which

represent the Querent, and are so arranged as to present a true 'personality profile' for him.

Serial Court cards are usually called Secondary Significators, and they are naturally much more difficult to spot than, say, randomly appearing or Primary Significators; but they are often the key to what would otherwise seem to be an appallingly complicated and difficult spread situation.

Secondary Significators can be cards of the same or another suit as that of the Primary Significator. Usually, the only indications that an otherwise unidentifiable Court card (or cards) in a spread is a Secondary Significator representing an aspect of the Querent himself, will be that the 'stranger card' will be of the same *gender* as the Primary Significator, and by position obviously attached and related to it; but so juxtaposed with other cards as to indicate that the Querent is responding to circumstance in ways that would be 'out of character' for him in his role of Primary Significator.

Single Secondary Significators frequently indicate immaturity in a particular area of life. Obviously, if the Primary Significator is a King or Queen, while the single Secondary Significator is a Knight or Page of the same suit, then this will usually indicate a *generalized immaturity* that is definitely *not* confined to one particular area; but it must be remembered in this context that this behaviour may nevertheless be a temporary *attitude* — a simple response to an isolated event or specific set of circumstances — and may consequently be a transitory rather than an enduring condition. It is worth noting, in fact, that single Secondary Significators of the same suit as the primary Significator are frequently indicative of such attitudes and therefore do not qualify as expressing character at all.

Single Secondary Significators taken from other suits on the other hand — and these may be reversed cards of the same 'maturity' (i.e. King for King) as the Primary Significator, or cards 'junior' to the Primary Significator (i.e. Knight or Page for King) — usually indicate *specific immaturity*. In this event, the area and degree of the immaturity involved are naturally indicated by suit and dignity, but in either case the bulk of the rest of the cards will indicate situations that the Querent has mishandled or circumstances with which he has proved incapable of coping in an manner suitable to his years or experience.

Secondary Significators do not, of course, always indicate immature behaviour patterns — and this is particularly unlikely if *several* Secondary Significators make their appearance, rather than just a single one.

The appearance of multiple Secondary Significators usually indicates a complex and intelligent personality that is undergoing an important period of personal growth and expansion, thus making the reading a psychologically-oriented one that necessitates the appearance of cards representing the whole character. Naturally, such spreads are usually multi-levelled, and it is quite possible to get a very full reading indeed by reading the entire spread as it relates to each individual Secondary Significator in it. This is obviously a time-consuming process, but it is interesting and informative — and highly accurate.

Very, very rarely serial Secondary Significators can indicate acute psychological problems. This, however, is very rare indeed, and you should obviously not jump to the conclusion that your Querent is a certifiable lunatic just because his spread is full of Court cards that are aspects of himself rather than individuals other than himself!

COURT CARDS THAT REPRESENT INDIVIDUALS OTHER THAN THE QUERENT

Court cards that definitely indicate individuals other than the Querent present less of a problem than those indicating aspects of the Querent himself, but they are still remarkably difficult to sort out. The grouping and juxtapositioning of cards — particularly the Small cards — provide the best clues to problems posed by the Querent's friends and relatives, because Small cards tend to group about these 'intruders' in such a way as to indicate the presence of opinions and feelings that are opposed to, or manifestly different from, those held by the Querent, and may in some instances disclose situations that do not relate to him at all. Most Tarot readers are familiar with Querent-unrelated spreads or portions of spreads — and this is particularly true of those readers who work frequently for elderly people, whose lives often revolve entirely around their various children, grandchildren, friends and neighbours.

Court cards nearly always indicate intimate relationship to the Querent by presenting themselves as being of the same suit. In this way, the wife of a Querent whose Significator is the King of Staves will often appear as the Queen of Staves, notwithstanding the fact that her own true astrological Significator might be something quite different. The child or children of the marriage will repeat this Stave pattern so far as possible, but the rule will be found to obtain, of course, only so long as no member of the family is at odds with the Querent, or is in some way an 'outsider' in the family circle, because if that happens, the antagonistic individual will immediately shed the 'Stave identity' and take on 'inimical suit identity' instead. To sort this out, one must, of course, turn to the rules of Resonance and Dissonance, rules based upon the interaction of the properties of the four elements, and explained more fully on page 222 of Chapter 9.

These same rules indicate the 'fors and againsts' of any of the personal relationships revealed by Tarot spreads, the dignity of the cards involved indicating *degree*. Thus a dignified Court card of a suit inimical to a similarly dignified and randomly appearing Significator will be indicating a simple clash of personalities or a misunderstanding, while a single reversal of either card may indicate a one-sided enmity or dislike. A double reversal, however, is nearly always an indication of a strong, mutual antipathy, the cause of which may or may not be obvious from the rest of the spread.

COURT CARDS AS INDICATORS OF SEXUALITY AND GENDER

All too often, Court cards are simply taken as indications of gender. Court cards *do* indicate gender, of course, but not exclusively. When they are used properly they also indicate *sexuality* — sexual problems or sexual preference, in other words.

Homosexual preference is a particularly interesting case in point. Male homosexuality is usually indicated in the Tarot by the presence of one (or even all) of three Major Arcana cards — the High Priestess, the Empress, and the Hierophant. Whichever, and however many, of these cards appear will always be ill-dignified — and it is important in this regard to remember that 'ill-dignified' does not equate with 'badly aspected' as it is often — and quite wrongly — assumed to do.

Roles within homosexual relationships, on the other hand, are usually indicated by the presence of one or two Secondary Significators. Interestingly, while the Secondary Significator of a 'negatively polarizing' role within a homosexual relationship can be a Page (or, more rarely, a Knight) of *any* suit, the Secondary Significator of a positively polarizing role will always be the King of Cups, which will always appear ill-dignified. This is not illogical, considering some of the basic characteristics of that latter card, but it is still surprising that its appearance is so very consistent.

Lesbian relationships are much more difficult to pinpoint, and much less easy to pin down, because the card indications are for some reason (and we do not yet know what it is) quite random. For example, positively polarizing partners in lesbian relationships often appear as Secondary Significators of masculine gender — or as another Major Arcana reversal, this time the Emperor. This 'gender jump' does not take place at all when the subject of the reading is a male homosexual — or at least does not occur in quite so marked a fashion, for — although negatively polarizing male homosexuals can be (and sometimes are) represented by Pages — they are never represented by cards of definitely feminine gender.

In addition, Pages rarely appear at all save as the living children of one of the partners in a lesbian relationship; and to make things even more difficult such relationships often follow the same pattern as those of the intimate relationship cards of heterosexual relationships, and consequently begin to 'follow suit'. This means that the positively polarizing partner will appear as the Knight (but rarely the King) of, say, Staves, while the negatively polarizing partner will appear as the Queen of the same suit.

Naturally, this makes it particularly important to look for Major Arcana back-up; for in all spreads revealing homosexual relationships of any kind, Major Arcana cards indicating anima/animus figures in an ill-dignified attitude will always appear with monotonous regularity.

Again we would stress that these reversals should *not* be read as being ill-dignified according to the usually understood meaning of that term, and it should be appreciated in particular that they do *not* occur because such relationships are in any way abnormal or 'bad', or because the people who enjoy such relationships are themselves 'wicked' or 'depraved'.

Homosexuality has existed for as long as man himself has existed. It is an aspect of man — an inherent part of the structure of the human psyche — and as such it cannot be categorized as 'abnormal' as we usually understand that term, despite the fact that such sexual orientation has frequently been condemned as 'unnatural' by some societies.

Homosexuality is as much of a vexed question in esoteric circles as it is in everyday life — and it must be said that these practices have in the past found as little favour with occult organizations as they have with the ecclesiastical establishment. However, a true understanding of the contents of Chapter 5 of this book must surely shed light on the factors behind the physical manifestation of homosexuality on this plane; and I feel that it is particularly important, in view of the events of the present day, to give thought to these factors — and render respect and understanding to those ones among us who are homosexual.

COURT CARDS AS SIGNIFICATORS OF EVENTS, THINGS, OR COMMERCIAL ENTITIES

Sometimes, Court cards signify events — like news — or corporate entities, and when this occurs, they are really acting as *emphasis cards*.

Usually, the news or corporate entity indicated by the Court card will be represented somewhere else by a Small card as well. The Knight of Swords, for instance, frequently appears as an emphasis card in a spread where events are moving swiftly and news is flying to and fro with great rapidity.

Additionally, of course, an emphasis card signifying news that is backed up by a 'message card' may well indicate in what manner the news will arrive, or what it is about. The Page of Staves, for example, might well back up the Eight of Staves to indicate 'Telex message delivered by office boy/girl' — particularly, of course, if the spread is business, rather than family, oriented.

Obviously all emphasis cards indicate that a certain amount of importance ought to be attached to the event they foretell, so it is worth examining the subjects highlighted by emphasis cards very carefully.

Chapter 7.

Graven Images

As stated in Chapter 5, Major Arcana cards are attributed to the Netibuth of the Tree of Life. The Netibuth are the routes along which energy flows from one Sephirah to another, and there are twenty-two of them altogether. Figure 12 shows how Tarot card/Netibuth attributions are made.

The attribution system used in this diagram is based upon that devised and practised by the members of the Golden Dawn — as, indeed, are *all* the attributions and meanings used throughout this book. But it is very important to realize that this latter system is not the *only* system there is.

Because both the Qabalah and the Tarot are remarkable for their flexibility, attribution systems are myriad. Indeed, they flourish like the green bay tree, and the published systems represent only a tithe of those that exist. *All* of these 'variations on a theme' are manifestations of the ideas of a particular person or group of people; *all* offer opportunities for personal research and personal growth (two things, incidentally, which frequently go hand-in-hand) and — most importantly — *all* work.

Different Tarot/Tree systems approach a very large subject from different angles. They do not vie with each other, and in essence rarely contradict each other very much when it comes to *results* — which is, of course, where it matters. None is therefore 'better' than any other, and *every* system of attribution — however apparently ridiculous or strange — has something to recommend it.

It is essential in the beginning, of course, to study and learn one system thoroughly; and for beginners, the Golden Dawn system is possibly the best there is simply because it is the most coherent and well-established of all systems, and provides a wealth of reference material. But when the initial learning period is over, it is just as essential to afford other systems at least a cursory examination, or even develop

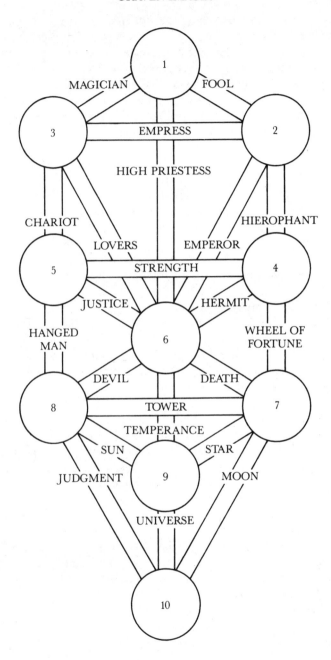

Figure 12: The Major Arcana and the Tree of Life.

your own personal one. Flexibility of mind is a fundamental of
Qabalistic training. It is 'required' — an essential element for success.
Obviously, a rigid adherence to a single system does not cultivate
flexibility of mind — and rarely proves to be a path to success either.

Like the Sephiroth, the Netibuth have certain Qabalistic attributions,
and these are listed as a preface to the text relating to each Major
Arcana card in this, as in many other books. The basic meaning and
purpose of these attributions is as follows:

The Title

This is the exoteric title of the card, and appears at the foot of each
card in capital letters, e.g. 'THE FOOL'. Each of these titles bears
some relation to the esoteric meaning of the card, but because card
titles are of necessity very short, and because they were allotted some
years (in some cases some *centuries*) ago, since when the common and
accepted usage of certain words has altered considerably, they are not
now as enlightening as they ought to be.

a) The Face Number

The face number is that number which appears at the top of the card
in roman numerals. It serves to identify the situation of the card within
the Tarot deck as an entity. Figure 13 opposite shows Tarot card/
Netibuth attributions by face number. Face numbers appear on this
diagram as white on black.

b) The Esoteric Title

This title does *not* appear anywhere on the card itself and was originally
conceived by those members of the Golden Dawn responsible for the
design and production of the Order deck. Like the Qabalistic title
(see below) it is essentially a 'meditation sentence' designed to enshrine
the entire meaning of the card in one short, memorable phrase.

c) The Qabalistic Title

Like the esoteric title, the Qabalistic title does *not* appear anywhere
on the card itself and is a 'meditation sentence'. The Qabalistic title
connects the cards with established Qabalistic principles.

d) The Key Number or Path Number

The key number indicates the situation of the card within the Qabalistic
system and can be arrived at by taking the face number of the card
and adding eleven; e.g. the Fool = 0. 0 + 11 = 11, and thus the
key number of the Fool is eleven. Key numbers do not appear on the

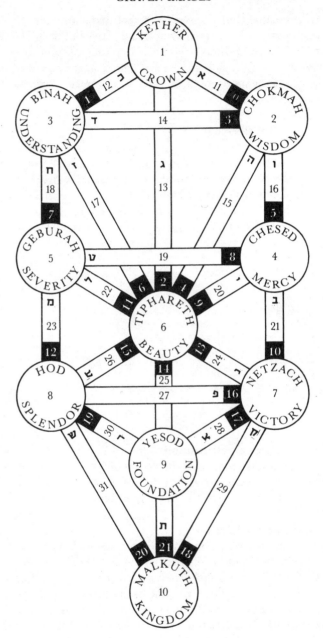

Figure 13: Face Numbers, Key Numbers and Hebrew letters on the Tree of Life.

face of the cards, but correspond to the path numbers that are frequently to be met with on diagrams of the Tree of Life in Qabalistic literature. Figure 13 shows how the face number, key number, and Hebrew letter of each path may be juxtaposed for reference purposes. The key numbers appear black on white in the centre of each Netibuth on this diagram.

e) Situation on the Tree
The situation of each card on the Tree is shown by a small boxed diagram that appears to the right of the list in each case. For the sake of clarity, the Sephiroth are numbered in these tiny diagrams. The path indicated in the example refers to the Fool and is therefore path number eleven and links the Sephiroth Kether and Chokmah. Diagrams that show the situation of each card on the Tree will look like this:

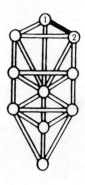

f) The Astrological Attribution
This attribution is reflected in the design of the card in some decks, but this is by no means always the case, and no astrological attributions are reflected anywhere in the Prediction Tarot.

g) The Hebrew Letter
Hebrew letters describe in one abstract symbol those principles described in the Tarot by pictures. There are three kinds of Hebrew letters: Mother letters, Double letters and Single letters. **Mother letters** are attributed to *primal forces*, i.e. Alchemical Air, Water and Fire. Earth is omitted because Major Arcana Cards are not considered to relate to this element. **Double letters** represent *opposing human conditions*, e.g. Life/Death. **Single letters** represent *senses* or *properties*, e.g. Smell or Work. (The distribution of the three types of Hebrew letter on the Tree of Life appears on Figure 14.) Hebrew letters do not usually appear

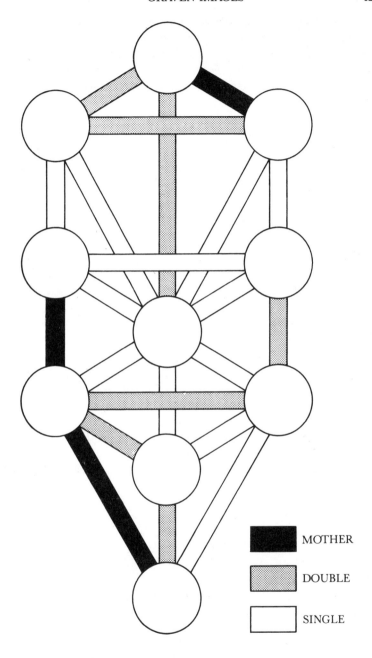

Figure 14: The Hebrew letters and the Tree of Life.

on the face of the cards themselves, and do not appear thus in the
Prediction deck. Each Hebrew letter is in fact a complete word.
ALEPH, for instance, is both the first letter of the Hebrew alphabet
and a word meaning *ox*. The meaning of each Hebrew letter follows
the letter and its transliteration in the list prefacing the text to each
individual card, e.g. ⊐ /ALEPH/Ox.

h) The Yetziratic Attribution

The Yetziratic attribution consists of the *primal forces, opposing human
conditions* and *senses or properties* mentioned above, e.g. the Hebrew letter
associated with the card the Fool is ALEPH which is a Mother letter.
The Yetziratic attribution is therefore a *primal force* which is, in this
case, Air.

i) The colour

As each Netibah naturally exists in all four worlds, there are four colours
to each path. These are listed in the text in the usual order, i.e. the
first colour listed will apply to Atziluth and the last to Assiah. The
remarks made about colour at the end of Chapter 2 naturally apply
here also.

As I have repeatedly stressed throughout this book, the Tarot is a 'multi-
purpose' esoteric tool. It is a divinatory device, and an initiatory device.
It can be used to gain insight into other people — to forecast the
ongoing pattern of their lives, the cause and effect of their existence
— or it can be used to teach the self about the self and, through the
self, about the cosmos, and the Creator.

Because the microcosmic self is an image of the macrocosmic whole,
every Tarot Trump takes on a dual relevance when it is used to
experience the realities and structure of the self. Deliberate subjective
journeys in consciousness through these keys to the Netibuth highlight
little segments of the self that mirror little segments of the greater whole,
so that factors both intimate and impersonal pass before the inner
eye. But it must be appreciated that *intimate* factors — the little segments
of self that are thrown into high relief through the medium of single
Trump cards — do not really exist in isolation, despite the fact that
they are *approached* in isolation. Rather, they exist as part of *you*, a fully-
functioning human being, a holistic entity; and the personal strengths
and weaknesses that are reflected through work with individual
Netibuth therefore resonate throughout the whole of the Tree of the self.

For this reason the Netibuth — like the Sephiroth — work best and reveal most when they too are examined *holistically*. Some paths — and so some parts of the self and the greater whole that forms an environment for the self on every level — are well known to be related in special and important ways.

Cards that represent *complementary opposites*, for instance, quickly reveal *specific* personal imbalance — areas that need development or control — when they are examined as pairs. And, of course, the reflective qualities of all basic Tree structures applies here also, so that one pair of complementary opposites can be usefully compared with its 'reflection'.

In the same way, the cards making up the Triads can be used to examine the structure of the personality (Astral Triangle), the individuality (Ethical Triangle) and the spiritual self (Supernal Triangle). All these 'selves' are, of course, ideally supposed to be perfectly balanced reflections of each other — and it is therefore particularly useful if work on the Triads is undertaken in conjunction with work on the cards that make up the Middle Pillar.

The Middle Pillar is the 'line of communication' between the separate parts of the self that are symbolized by the Triads, and thus work with these cards quickly reveals the 'breakdowns in inner communication' that make the 'alienation' of one 'self' from another more serious than it need be.

These examples of related paths are not, of course, the *only* useful working groupings the Tree has to offer; but they can certainly be used to make a start at least on the all-important process of *synthesis*, which — as you might surmise from my comments on Chokmah in Chapter 4 — is the ability that makes a Tarot reader into a Tarot master; a Neophyte into an Initiate. You will certainly not find it difficult to discover other groups for yourself as — as you can see for yourself from the suggestions made here — one working group both suggests and accesses another.

Work with groupings is, of course, always experimental, but — like most other esoteric tools — the Tarot responds best to experiment, and reveals most to the person who is prepared to experiment. It is therefore to experiment (on yourself, please!) that I would urge you to turn in your journey through the branches of the Tree, the halls of the Citadel of the self.

Chapter 8.

Archetypal Images

Because both the Tarot deck and the Tree of Life were designed to mirror every aspect of life on every level of being, the very structure of each of them copies the structure of the cosmic whole. Thus, both systems are, in effect, *Paper Microcosms* — working models, in fact, or sophisticated educational toys — which strive to illustrate an identical truth in very different ways.

As is amply illustrated in previous chapters, the conjunction of these two separate 'universes in miniature' produces a system that is many times greater than the sum of its parts — a system that is strong, flexible, universally appealing, and much more useful and comprehensive than either of its individual ingredients. Indeed, this Tarot/Tree combination — in any one of its many forms — is one of occultism's better 'marriages', since there are very few substantial grounds for disagreement between the systems involved. Still, however, the Tarot/Tree system is not perfect, and there remain some few areas where it becomes necessary to employ a 'third party system' as an aid to comprehension.

One such 'third party system' is the *Cube of Space*, which is a 'model' of the cosmos as described in the Sepher Yetzirah. This system allots a direction on a cube to each of the Hebrew letters, and thus illustrates the relationships that exist between them — relationships that are not at all obvious from an examination of the mandala of the Tree of Life as it usually appears, flat and two dimensional on the printed page.

The Cube system looks, at first glance, to be a very complex and difficult way of working; but in fact it is a very simple and practical one.

The trick of coming to terms with the Cube of Space is either to imagine that you are sitting inside it — a trick that is best brought off simply by sitting in the middle of an ordinary room and mentally superimposing the diagram over its salient features — or to buy a cheap clear plastic box (with lid) and paint the

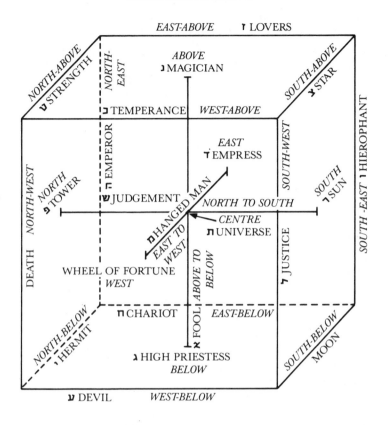

Figure 15: The Cube of Space.

various directions onto its inside surfaces.

Either of these methods allows the areas of influence of each separate card — and, more importantly, the points where those areas of influence converge — to be quite clearly seen and evaluated; and will thus reveal how the qualities of two cards blend together to produce an effect that is demonstrated by a third, and so on.

The Cube of Space illustrates the action and relationship of the various forces symbolized by the Hebrew letters and their associated Major Arcana cards more obviously and more efficiently than any other method, and it is therefore naturally well worth going to some time and trouble to come to terms with its construction and use. I would point out, however, that it would be unwise to attempt to take the process of system synthesis through to what would appear to be its natural conclusion, and so go on to relate the Cube of Space to the Tree of Life. The two systems of symbolism are very different. They do not parallel each other precisely and, indeed, in some instances do not parallel each other at all.

There is, in any event, no real reason for the average person to attempt such a synthesis, the only purpose of which would be very, very advanced esoteric research of doubtful value. The Hebrew letters link the three systems involved, and for all normal and usual purposes that is enough. All three systems have specific uses, strong points and weaknesses — and all are merely a means to an end, paper models of a whole that must be experienced in its real self if it is to be understood.

In the work that we have done so far in this book, we have followed the Path of the Lightning Flash *down* the Tree, allotting the cards of the Minor Arcana to the Sephiroth according to face number or elemental attribution. In our work with the Major Arcana, however, we shall be following the path of the *Serpent of Wisdom* — a path that meanders back *up* the Tree in a fashion far removed from the neat and straightforward pattern described by the Lightning Flash.

The Serpent of Wisdom is usually depicted as an actual snake like the one in Figure 16 which follows the course of gradually expanding consciousness *away* from 'the norm' — although some of the forms of consciousness symbolized by the paths abutting Malkuth and travelled by the Serpent's coils are in fact constructive parts of 'normal' consciousness. Thus, and despite the fact that the numeration of the Major Arcana cards commences in Kether at the top of the Tree with Path Number 11, we shall be commencing our examination of these paths with Path Number 32, or that path which is closest to us and our 'normal condition' of consciousness.

It must be remembered, to avoid any unnecessary confusion, that these pathways are subjective routes of consciousness that underlie the 'energy centres' represented by the Sephiroth, and that they are therefore symbolic of many different ideas. They are, for instance, the struts upon which the human psyche and the cosmos are built. They are the roads upon which we travel in dreams — and in those waking dreams we call 'pathworkings' — and they are roads along which we travel to 'die' and to be 'born'. It is essential *not* to limit the explanations of the various attributions of the paths given in this chapter to any single one of these functions, but to strive to relate them to *all* the functions of which they are capable.

Like the Pillars, the Sephiroth and the Triads, the Netibuth can be categorized as to energy type: that is to say, a given path can be *positive*, *negative*, or *equilibrized*. Because this information is obviously

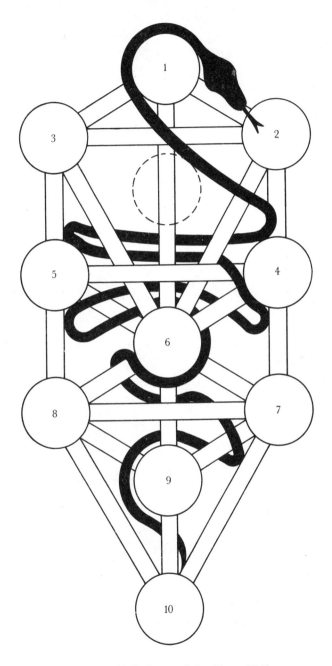

Figure 16: The Serpent of Wisdom and the Tree of Life

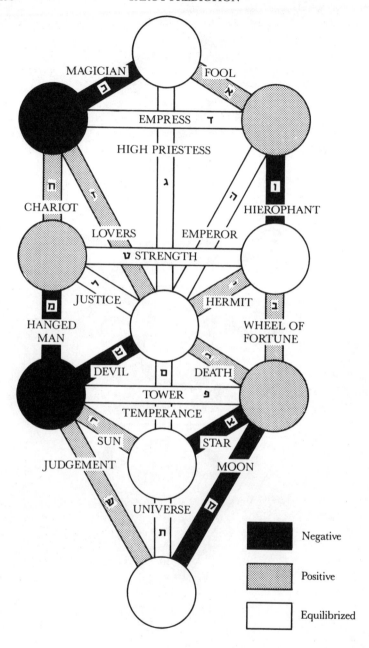

Figure 17: The 'Energy Patterns' of the Tree of Life.

germane to the nature and function of the individual paths, Figure 17 shows these 'energy patterns'.

Obviously, and because of the basic nature of the Tree, all the Netibuth are interrelated. However, some of these relationships are 'closer' than others — and I am thinking particularly here of those Netibuth which form individual Triads. When this is the case, the reader is advised to refer to Figure 17 and make himself aware of the basic function of a given path within the context of its 'group'.

THE WORLD

a) Face No. **21**.

b) The Great One of the Night of Time.

c) The Foundation of the Cosmic Elements and of the Material World; Luna acting through Saturn upon the Elements.

d) Key No. **32**.

e)

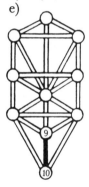

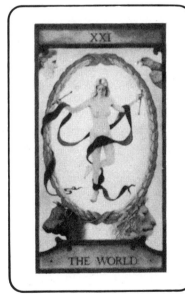

f)

Saturn.

g)

Tau — a Cross or Mark.

h) Opposing Human Conditions — Dominion and Slavery.

i) Indigo; Black; Blue black; Black, rayed Blue.

The 32nd Path is the *Administrative Intelligence*, so called because it directs and associates the seven planets in all their operations, even all of them in their own due course.

'The World' is the last of the Major Arcana cards according to the system we are using here. It portrays a naked figure that holds two wands, one in each hand. The figure is draped in a long scarf, and encircled by a wreath of leaves, which are bound top and bottom with the symbol of infinity. The four corners of the card depict a bull, a lion, an eagle and a man.

The exoteric title of the card — 'The World' — has of course reference to the planet Earth, since the two terms 'earth' and 'world' are sometimes used interchangeably. Within the last hundred years or so, this card has been retitled 'the Universe' by some occult sources, but the implied meaning remains the same, and refers to that level of manifestation wherein all four elements are blended and active. More recently, the title has been updated again — this time to 'The Cosmos', a change necessitated by the constant misuse of the word 'universe' to mean our own solar system only. However, it should be remembered that although there is a link between this card and the solar system (as revealed by the Yetziratic Text which refers to the components of the solar system as the Ancients knew it), there can only be one *uni*verse, as that word implies.

The card is allotted to Path Number 32, which connects the sphere of *Yesod* with that of *Malkuth*, and is therefore the path which connects Microposopos with the Bride. This is the only path of the Tree where all the energies that make up the manifest whole are present in a balanced condition; because of this, much of the symbolism of both path and Tarot card is either four-fold or refers to the qualities of completion and limitation.

The figures that appear in each corner of the card are the four Holy Creatures that are mentioned in Ezekiel and in Revelations. They represent the fixed signs of the Zodiac (i.e., the bull is Taurus — Earth, the lion is Leo — Fire, the eagle is Scorpio — Water, and the man is Aquarius — Air) and thus symbolize the fixed modes of the cosmic whole, or those which are permanent, eternal and immutable. These four creatures and their positioning on the card are an indication of the limitations within which material reality must function, for they are at once the parameters of manifestation, and its basal elemental constituents. The four Holy Creatures, indeed, symbolize the four elements in both their densest and their most tenuous form — and hence, of course, the Qabalistic title of the card: the Foundation of the Cosmic Elements *and* of the Material World.

It will be noted that this Qabalistic title also refers to Saturn (which is the astrological attribution of the card) and in particular to the action of that force upon the elements; and further that the esoteric title of the card emphasizes the Saturnian qualities of the path by its reference to time, the ruler of which is Saturn.

Time is a phenomenon of mass and motion, and — as we are all only too well aware — time is a limiting factor. All creation naturally falls under the dominion of time, because creation is itself finite; but it must be understood that time's grip is tightest and its rule most tyrannical where matter is densest and velocity highest. In this regard, indeed, it is interesting to note that it is in fact quite possible to plot the stages whereby time tightens its grip on an increasingly dense manifestation through the medium of Tarot cards and their symbolism; for the 'natural breaks' in the free flow of force on the Tree symbolized by the Three Veils are always surrounded by cards referring either directly or obliquely to time and/or material conditions. The card 'Temperance', for instance, stands directly below such a Veil that is straddled on its farther side by the cards 'Death' and 'The Devil'. All three cards carry symbology relative to the twin concepts of time and matter, and 'Temperance' in particular bears the figure of an Angel on its face that is sometimes dubbed 'the Angel of Time'.

The finite nature of matter *in a particular form*, and the arena in which time may operate *in a particular manner* is thus also signified by the allocation of Saturn to Path Number 32 and to the card 'The World' — as is the cycle of 'birth' and 'death' to which all things are subject; for mythology tells us that Saturn (whose Greek name is *Chronos*) ate his children, which story is a symbolic description of the manner in which the various expressions of matter (or the forms taken by matter) are absorbed back into the greater whole in due season preparatory to transmutation into a further and different form.

This oblique reference to the cyclic nature of the life force is borne out by the very positioning of the path itself. It is the point of conjunction between manifestation and those processes which precede and follow it, and it is thus the path along which we must travel in order to enter and exit manifestation during the events we call 'birth' and 'death'. It is therefore quite logical to say — as Robert Wang says in his book *Qabalistic Tarot* — that the dancer shown on the face of the card is an aspect of the Great Mother, who dances the eternal dance of life, channelling and transmuting the life force.

This latter attribution is to some extent born out by the presence of the symbols of infinity that bind the wreath that surrounds the dancer, and also by the interpretation that is generally placed upon the wands carried by this figure; for most sources agree that these latter symbolize the circular and perpetual motion of the life force in its active and passive phases, as well as evolution and involution.

The matter cannot, however, be left there; for the identification of this figure with the Great Mother it is not one with which all authorities would wholeheartedly agree.

Paul Foster Case, for example, never mentions the Great Mother at all in his interpretation of this card, and further states quite categorically that the dancer is an androgenous figure whose ambivalent nature is concealed by the positioning of its scarf, and that what it is intended to symbolize is superconsciousness — a quality which necessarily has no sense either of separate sex or separate personality. Case also states that the dancer is 'the Bride and the Bridegroom, the Kingdom and the King' — a remark which becomes logical only when it is remembered that the path itself is a path of *consciousness* which *connects* the Bride and the Bridegroom.

Although it may not be immediately obvious, both of the very different interpretations endorsed by the well-known and well-respected Qabalists mentioned above are quite valid — certainly neither is wrong. The dichotomy of opinion is probably rooted in the emphasis of one authority on the fundamental nature of the Pillar upon which Path Number 32 is to be found, as opposed to the emphasis of the other on the underlying nature of the path as the Gateway of Life.

Tau is the Hebrew letter assigned to this path, and it means 'cross', 'signature' or 'mark'. The letter thus synthesizes much of the symbolism already discussed here very neatly indeed, for the cross referred to is the equal-armed 'Cross of the Elements', while a signature (being that which at once completes a document and renders it valid) is something that both signifies completion and limitation, and — most importantly — infers a covenant of some kind.

The Hebrew letter is the only piece of symbolism allotted to this path which refers to this last concept in any obvious way at all; but there can be no question of its validity — particularly if reference is made to the relationship that exists between the Creator and Creation as this is explained by the Bible and other Qabalistic literature, which relationship does indeed involve a covenant.

The area of the Cube of Space allotted to this card is *centre*, or that point at which the three Maternal letters (which themselves symbolize the forces of which manifestation is created) meet.

The word 'centre' implies place of stillness and place of holiness as well as the point of culmination which we have referred to in Chapter 5 as 'the point of completion'. Indeed, Qabalistically speaking, the attribution of this card to the letter *Tau* and thus to centre, places it and its associated symbology as 'the Palace of Holiness, sustaining all things'. This 'Palace of Holiness' is *Zion* or Jerusalem, but it must be remembered that these terms do not, in this context, refer to a physical *place*, but are only representative of a perfect *state*, a 'nirvana', where man can commune with his Creator — a 'state' which can, of course, only become a 'place' when the process of *Yichud* is completed.

Yichud, too, has much to do with the form of consciousness associated with this path (as is implied by the Yetziratic Text) and amply bears out the explanation of man's purpose given in Chapter 5; but it must be understood in this regard that the word *administrative* implies many things, only one of which is at all straightforward and obvious.

Administrative Intelligence exists in two forms. Firstly and primarily it is a separate entity outside of mankind and superior to it — the Intelligence that directs all force to a single end, and knits it into a coherent whole. Secondly, it is that which exists within any human being who has managed to re-forge the links between his own conscious and subconscious levels, and who has thus become consciously aware of his cosmic duty to be an administrator of the physical plane working under and through the Administrative Intelligence.

This path is the first step towards forging such a link, for — on a personal level — it is the first descent into the subconscious. On quite another level, however, it is the first step out onto another plane of being where the limitations imposed by manifestation do not apply, and where the uses and purposes of those limitations can be first recognized and then realistically understood.

It is also, of course, the path where the traveller first becomes unmistakably aware that an Administrative Intelligence exists — and hence its unofficial title of 'the Path of the Terrible Tau' — the word 'terrible' in this particular context meaning 'awe-inspiring' rather than 'horrifying'.

JUDGEMENT

a) Face No. **20**.
b) The Spirit of the Primal Fire.
c) The Splendour of the Material World;
   Mercury acting through Fire upon the
   Cosmic Elements.
d) Key No. **31**.

e)

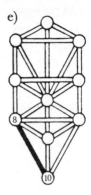

f)

Pluto; the North Node.

g)

Shin — Tooth.

h) Primal Force — Fire.

i) Glowing Orange Scarlet; Vermillion; Scarlet-flecked Gold; Vermillion-flecked Crimson and Emerald.

The 31st Path is the *Perpetual Intelligence*. but why is it so called? Because it regulates the motions of the Sun and Moon in their proper order, each in an orbit convenient for it.

'Judgement' depicts three naked figures — a man, a woman, and a child — who are shown rising from neatly-cornered holes in the ground in answer to the trumpet call of the Angel who hovers in the clouds above them. Thus, although no actual coffins appear on this card — as they do in older and more conventional decks — the effect of resurrection from the grave remains unchanged.

The exoteric title of the card — 'Judgement' — when allied with this picture, naturally recalls to mind the last Judgement; but it is important in this regard to bear in mind what we have said at the beginning of this chapter; i.e. that each of the Major Arcana cards refers to many concepts rather than to just one. Thus although this card is relevant to the concept of resurrection from physical death — and, indeed, has much to say about the nature of that process of resurrection — this is not by any means its only meaning.

The 31st Path joins *Malkuth* with *Hod* — the latter being the sphere of the mind and the intellect that stands at the base of the Pillar of

Severity. Because the sphere of Hod is representative of mental action, this path is primarily one of intellect — a fact that is emphasized by the Hebrew letter attributed to it and also by its Qabalistic title which refers to Mercury the Messenger God, one of whose spheres of influence is the mind.

The Hebrew letter associated with the 31st Path is *Shin*, which means 'tooth' or 'sharpness'. Teeth are used to break down food into fuel for the body. They are the first stage in the process of converting matter into energy. Thus this letter symbolizes the power which tears down the limitations of form — releasing the spirit from the body during the process we call 'death' and, on another level, assisting in the inner process of self-judgement that we all go through as we strive to come to some understanding of our true selves. It is that, in other words, which breaks down the walls of the false personality and sense of separateness to reveal the true individuality within — a process that naturally involves the breaking down of old beliefs or habit patterns and the release of the energies tied up in those patterns for use elsewhere. On a more mundane level, of course, this is also the force that is used to break down sensory experience for the use of the mind on a daily basis.

As in the previous card, 'The World', the inference is, of course, that nothing is ever actually destroyed, but is only transformed or transmuted into another state. This is, in fact, the inner meaning of the name allotted to the mode of consciousness represented by this path: *Perpetual* Intelligence, for the word 'perpetual' means 'everlasting', 'infinite', 'eternal' and implies 'that which survives'.

It is interesting, in this regard, to note firstly that the teeth are the hardest and most enduring constituent of the human body, and secondly that the word from which the translation 'perpetual' is derived itself comes from a root word meaning 'to stretch' — the implication here being that consciousness itself is something that 'stretches' or grows; and further that it is only when it is so 'stretched' that it becomes consciously aware of its own enduring nature.

The attribution of the element of Fire to Path Number 31 and the Major Arcana card 'Judgement' only serves to emphasize the concepts represented by the symbols we have already discussed; for the action of Fire, and the transformation of being it creates, illustrates the durability not of form, which is finite, but of consciousness, which is not. When a material object is placed in a fire, for example, its physical form is utterly destroyed; but its non-material constituent (which is represented in the Prediction Tarot and other decks by the child on the right hand side of the picture) is both liberated and transformed — it is freed, in fact, to act upon another level and its consciousness is thus stretched or extended beyond the limits imposed by its original form.

Again, I would here impress upon you the importance, when assessing the Tarot keys, of remembering that all Major Arcana cards have several levels of meaning; and would further ask that you bear in mind that the physical plane and the physical body play a vitally important role upon all those levels.

'Judgement' shows a resurrection — a rebirth — on its face. On one level this is indeed the rebirth of the spirit upon the death of the body, and its corresponding expansion of consciousness. However, it is also, and on quite another level, the refinement of consciousness which takes place through the inhabiting of the physical form which lends it a vehicle of expression, and the changes which take place in the physical body of a living person when he deliberately expands his consciousness by way of meditation.

Meditation is the key and the gateway to other realms of being, other levels of consciousness. It is a search for the hidden splendour that lies immanent within the material world, and for contact with the soul that lies 'within' (metaphorically speaking) the physical body. It alters consciousness, and in the process alters and transmutes the self in all its aspects, including that of the physical body. Indeed, the physical body is of vital importance to the entire cosmic process, and this fact is expressed in the Qabalistic title of this particular path which refers to 'The Splendour of the *Material* World'.

Paths 30, 31 and 32 are all aspects of normal consciousness. They represent not only routes of ingress and egress to and from the material world, but also methods of altering consciousness which facilitate understanding of the self and the environment in which the self exists. Thus the figures on this card are not only indicative of resurrection following physical 'death', but of the blending of the properties of self-consciousness and subconsciousness and the birth of superconsciousness which is in itself a form of resurrection. As is usual in Tarot symbolism, the woman on this card represents subconsciousness in this context, the man consciousness, and the child the insubstantial and non-material aspect of this union, the regenerated personality.

The spiritual condition denoted by the card is therefore perhaps best described as 'reconstitution following apparent death and dissolution' — a description that is of course born out by the attribution of Pluto, Lord of the Underworld, to the card, for Pluto is, of course, the husband of Koré whose return to the upper regions heralds the coming of spring and the re-birth of the land.

There is some controversy about the identity of the angel on this card. Case insists that this is Gabriel, and that what is pictured is the Last Judgement. Other sources, however, state that the angel is Michael, ruler of *Hod* and solar fire. Either attribution would certainly seem to be logical in view of the other symbolism and attributions of this card, and thus — as is often the case — the identification of the angel is really a matter of personal choice.

THE SUN

a) Face No. **19**.
b) The Lord of the Fire of the World.
c) The Splendour of a Firm Basis, the Glory of Fundamental Strength; Mercury acting through the Sun upon the Moon.
d) Key No. **30**.
e)

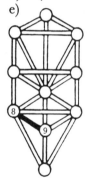

f)
The Sun.
g)

Resh — A head, face, or countenance.
h) Opposing Human Conditions — Life and death.
i) Orange; Gold Yellow; Rich Amber; Amber, rayed Red.

The 30th Path is the *Collecting Intelligence* and is so called because astrologers deduce from it the judgement of the stars, and of the celestial

signs, and the perfections of their science, according to the rules of
their resolutions.

'The Sun' is one of the three cards that make up the Astral Triangle
and is therefore representative of one of the primary struts of the human
personality. The card depicts a bright landscape dominated by a Sun
in splendour with a human countenance, whose wavy rays and brilliant
nimbus suggest heat, energy, and light. In the foreground of the picture,
a boy and a girl sit facing each other on the parapet of a low wall.
Their mouths are open in laughter or song; their faces tilted to catch
the warmth of the sun. Behind these figures is a field of corn that
stretches as far as the foothills of the low mountain range on the distant
horizon.

The 30th Path joins *Hod* with *Yesod*, and 'The Sun' is thus — like its
predecessor 'Judgement' — a card that deals with the intellect. In
so far as this card is concerned, however, it is not the eternal nature of
consciousness or its capability of transmutation that is at issue, but the
realization of the true limitations of the intellect, and of the synergic link
that exists between the mind and its essential vehicle, the physical body.

The identification of 'The Sun' and the 30th Path with these
particular factors is emphasized by the Hebrew letter attributed to
the path, which is *Resh* and means 'countenance' or 'face', thereby
implying self-consciousness or that aspect which is outermost; and
the relevant text from *Sepher Yetzirah*, which calls this path 'the Collecting
Intelligence', and which by its use of the word 'collecting' infers a process
of 'bringing together', 'uniting' or 'synthesizing'.

The Yetziratic Text, however, in its reference to 'celestial signs', also
introduces (albeit obliquely) the interesting concept of incarnatory
memory, thus hinting that this card links not only the mind and the
body, but also the mind and the higher self — which is, of course,
the repository of such memory.

The Sun exercises control over the signs of the Zodiac which in
turn govern birth and the course of life. The signs of the Zodiac
represent both the planetary influences that act upon the physical world,
and twelve separate aspects of the personality, each one of which governs
each separate incarnation. Thus the Sun can be seen to be both a
directive force (as, indeed, intellect itself is a directive force) and a
link between separate incarnations — a point of connection and
collection that concentrates all that has gone before into a new form.

The importance of the relationship of the Sun to the Zodiac can
be readily seen on the Tree of Life, for upon that mandala it becomes
obvious that it is from *Chokmah* (one attribute of which is The Zodiac)

that this path derives all its power; the constituent elements and nature of which power are illustrated on the face of the card by the presence of two different kinds of ray — wavy and straight (being negative and positive respectively) — emanating from the solar disc.

The card occupies the position of *south* on the Cube of Space. This is the place of greatest power, and in this regard it will be remembered that the Sun is associated with *Tiphareth* on the Tree, the sphere which is both the seat and centre of perfected man, and the connecting point between the Astral and the Ethical Triangles. Thus it can be seen that this Path is indeed the point which links the human intellect with its higher counterpart; the personality with the individuality, or higher self.

The mode of consciousness represented by 'The Sun' is therefore an integrating force that recognizes both the necessity of working in harmony with its associated aspects of consciousness and with its physical vehicle and, indeed, its own power to achieve this end. It is intellectual power in its highest manifestation — the sun of human consciousness.

The exoteric title of the card is identical with its astrological attribution, and its Qabalistic title is consonant with the ideas expressed by both these attributions and those we have examined above. This title is 'The Lord of the Fire of the World', the dispenser of life or death, fertility or barrenness, simply because the Sun has the capacity to create both gardens and deserts. When dealing with the 'Fire of the World', therefore, neither an access nor a deficiency of its qualities is beneficial — a fact which further emphasizes the need for inner harmony and balance referred to above.

All the concepts we have discussed here are symbolized on the face of the card 'The Sun' in the most straightforward way for, as is usual in Tarot symbology, subconsciousness is represented by the woman, consciousness by the man, and superconsciousness by The Sun. The fact that on this card man and woman are facing each other — and are thus able to see each other's 'countenances' directly and full on — while singing or laughing together in harmony is indicative of the unity of the forms of consciousness they represent, with the result of course that the sun of superconsciousness shines equally upon them both, illuminating their countenances with its own.

THE MOON

a) Face No. **18**.
b) The Ruler of Flux and Reflux; the
   Child of the Sons of the Mighty.

c) The Victory of the Material; Venus acting through Pisces upon the Elements.

d) Key No. **29**.

e)

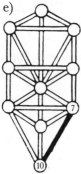

f)

Pisces.

g)

Qoph — An Ear, the Back of the Head.

h) Sense/Property — Sleep.

i) Crimson; Buff, flecked silver-white; Light translucent pinkish brown; Stone.

The 29th Path is the *Corporeal Intelligence* so called because it forms every body which is formed beneath the whole set of worlds and the increment of them.

The Moon is the last of the three cards that link the Kingdom with the Pillars of the Tree, for the 29th Path joins *Netsach* and *Malkuth*. It is Nature's Path, and that of the subconscious mind and the emotions, and is one of the most misunderstood symbols in the whole of the deck.

The card itself depicts a bleak lunar landscape dominated by a large round moon whose unsmiling human countenance stares with pupilless eyes at its own milky reflection in the waters that form the foreground of the card. Within this reflection a pale crayfish rises, pincers outstretched to touch dry land. In the middle distance, two large dogs — one black and one white — face each other over a path that meanders between two towers before disappearing over a dark and distant horizon.

The 29th Path is called the 'Corporeal Intelligence', which infers both 'body consciousness' and 'body building' on an etheric level — the organization of body cells that lies behind all healing and repair work, and indeed, behind actual physical incarnation itself. It therefore represents the mental power that resides in, and indeed forms in the first instance, the physical body.

The Hebrew letter attributed to the path is *Qoph*, which means the 'back of the head', and denotes that area of the skull which contains the cerebellum and the medulla oblongata — those parts of the brain, in fact, which remain active even while we sleep. Not surprisingly, therefore, sleep is the human function assigned to 'The Moon' by the *Sepher Yetzirah*.

Sleep constitutes an aspect of deep meditation — the mode of consciousness that is attributed to the next card, 'The Star' — and is a function which emphasizes those concepts symbolized by the words 'the Corporeal Intelligence'; for it is during sleep that physiological and psychological repair takes place. It is worth remembering here too, that it is during the latter part of the 'sleep' we call 'death' that the building of a complete new body takes place preparatory to a new incarnation.

The 'back of the head' is, of course, quite literally behind the countenance. Thus this Path and its associated card 'The Moon' represent the subconscious counterpart to the bright face of intellect represented by the previous card 'The Sun'. The position allotted to 'The Moon' on the Cube of Space — *south below*, or the southern end and lower face of the Cube — serves to emphasize the fact that this card is intended to represent that form of consciousness which reflects the solar radiance of the intellect.

Perhaps the most important symbol on the card 'The Moon', however, is the pool that lies in the foreground. This pool is primal 'water' or Astral Aether — the mind stuff out of which all manifestation emerges — and is also symbolic of the Universal Unconscious, in which all that was, is and will be is recorded.

The crayfish that is shown in the act of climbing out of this primal 'water' represents the early stages of consciousness unfoldment, and those purely organic evolutionary processes that accompany and keep pace with it; while the ready access to this pool of knowledge and life that is available to the subconscious mind is illustrated on the card by the fact of the reflection of the Moon on the face of the water.

The towers that guard the path that wanders from the foreground of the card to the horizon mark the boundaries of that which is known, while their battlements guard the narrow pass into the broad realms of the unknown that lie beyond. Effectively, too, they form a demarcation line between that section of the Astral Aether which has been utilized or 'shaped' and that which has not.

The path itself continues on past these towers, and out onto those planes of consciousness we can only access through sleep, or trance, or death. It is consequently guarded by two dogs that most occult sources agree are intended to represent the Jackals of Anubis, the Opener of the Ways, the Egyptian god of death and resurrection — an attribution that emphasizes once again the fact that all paths to *Malkuth* are routes of ingress and egress to and from manifestation.

Indeed, the concepts of birth, death, and resurrection and the cyclical nature of these biological events are fundamental to this path — which is basically a very primitive one representative of the continuing process by way of which our bodies develop, live, and finally die, and also of the uncontrolled animal nature and instinct for survival and perpetuation of the self, the tribe, the race, that are usually repressed by social *mores* and which have nothing to do with either morals or ethics.

It is primarily because of these latter factors that the mode of consciousness allotted to 'The Moon' is sometimes called 'the automatic consciousness' since its fluctuations — its positive and negative phases — are not under the individual's conscious control any more than the cycles of the body (like, for instance, menstruation) are under his conscious control.

At the beginning of this section, I referred to the card 'The Moon' as being one of the most misunderstood symbols of the deck — and now that all its symbolism has been discussed it is easy to see why this is so. The path is a primitive and violent one. It is the path of sleep and death that accesses the deepest reaches of our consciousness. It is Nature red in tooth and claw who ruthlessly discards that which fails to adapt. It is the Dark as well as the Bright Mother; at once the Black and the White Isis. Above all it is *dark* — a place of mysterious and powerful forces. All too often, therefore, every emphasis is placed upon its illusory and frightening qualities and none at all upon its potential for construction, growth, healing and learning. It should be remembered, therefore, that while this path is indeed 'the stuff that dreams (bad dreams, moreover!) are made on', it is also the stuff that we — and evolution — are made on too.

THE STAR

a) Face No. **17**.
b) The Daughter of the Firmament; the
   Dweller between the Waters.

c) The Victory of the Fundamental Strength; Venus acting through Aquarius upon Luna.

d) Key No. **28**.

e)

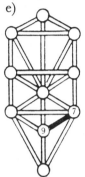

f)

Aquarius.

g)

Tzaddi — A Fish-hook.

h) Sense/Property — Meditation.

i) Violet; Sky Blue; Bluish Mauve; White, tinged purple.

The 28th Path is the *Natural Intelligence* and it is so called because through it is consummated and perfected the Nature of every existing thing beneath the Sun.

'The Star' is the second of the three cards which go to make up the Astral Triangle and, consequently, the human personality also. It depicts a woman who kneels on rocks beneath a skeletal tree, in which a bird sits silhouetted against a bright evening sky. The woman is partially disrobed and holds a jug of water in each hand, the contents of which she is pouring onto the rocks at her side and into the pool at her feet. From her stance, it can be seen that although one of her knees rests firmly upon dry land, the toes of the other foot rest in the water of the pool. Over the woman's head, seven small five-point stars and one large eight-point star are arranged in a pattern reminiscent of the Tree of Life.

The 28th Path is the path of intuition that joins *Netsach* with *Yesod*, and is thus a very powerful path indeed — a fact that is born out by the use of the words 'Natural Intelligence' in the Yetsiratic Text, for these words imply the vital forces of nature associated with these two Sephiroth.

Tzaddi, which means 'fish-hook', is the Hebrew letter allotted to this path. A fish-hook is obviously an instrument which is used to draw forth fish from water — but it must be remembered that we do not use the word 'fish' solely to indicate this pursuit.

We say that we are 'fishing' for all kinds of things in daily life, when what we really mean is that we are looking, — questing, searching — for we know not quite what, often in the dark, or the unknown. In the context of this particular path, therefore, the 'fish-hook' referred to is *meditation*, which is a process of searching or 'fishing' for enlightenment and understanding in the waters of the universal Unconscious.

This latter interpretation of the Hebrew letter *Tzaddi* is amply born out by the fact that the letter itself is one of a group of letters with interconnected meanings, the other two being *Mem*, which means 'water', and *Nun*, which means 'fish'.

All water, in the symbology of the Tarot, refers to cosmic mind stuff — the Astral Aether referred to in the previous section, 'The Moon' — while fish represent not only the fusion of self-conscious and subconscious characteristics, but also reproductive energy.

This latter point is a particularly important one, for it must be realized from the outset that meditation is not a passive exercise, but an active one; and further that it is an exercise that utilizes sexual energy.

All the regenerative and creative processes that meditation calls forth within us (and which are referred to in the cards which precede and follow this one) are therefore fired by the Kundalini force, or sexual energy, which is usually symbolized by a serpent — as indeed it is so symbolized on page 135 of this chapter — for Kundalini is the Serpent of Wisdom which, although it is sometimes referred to as being 'coiled in Yesod' (the Sephirah which, you will recall, rests at the genitals of Adam Kadmon), in fact touches every path of the Tree of Life.

Meditation is a special form of concentration that is closely linked with the imagination. It is symbolized on the face of the card by the bird which rests motionless in the Tree (which latter represents the brain and the nervous system), and thus symbolizes the stilling of the conscious mind that is essential to this particular form of concentration.

The basic nature of meditation and the form of concentration it demands is very well symbolized also by the position allotted to the card 'The Star' on the Cube of Space — *south above* — for that position combines the energies of the sun (*south*) with those of Mercury (*above*) and thus infers controlled, directed (Mercury) energy (Sun).

The aim and purpose of meditation, and its sphere of influence, are all illustrated by the Yetziratic Text, which states of the 'Natural Intelligence' that: 'through it is consummated and perfected the nature of every existing thing beneath the sun'.

This latter sentence is one of the most important and enlightening of all Yetsiratic Texts — a masterpiece of brevity that provides the key to the whole meaning of the 28th Path and so of 'The Star'. It infers, of course, that the 'Natural Intelligence' contacted during meditation is capable of perfecting nature and bringing it to its full potential, and goes on to neatly identify the 'nature' referred to as that which is below the sphere of Tiphareth; thus making it perfectly clear that it is the personality *and* its vehicle the physical body that is referred to here.

We have previously remarked upon the very profound effect that meditation has upon the physical body, in which it causes changes that are in fact quite physiological in nature. Indeed, Case goes so far to say of the adept: 'He is chemically and structurally unlike *genus homo*. There are different constituents in his bloodstream. Through his nervous system pass currents of force not present in most human bodies because in his organism channels are open which are closed in the physical vehicles of most persons.'

The channels referred to in this passage are represented on the face of the card by the seven smaller stars, for these symbolize the Chakras, or interior 'stars', which correspond to the seven planets of astrology and the seven metals of alchemy, and which are used in and activated by meditation.

It is important to understand also that meditation is not a one-sided process. Case puts this over very clearly when he says '. . . when we really succeed in meditation we discover that what happens is not that we meditate, but rather that we are meditated'.

This concept is not an easy one to understand and come to terms with, but it is certainly an accurate one that is amply born out by the attribution of the letter *Tzaddi* and the astrological sign of Aquarius to this path, both of which symbols are primarily representative of the inner alchemical changes (both physical and psychological) that are the result of meditation. The act of dropping a fish-hook into water implies the coming together of two separate things which of necessity interact and thus alter each other, while the symbol of Aquarius ($\approx$) is also the alchemical symbol for dissolution — the state which must occur before regeneration can take place.

The mode of consciousness represented by this card is therefore an evolutionary one which seeks to perfect itself and its vehicle by seeking access to the Universal Unconscious and the memory of nature; while the card itself reveals the method whereby this may be achieved.

THE TOWER

a) Face No. **16**.
b) The Lord of the Hosts of the Mighty.
c) The Victory over Splendour; Venus acting through Mars upon Mercury.
d) Key No. **27**.
e)

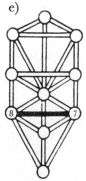

f)
Mars.
g)
Peh — A mouth.
h) Opposing Human Conditions — Peace and War.
i) Scarlet; Red; Venetian Red; Bright Red, rayed Azure or Emerald.

The 27th Path is the *Active or Exciting Intelligence*, and it is so called because through it every existing being receives spirit and motion.

'The Tower' is the last of the three cards that go to make up the Astral Triangle, and depicts an isolated granite tower standing alone on a grassy mound. The tower is in the process of being shattered by lightning, and two figures can be seen plummeting from its summit head first towards the ground.

The 27th Path is the reciprocal path that joins *Netsach* with *Hod*, the emotions with the intellect. It is thus the path which balances and harmonizes these two fundamental elements of the personality, and one upon which a pair of complementary opposites must necessarily meet and meld into a coherent whole.

The card 'The Tower' has had various titles over the years, all of which hint at its meaning, and some of which, indeed, are much more evocative than the simple title 'The Tower' by which we know the card today. Under whatever title, however, the tower depicted on the card refers traditionally to the Tower of Babel where human speech was confounded.

The oblique reference to 'speech' provided by the identification of the tower on the card as the Tower of Babel is one of the most important of all clues to the fundamental nature of the 27th Path; for 'speech' implies language, expression, and communication — all of which are *formulating*, socializing, principles. Without words, no concept can take shape in the mind: without speech, none but the most rudimentary expression can take place between individuals — and consequently none but the most rudimentary form of society be built up either, for communication is the basis of co-operative action.

It is therefore man-made social structures like religion, law, government, and so on — and their destruction — that are initially symbolized by the shattered granite tower on the card, a fact that is made rather more obvious by one of the alternative names for the card, 'The House of God', for this title refers quite unambiguously to the strong and unyielding structure of exoteric religious belief.

Thus the association of the Tower of Babel with this path and the card 'The Tower' — which depicts a strong and apparently impregnable structure shattered by 'The Fire from Heaven' (which is a further alternative title for the card, incidentally) — shows that the path itself is primarily representative of a force which causes established form to break down or disintegrate.

However, and as I have several times previously remarked, the meanings hidden within the symbolism of the Tarot are multi-levelled, and have reference not only to the environment in which man lives, but to those corresponding factors within his own psyche. Thus the card 'The Tower' symbolizes not only the social structures that man builds and organizes outside himself, but corresponding edifices within him.

To accept the idea that this path is expressive of a single concept of whatever nature, however, would be to ignore the fact that it is a *reciprocal path*, or one which reconciles opposing (or rather, complementary) principles, and therefore although the idea of disintegration and destruction symbolized by the name of the card and the picture on its face is emphasized by both the Yetsiratic and astrological attributions of Path No. 27 and its associated Hebrew letter all these latter symbols also introduce different and contradictory ideas that throw new light on the original concept and allow a much greater understanding of it.

Of the three different symbols mentioned above, the Yetsiratic attribution is the most straightforward, and the one which most clearly expresses the duality that is inherent in this path and its associated card, for it sets forth a pair of opposites — peace and war. The concept of duality thus baldly introduced is emphasized, albeit rather less obviously, by the astrological attribution of the path, which is Mars, for Mars is sometimes entitled 'The Contradictory Lord' and — despite his reputation as a destructive force — is a god of agriculture as well as a god of war.

These ideas are naturally carried through by the Hebrew letter allotted to the path; but although this letter is possibly the most revealing of all the symbols we have dealt with so far, it is easily the most difficult to understand; for *Peh* is a double letter which means 'mouth'.

The mouth is the organ of speech and the means whereby sustenance is taken into the body — the inference being that what is taken in is given out, or that what is perceived is expressed — and the mechanics of the function of speech serve to emphasize the ideas of rigid organization and duality of purpose introduced by all the other symbolism related to this path.

Both words and sound are singularly important esoterically, and both are produced in the same way. Air is taken in, and thereafter expelled. The diaphragm, larynx, mouth, tongue, and facial muscles all conspire — by the adoption of rigid forms — to produce either sound pure and simple, or alternatively differentiated sound, which is speech.

Sound is a force which can be felt in and has a definite effect on the body. It can alter the body constructively or destructively, for it is both a disintegrating and a creative force. Sound can kill (a fact which has been demonstrated accidentally and, alas, deliberately) and cure. It achieves both these very different effects by identical means — sympathetic vibration.

Speech is, as we have said, an enormously powerful tool; for words identify concepts, things, or people, and allow us to communicate our thoughts to others. It can be used truthfully or not, to calm or to enrage — constructively or destructively.

Thus, when the two separate factors of speech and sound are united, and words vibrated so that they echo through the body, the effect can be shattering — again, for better or worse.

From an interpretation of all of the foregoing symbols, it can be seen that the force associated with this path is both destructive and constructive, and moreover that these two qualities are complementary opposites, two sides of the same coin, *necessary* to each other. This implies that old forms must be destroyed or broken down to make room for new ones, and further that this process must be an unceasing one.

Since this path is one of the three that make up the Astral Triangle, some of the forms referred to are obviously ideas or psychic edifices that impede the development of the personality — internal structures that are often too rigid to permit of any real inner communication or harmony. On a wider spectrum, the path refers to all forms, and in particular to that which is inclined to become over-rigid or over-formulated, like the social structures mentioned above.

When form is broken down, two things happen. Firstly, energy is released for use elsewhere in the building of new and more useful forms. Secondly, perception changes.

This implied change of perception is extremely important and very well illustrated by the design of the card, for the figures falling from the tower have literally been 'turned on their heads', with the result that their ideas and perception of things have been reversed, and thus drastically altered or transformed — transmuted, indeed, into something quite different.

Every path on the Tree of Life refers to an alchemical transmutation of some kind, and the symbols associated with every path hint at the method whereby such transmutation may be achieved. All such methods are different, for each are designed to react on separate sections of the self which respond to different stimuli. To get at the method hidden in the symbolism of this particular card we must return to its astrological attribution, Mars, and contrast it with some of the other available symbolism.

The Qabalistic title of this card is perhaps the most useful piece of symbolism in this context, for its comment 'Venus acting through Mars upon Mercury' is really a very explicit explanation of the mechanics of this path.

Venus is an emotional force, while Mercury is an intellectual one — that which builds concepts and rules communication, both of which in turn channel and influence perception. Mars, on the other hand is a force that finds expression in reproduction. It is the sexual force of Microposopos, and is thus — like many of the symbols on the card

— a masculine one, for the tower itself is obviously phallic, while the lightning flash which appears in the corner of the card and is seen striking the tower is the masculine force which creates the Sephiroth.

The key to understanding what is implied by this symbolism lies in recognizing that the self has many levels, each of which perceive the truth of their existence and function differently and with varying degrees of accuracy.

When viewed in this context, the phallic symbol of the tower represents the primary formulating factor of the human identity and the source of all its power — its sexuality.

Biological sexual differentiation plays a very large part in the view we form of ourselves. It determines self-image and channels all our thinking. Consequently, if that view of self is wrongly aligned, the entire psyche exists in a condition that is also distorted, and the power that is centred in the subtle levels of sexuality cannot function correctly. As must be obvious by now, we use this force in all manner of ways, and for all manner of purposes: its failure of function is therefore a crippling disability.

The need to review the fundamental image of ourselves created by biological sexual function, and the uses to which we put this function — to turn ourselves around and see these things from another angle — is symbolized on the card 'The Tower' by the fact that the potently sexual symbol of the tower pictured on the card itself is being destroyed by the lightning flash, which is itself representative of a much more powerful but similarly masculine, potent, and creative force.

This is a picture of the physical destroyed by the subtle, but it is also a picture of the physical *informed* by the subtle; and the experience of the path is therefore one of being informed by the subtle at the most fundamental and powerful level of being — an experience which naturally drastically changes the perception of the self, and thereby the self's perception of its environment.

The place assigned the card on the Cube of Space is *north* — the place known in the Mysteries as 'the place of greatest darkness'. It would be unwise, however, to take this statement at face; for it is in darkness that things germinate and grow, and it is out of darkness that light and life comes — as will already be clear from the remarks we have made earlier about 'The Moon'.

THE DEVIL

a) Face No. **15**.
b) The Lord of the Gates of Matter; the

Child of the Forces of Time.

c) The Sovereignty and Beauty of the Material Splendour; Sol acting through Capricorn upon Mercury.

d) Key No. **26.**

e)

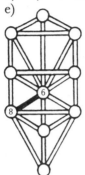

f)

Capricorn.

g)

Ayin — An Eye.

h) Sense/Property — Mirth.

i) Indigo; Black; Blue-Black; Cold dark grey, approaching black.

The 26th Path is called the *Renovating Intelligence* because the Holy God renews by it all the changing things which are renewed by the creation of the world.

The card 'The Devil' depicts a stylized demonic figure who stands balanced on a stone plinth. A pair of antlers are bound to its brow by a metal crown, and behind it, huge leathery wings can be discerned against an angry purple sky. The devil clutches a blazing torch in its left hand, and holds its right hand up, palm outwards. Its face and upper torso are humanoid, its lower body and legs are covered with shaggy hair, its feet are eagle's claws. A long beard spreads across its chest and shoulders. Chained by the neck to the plinth at its feet stand two naked human figures, a man and woman. Both of these figures hold a tall staff.

The 26th path connects *Tiphareth* with *Hod*, and is the first of three paths — the 24th, 25th and 26th — that link the personality (an aspect of normal waking consciousness) with the individuality ('spiritual' or higher consciousness) through the medium of the Sephirah Tiphareth. All three paths represent different aspects of a state of consciousness that is called 'The Dark Night of the Soul' and all are therefore aspects of a single thing. Each tests the traveller on the Tree on one of the triad of components that go to make up his human nature — love, wisdom, and power. The aspect represented by this card, 'The Devil', is an intellectual one.

The Dark Night of the Soul is a condition of consciousness in which everything that is worthwhile ceases to have value or meaning, and the individual develops a complete disinterest in everything. It is, in fact, a form of acute clinical depression, the nature of which is determined by the nature of the path involved.

The Hebrew letter attributed to the 26th Path, is *Ayin* which means 'an eye'.

The eye is the organ of sight, and sight is at once the most vital and reassuring of all human senses. Indeed, because sight is so predominantly important to man, the eye which makes sight possible has come to symbolize not just the visual, but all the human sensory equipment, and human sensation generally.

The human sense organs are miraculously efficient pieces of equipment — so efficient, indeed, that although we may sometimes think of them as being limit*ed* in comparison with those enjoyed by most animals, we rarely or ever think of them as being limit*ing* to us. In one respect, however, human sensory equipment is both limited and limiting, for its very efficiency in its own material sphere leads us to forget that its operation is necessarily confined to that sphere, and so to believe that what we cannot experience through it does not exist.

Practically all of the symbolism attached to this card and portrayed on its face is intended in the first instance to emphasize the limitations of the human senses and the limiting effect those senses have upon human consciousness — an effect which, to all intents and purposes, binds man to the material world, and keeps him in ignorance, not only of all that exists beyond the material, but of the very laws that govern it.

The background of the card itself, for instance, is dark: full of misty, half-seen shapes too dim to be recognizable. The torch held by the central figure is blazing, but it throws no light. The uplifted right hand and open fingers of the same figure are saying 'Look! What you see is all there is', and indeed the figure itself is indicative of one of man's most serious misconceptions, for even the appearance of this figure is what man has made it, and is by no means indicative of the force it truly represents. Ignorance alone has led man to postulate *Pan Pangenetor*, the 'All Begetter' — a figure which symbolizes creative energy at its most material — in such an aspect.

The position allotted this path on the Cube of Space — *west below* — reinforces these same ideas of ignorance and bondage, but gives them a new and even less palatable dimension by introducing the concept of man not only bound to the material, but powerless in the hands of fate. *West below* connects *west*, the placement for 'The Wheel' which symbolizes fate and circumstance, with '*below*', the place allotted to the High Priestess which card is one of the most important symbols of the subconscious, and thus infers that fate reacts upon human consciousness, rather than vice versa, and indeed that free will does not exist.

These latter unpleasant concepts are yet further emphasized by the human figures that stand at the feet of the central demon, for these figures represent self-consciousness and subconsciousness, and their condition — they are horned and chained — is intended to show that when reason takes its cue from surface appearances alone, then human consciousness, trapped in illusion, becomes both bestial and enslaved.

The idea that man is bound to material conditions and the limitations of those conditions (as he perceives them by way of his sensory equipment) is illusory, despite the fact that the material is indeed subject to certain limitations (hence of course the reference in the esoteric title of the card to 'the Gates of Matter' and 'the Forces of Time', both of which factors are limiting ones — which has already been discussed relative to the card 'The World'). Man has free will; his bondage to the limitations of the material as he usually perceives them — symbolized here by the chains that bind the two little figures on this card to the plinth at the demon's feet — can be quite easily removed if he will only avoid the traps set for him by his own senses, and seek to explore and so understand the material and its limitations better. Man, indeed, can make no effort to be free of those limitations until he does understand them — a fact that is very well illustrated by the allocation of Capricorn as the astrological attribution to this path, for Capricorn governs *mastery* over mundane conditions.

From what we have said above, it can be seen that this card, like its predecessor, 'The Tower', represents a force that alters perception so that reality can be seen more clearly. It is indeed a *renewing intelligence* — something that allows us to renew our perception of what reality is and how we stand in relation to it. Thus the allocation of the property of mirth to this path is particularly applicable, for not only is laughter a cleansing agent, it is also a great corrective that allows us to modify our perception of ourselves and things outside ourselves and bring them into a more reasonable perspective. Laughter, after all, is usually provoked by the ridiculous or the incongruous — and ridiculous or incongruous things make people think again, and so to adapt their ideas or come up with completely new ones. Incongruity, in fact, is what makes it obvious that a given fact does not fit a given theory, and so gives rise to analysis and revision.

The mode of consciousness symbolized by the 26th Path is therefore that which, by turning the inner 'eye' (as opposed to the eyes of the senses) onto the external and internal limitations set by manifestation, analyses the individual components of which those limitations are made up so that they may be understood — after which, of course, they can be overcome.

TEMPERANCE

a) Face No. **14**.
b) The Daughter of the Reconcilers; the Bringer Forth of Life.
c) The Beauty of a Firm Basis, the Sovereignty of Fundamental Power; Sol acting through Sagittarius upon Luna.
d) Key No. **25**.
e)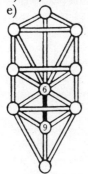

f)

Sagittarius.
g)

Samekh — Prop.

h) Sense/Property — Anger.
i) Blue; Yellow; Green; Dark Vivid Blue.

The 25th Path is the *Intelligence of Probation*, or is tentative, and is so called because it is the primary temptation, by which the Creator trieth all righteous persons.

'Temperance' depicts an angel stading near a stone well who pours water from one large jar into another. Two other jars stand nearby, and all are linked together at the neck by a hempen cord. The angel is dressed in a long white robe, and two golden wings can be discerned against the cloudy background of the sky. At the right of the figure runs a small clear stream that gathers into a pool at the angel's feet, one of which rests on the stone plinth at the foot of the well, while the other rests in the water.

The 25th Path leads from *Yesod* to *Tiphareth*, and thus links the personality to the Higher Self, and the moon to the sun by way of the Middle Pillar, or Pillar of Consciousness. The direct link thus formed between higher and lower, consciousness and subconsciousness, is called 'The Path of the Arrow' and passes through the veil called *Qesheth* that spreads beyond Yesod. 'Qesheth' means 'bow', and the bow in question is formed by the three lower paths on the Tree that are symbolized by the Hebrew letters *Qoph*, *Shin* and *Tau* — which letters together (*Qshth*) spell 'Qesheth'. It is the bonded power of these three paths which constitute the 'Firm Basis' referred to in the Qabalistic title allotted to this card; the 'Fundamental Power' referred to in the same source being the Sephirah Yesod, the name of which is usually translated as 'foundation'.

This veil of Qesheth is sometimes referred to as 'the Bow of Promise', but it nevertheless represents a barrier to the free passage of consciousness up and down the Tree. The 25th Path is therefore a difficult one of trial and temptation and, indeed, has been called the primary path of 'the Dark Night of the Soul', which term represents, as stated with reference to the previous card, a condition of inner darkness that must be experienced in the faith that light will eventually dawn at the end of it. Passage through this state is a necessary preliminary to further spiritual progress, and is therefore the foundation upon which such further progress is built. This concept of a firm and stable foundation is expressed not only by the Qabalistic title allocated to this path, but also by its Hebrew letter, which is *Samekh*.

Samekh means 'prop' or 'tent peg' — both of which objects are things that secure other things in place. The meaning 'tent peg' is particularly applicable in this context, for a tent peg stands in relation to a tent as foundations stand to a house.

The esoteric title of the card — 'The Daughter of the Reconcilers, the Bringer Forth of Life' both emphasizes and adds to the idea expressed by the Qabalistic title and Hebrew letter, and in the process gives an important clue to the real nature of the path represented by the card 'Temperance'; for it at once identifies the mode of consciousness expressed by the path and the method of attaining it.

The words 'The Bringer Forth of Life' in the context of this path refer to the Great Mother, and in this regard it is interesting to note that the figure of the angel on the card in the Prediction Deck is quite obviously a female one that is, I believe, representative of Gabriel. This is not, however, the case in many other decks — and, indeed, Paul Foster Case quite categorically identifies the angel as being Michael, and makes no mention of the Great Mother at all.

As is usual with Tarot symbolism, a very good case can be made out for both these theories, but I believe that the allocation of Sagittarius as the astrological attribution to this path ratifies the figure as being Gabriel rather than Michael, simply because Gabriel is the archangel of the moon, and Sagittarius (which is a fiery sign the Hebrew word for which is 'Qesheth') also represents Diana the Huntress, the moon goddess considered to rule Sagittarius.

The moon, as I have said, governs all tides, inner and outer, and thus controls the waxing and waning of all cosmic energies. She is, indeed, the 'prop' that provides the foundation for a particular aspect of the life process, just as the Great Mother is the 'prop' of another, quite different aspect.

The mode of consciousness represented by this path is therefore that which must support the whole edifice of the self. It is not the path of greatest power, but it is certainly the path of greatest pressure at this level of the Tree.

The words 'The Daughter of the Reconcilers' which form part of the Qabalistic title are the clue to the method whereby the 'prop' may be made strong enough to withstand this pressure — a clue that is illustrated by the action and stance of the central figure on the card, and by the very name of the card itself.

The angel, for instance, pours water from one vessel to another and thereby intimates action and reaction, for when one vessel is full the angel will obviously reverse the position, and begin the process again. The idea that this process subtly changes the nature of the water and the vessels themselves — and indeed that the vessels represent differing states — is inferred by the fact that while the left foot of the angel rests in the water, symbol of cosmic mind stuff, the other is placed firmly on land, the symbol of concrete physical manifestation.

The idea of the modification of one thing by the action of another, and the results obtained by such modification, is further emphasized by the word 'temperance' that supplies the name of the card; for 'temperance' means 'tempering', 'adapting' or 'modifying', and derives from a verb which means 'to bring to a proper condition'.

Of all these meanings the word 'tempering' is possibly the most enlightening, for it is usually applied to metalworking and refers to a specific process that involves the application of fire and water.

The oblique reference to the element of Fire contained within the name of the card is extremely important — indeed, it is vital to a correct understanding of the method of alchemical transmutation represented by this card. The presence of the element of Fire in the personal equation represented by 'Temperance' is, alas, inadequately represented on the face of the card itself, although the positioning of the path — a link between the fiery power of the sun and the watery influence of the moon — make it obvious enough. However, it seems reasonable to postulate that the four linked jars are intended to symbolize the four elements — which are, of course, interdependent — and the actions of the central figure then make it perfectly obvious that two of those elements are interacting on this path. Whether this is a reasonable interpretation or not, however, the fact remains that it is indeed the action of Water on Fire and vice versa that is intended to be symbolized by the stream of water that is poured back and forth between one vessel and another in a process whereby one element tempers and modifies the other.

As the element of Water in this context symbolizes the waters of consciousness, while the element of Fire symbolizes the fiery energies of spirit emanating from Tiphareth, this would infer that spirit tempers and tests and is tempered and tested by consciousness.

Thus it can be seen that the secret of the method of strengthening the 'prop' or mainstay of the self lies in the deliberate interchange of two opposing forms of energy within the body. In addition, it is made quite clear by the picture on the face of the card that it is the Higher Self that initiates this process, for the angel that is the central figure on the card is the Higher Self as well as the natural force usually represented by Diana the Huntress or the Archangel Gabriel.

The fact that this process is initiated by the Higher Self clarifies the meaning of the Yetziratic Text, which states that this path is that of the Probationary or Tentative Intelligence — although in fact two quite separate concepts are dealt with by this text.

The first, which is signified by the use of the word 'probationary', refers to the testing process initiated by the Higher Self which, by tempering its lower vehicle (the personality), also tests the strength of that vehicle, and measures its progress — a process that obviously continues until the vehicle is ready to stand the influx of light and enlightenment that will represent the end of the 'dark night of the soul'. The temptation of the personality to use the skills it has learned on the preceding paths, or to turn away from the contest altogether and accept defeat is the 'primary temptation' referred to in the Text — primarily because it is only the first of many such tests.

The second concept introduced by the Yetziratic Text is that signified by the use of the word 'tentative', which implies a mode of consciousness whereby experience becomes the test of ideas. This particular aspect of the Yetziratic Text is further illustrated by the position allotted this path on the Cube of Space, which is *west above*, a position that conjuncts the card 'The Wheel' with that of 'The Magician' and thus links the idea of the rhythmic rotation of ideas with that of concentration and acute observation of physical experience.

The idea of rhythm introduced by this last allocation is born out by the property attributed to this path, although this is by no means obvious at first glance, for the property in question is 'wrath' or 'anger'.

Robert Wang puts forward the idea that the 'anger' referred to is 'Divine rage, a passion so overwhelming that its force draws the bow and releases the arrow of Sagittarius up the Middle Pillar', thus of course, allowing the individual to break through the barrier represented by the veil and come out on the other side of his personal 'dark night'.

Case offers a more viable attribution by treating the original Hebrew word that translates as 'wrath' not as a verb, but as a noun. The literal meaning of that Hebrew noun is 'quivering' or 'vibrating'. Vibration is the basis of manifestation and is a fluctuating wave-like motion, pulsation, or alternation, and its applicability to the many facets of meaning symbolized by the card 'Temperance' and the 25th Path is obvious. Certainly the interchange of opposing energies within the self mentioned above would create a rhythmic 'vibration' strong enough and sympathetic enough to allow free passage through the Veil of Qesheth.

It is important to realize, of course, that although the elements referred to with reference to this path are alchemical ones, the effect of the deliberate interchange of these opposite elements within the body results in physical effects as well as alterations in consciousness. As I have said before, the subtle and physical 'selves' and 'bodies' of man are inseparable, so what affects and changes one actually affects and changes all. It is worth remembering in this context that it is the physical body — the foundations of which lie in Yesod — that is the 'prop' for the complete whole of the self, for it is the physical body that provides the self with a mode and vehicle of expression.

DEATH

a) Face No. **13**.
b) The Child of the Great Transformers; the Lord of the Gates of Death.
c) The Sovereignty and Result of Victory; Sol acting through Scorpio upon Venus.
d) Key No. **24**.
e)

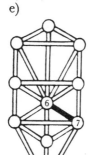

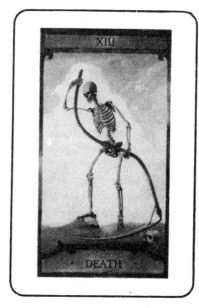

f)

Scorpio.

g)

Nun — Fish.
h) Sense/Property — Movement.
i) Green Blue; Dull Brown; Very Dark Brown; Livid indigo brown (like a black beetle).

The 24th Path is the *Imaginative Intelligence,* and is so called because it gives a likeness to all the similitudes which are created in like manner similar to its harmonious elegancies.

The card 'Death' depicts a bleached skeleton outlined against a pale and featureless sky. The figure stands in a hummocky field of bare earth, and keeps a two-handed grip on a long-handled scythe, over which it is poised workman-like for the swing. It right foot rests carelessly upon a half unearthed skull, and another such skull appears in the foreground and to the right of the picture.

The 24th path is the last of three paths that link the personality directly with the higher self through the medium of Tiphareth, the central sphere of the Tree. It is also therefore the last of the paths that constitute the 'Dark Night Trio' that commenced with 'The Devil'.

The importance of this path is stressed by many authorities on Tarot (Crowley, for instance, states that it '. . . resumes the whole Secret Doctrine') and is, indeed, made obvious by its very positioning on the Tree; for the 24th Path links *Tiphareth* with *Netsach* along the Path of the Lightning Flash.

As is suggested by the title of its associated Tarot card 'Death', the 24th Path is that along which the soul travels as it journeys towards or away from physical incarnation. Less obviously, it is also the path which the personality must take to achieve initiation — an experience that is a 'little death' involving many of the same processes as those associated with physical death. In physical death, for example, the material body is broken down into its component parts to allow its essence to commence another energy cycle in a new and different form. The 'death' experienced by the initiate, on the other hand, involves the dissolution of the personality, which is broken down into its component parts and reassembled in a new form. In both cases, of course, the essence of the self, which is the soul, remains intact, for the soul is the seed and core of the self.

This 'seed of self' is symbolized in the Tarot both by the skeletal central figure on the card itself, and by the Hebrew letter associated with the card — *Nun* — for one of the meanings of that letter is 'sprout' or 'grow', both of which obviously have reference to seeds.

Seeds are considered to be the central core of every living thing, the source of all fecundity, fertility and productiveness. They also naturally represent a form of immortality, for a plant, in producing seeds, effectively pours its essence into another vessel, which vessel again becomes a plant that is in reality *the* plant simply because the seed from which it grew held the essence of its own being.

Here is an obvious link between death and reproduction — a link that is symbolized by the allocation of the astrological attribution of Scorpio to this path, for Scorpio rules the sex organs (and is therefore closely associated with reproduction) and is connected with the 8th house of the horoscope, which is the house of death.

The implication hidden in these apparently ill-assorted linkings of meaning is that death is a form of reproduction; a concept that can only be appreciated if it is accepted that the apparent nature of life and death are illusory, and that both are in reality cyclic events in an eternal process of change and growth. The same inference of change of state is symbolized by the skeleton on the card. The skeleton of any living creature is obviously central and essential to its being. It is the core that provides the body both with a basic supportive framework and — most importantly — with the ability of movement that is the property associated with this path. The Hebrew word for 'movement' has a primary meaning of 'to walk' — a meaning that infers both 'travel' and 'departure' and thus also indicates change.

All these ideas are implicit in the position allotted to this path on the Cube of Space, which is *south west* — a position that links the card 'The Wheel', an obvious symbol of rotation and circular movement, with 'The Sun', a card that symbolizes energy and growth; and also in the esoteric title of the card, 'The Child of the Great Transformers; the Lord of the Gates of Death'. Obviously this latter title similarly refers to a transformation of being, and in addition makes it quite clear that the path itself is not death — a permanent state of non-being — but simply a gateway to another state of being.

Thus what is initially symbolized by this path is not final destruction but only the destruction of one phase of energy as a necessary preliminary to its transformation into something else — an idea that is symbolized on the card itself by the scythe which is a symbol of time and therefore of the Great Mother, giver of life and death.

It is the capability of seeds to produce what is to all intents and purposes a perfect image of the parent plant that is referred to in the Yetziratic Text, which states that the Imaginative Intelligence is that which '. . . gives a likeness to all the similitudes which are created in like manner similar to its harmonious elegancies'; but it must be remembered that, since the seed holds the 'essence' of the parent plant, it does not only reproduce a perfect image of it, but effectively resurrects it. In addition, it must be understood that seeds are not just a means of perpetuating life. They are also the method whereby all living things *change their nature.*

Obviously, the Yetsiratic Text refers in the first instance to the processes of reproduction and resurrection; but it also refers to a change of state that is not either of these things, but something quite different, and additionally sets forth quite clearly the method whereby all these transformations may be achieved.

The Yetsiratic Text calls this path 'The Imaginative Intelligence' — a fact which links the path with that symbolized by the letter *Tzaddi* which seeks to develop the tool of the imagination through a process of meditation, designed to contact 'The Natural Intelligence' which controls the evolutionary processes. The mode of consciousness referred to by this path is therefore that which uses the developed imagination as a tool to bring about certain transformations of being at will.

As I have now many times remarked, meditation effects changes within the physical body. On this path, we see the true source of these changes. As Paul Foster Case puts it:

'Change your ideas, and your old conception of personality changes. Every few years you have a new body, made up of trillions of tiny beings, or cells. Change your intellectual patterns, and with the passing away of the present generation of cells new ones will come to take their places. In the mental nucleus of each cell, implanted there by subconscious response to your new patterns, will be an impulse to realize the new thought in body structure, in function, and in external action.'

On a personal level, this means that the old 'I' dies, and is replaced by a new one. On a wider spectrum, it is the reason behind one of the phrases used in the first chapter regarding evolution, when I said that 'force determines form' — force, of course, being consciousness.

The experience of the 24th Path very adequately sums up the aggregate experience of all three paths that constitute the 'Dark Night Trio'. All these paths demand a fundamental alteration in the concept of what actually constitutes the self and the nature of life, and all strip away the trappings of the various aspects of the self — reduce them to a skeletal state, in fact, so that the process of rebuilding may begin. All, too, demand acceptance and understanding of the fact that change — continual transformation and transmutation — is the 'skeleton' or 'seed pattern' of the cosmos, its mode of growth and evolution.

The 'Dark Night of the Soul' is not a pleasant process to undergo. It deadens the life force — induces a complete disinterest in everything and everyone. A seeming void develops within the self — a dreadful emptiness of being. Everything seems useless, purposeless, hopeless, devoid of meaning. Faith is the only road through such an experience, and while it is true that the travelling of these three paths induces all the unpleasant feelings and effects outlined above, it is also true that the journey is productive of the faith necessary to see it through.

It should be understood also that although the experiences of this initial journey are reflected again and again on different and higher levels as one ascends the Tree, it need never again be assayed in such unpromising circumstances or while the self is in such a state of unreadiness. The journey is fundamental to spiritual progress; but it bestows a formidable strength and purpose on the successful traveller.

THE HANGED MAN

a) Face No. **12**.
b) The Spirit of the Mighty Waters.
c) The Severity of Splendour; Mars acting through Water upon Mercury.
d) Key No. **23**.
e)

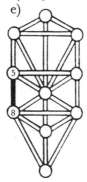

f)

Water.

g)

Mem — Water.

h) Primal Force — Water.
i) Deep Blue; Sea Green; Deep Olive Green; White flecked purple (like Mother of Pearl).

The 23rd Path is called the *Stable Intelligence* and it is so called because it has the virtue of consistency among all numerations.

The 23rd Path links *Geburah* with *Hod*, and is the first of two paths that link the personality with the individuality indirectly and through the medium of the Pillars of Function. Its associated card, 'The Hanged Man', depicts a man who hangs by his right foot from a shaped cross beam balanced upon the branches of two living trees. The pattern thus formed in wood resembles a Tau cross. The man's hands are tied behind his back, and his long scarf trails on the ground beside his head. Stones fall from his pockets to join a heap of similar stones beside him. The figure's legs are so arranged as to form a cross. His face is twisted into a tragi-comic mask.

'The Hanged Man' is called by some authorities 'The Drowned Man', a title that is in many ways more applicable to this path than the more usual one, and one that accords very well with the Hebrew letter associated with the 23rd Path, which is *Mem*, meaning 'water'.

In Tarot symbolism, water is consciousness, Astral Aether, Cosmic Mind Stuff, and — as is implied by the Yetziratic Text associated with this path, which states that the 'Stable Intelligence . . . has the virtue of consistency among all numerations' (for the latter word read 'Sephiroth') — consciousness is the underlying basic substance of all things; something that is always, or consistently, present.

The inference of the title 'The Drowned Man' is therefore that the figure depicted on the card to which it belongs is immersed in the 'waters' of universal consciousness as a person who drowns is immersed in ordinary common or garden wet water; and further that that figure is 'drowned' in that consciousness.

Obviously, the word 'drowned' is used figuratively here. The 'water' referred to is *not* wet water of the sort that, when consistently inhaled, causes death by drowning, but is consciousness. Thus it is not the figure himself that is 'drowning' but an aspect of his consciousness instead. That aspect is the essential 'I' referred to in the previous card 'Death'.

Jung describes the essentials of this 'drowning of the essential I' very well when he speaks of his experiences with what modern psychology calls 'the Collective Unconscious' in the following terms:

'. . . a boundless expanse of unprecedented uncertainty, with apparently no inside and no outside, no here and no there, no mine and no thine, no good and no bad. It is the world of water, where all life floats in suspension; *where the realm of the sympathetic system, the soul of everything living begins*; where I am individually this and that; where I experience the other in myself and the other-than-myself experiences me . . .' (Author's italics.)

From this really excellent description, it becomes obvious that the use of the word 'drowned' in the context of this path is not only figurative, but is somewhat ambiguous as well because it implies loss of life in a way that is not at all representative of the concept intended to be conveyed.

A more realistic and precise understanding of what is really meant can be arrived at only by returning to the present title of the card — 'The Hanged Man' — and replacing the word 'hanged' with its synonym 'suspended' (a word that Jung does in fact use in the above passage), and the word 'man' with another derived from the same Sanskrit root, 'mind'; thus producing the phrases 'the suspended mind' or 'the suspended consciousness'.

The phrase 'suspended consciousness' has two basic meanings, and both are referred to in Jung's description of his experiences.

The first of these meanings is the obvious one of the 'I' suspended in the consciousness of the 'All', which Jung calls 'the realm of the sympathetic system, the soul of everything living'.

This 'sympathetic system' is obviously the Universal Unconscious, and the suspension or submersion of the essential 'I' within it is indeed a form of 'death' for that 'I', simply because its image of itself as being something apart from the whole is lost. This 'death', however, is obviously not the 'loss of life' we usually associate with that term, but only a loss or blurring of the boundary line that usually separates 'self' from 'non-self'. Since, on the other hand, the self immediately becomes aware of itself as part of a greater whole when true self-consciousness is lost — thus effectively undergoing an expansion of consciousness — the 'death' referred to is less a loss than a gain.

The second of the meanings inferred by the words 'suspended consciousness' is that of an actual suspension of personal consciousness — the cessation of any action of the personal consciousness.

'Suspended mind' or 'suspended consciousness' is a state achieved with varying degrees of success in any kind of meditation, all the way from a lightly altered state through to deep trance, and this secondary meaning of the words 'hanged man' is therefore indicative of the method whereby the underlying meaning of those words may be experienced.

This experience is that of a state of union with the 'All', and 'The Hanged Man' represents the first of a series of such states, all of which are similar and yet subtly different, and all of which echo the states of union achieved between the lower vehicles of the self on the lower paths of the Tree.

The immediate result of this particular suspension of personal consciousness and entry into union with the All is a complete reversal of normal perspective — a condition very adequately symbolized by the picture on the card 'The Hanged Man', and is referred to by Jung thus: 'There I am the object of every subject, in complete reversal of my ordinary consciousness . . .'

What 'complete reversal of . . . ordinary consciousness' primarily entails is the willing sacrifice — the complete surrender — of the 'I' and the will of the 'I' into the 'All' and the will of the 'All'. That an implication of willing sacrifice (and so a form of death), followed by an expansion of experience of life and understanding (and so a form of resurrection), does indeed underlie the mode of consciousness represented by the 23rd Path is emphasized by the figure on the face of the card itself. There can be no doubt that this figure is the Norse God Odin — a dying and resurrected god like Osiris — who hung from the World Tree and flung down from thence the Sacred Runes. These latter are symbolized in the Prediction Deck by the stones falling from the figure's pocket, and represent one aspect of the increase in knowledge and ability that are purely personal 'side-effects' of work with the paths of the Tree of Life.

The immediate result of the sacrifice of the 'I' perspective in purely human terms is a true understanding of the nature of the 'All' and the 'I''s relationship to it, and a realization of the 'I' as a unique being with a free will that is synonymous with the will of the 'All'.

This latter is a seeming paradox which is much clarified by various other of the paths higher up the Tree, and in particular by the 20th Path, and its associated card 'The Hermit'. Some light can be thrown upon this mystery here, however, by the position allotted *Mem* on the Cube of Space, for this is the inner axis of the Cube, connecting the centre of the eastern face with the centre of the western face. This allocation places *Mem* at the exact centre point of the Cube along with the letter *Tau* with which it enjoys a symbolic relationship that is inferred on the face of the card by the shape of the gallows from which the central figure is hanging. As Robert Wang says in his book *Qabalistic Tarot* the implication of this attribution is that 'the completion of *Mem* is *Tau*'.

This idea, when examined in the light of the mode of consciousness associated with this path is obviously in accord with what we have said in Chapter 5 concerning the nature of man and his purpose within the larger scheme of things, and has much to say about the vexed question of 'free will'.

JUSTICE

a) Face No. **8**.
b) The Daughter of the Lord of Truth;

the Holder of the Balances.

c) The Severity of Beauty and Sovereignty; Mars acting through Libra upon Sol.

d) Key No. **21**.

e)

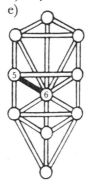

f)

Libra.

g)

Lamed — An Ox-goad.

h) Sense/Property — Work.

i) Emerald Green; Blue; Deep Blue Green; Pale Green.

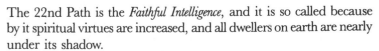

The 22nd Path is the *Faithful Intelligence*, and it is so called because by it spiritual virtues are increased, and all dwellers on earth are nearly under its shadow.

The 22nd Path links *Tiphareth* with Geburah and is one of the most important paths on the Tree because its symbols encompass not only all of the 22 paths of the Tree, but the ten Sephiroth also. The card associated with the path is 'Justice', which depicts a woman, crowned and robed, who holds a sword in her right hand and a pair of balances in her left. Behind the figure, a further and much larger set of scales appears etched against a cloudy sky.

In dealing with the card 'Justice', we follow not the numeration of the cards within the deck, but that of the paths on the Tree.

The card numeration of the Prediction Deck follows a tradition that predates the Golden Dawn System. Consequently, the Prediction Deck differs on this point from the deck put out by that Order and from those that follow — however loosely — Order principles and precepts. Thus in the Prediction Deck, 'Strength' is card number 11, and 'Justice' is card number 8, while in other decks these two cards are transposed as to face number.

The transposition came about because it was discovered that if the cards were placed on the Tree according to their traditional sequence, card number 8 — 'Justice' — fell upon the 19th Path, and thus under the dominion of the astrological sign of Leo, while 'Strength' fell upon the 22nd Path, to which is allotted the astrological sign of Libra. In view of the symbology of the two cards involved, these allocations seemed obviously incorrect, and so they were transposed both on the Tree and within the deck.

Leaving aside the question of the alteration of the face numbers of the cards involved — which would appear to have been quite unnecessary, and which seriously disturbed the integrity of the deck as an entity quite apart from the Tree of Life — the transposition is, of course, an eminently logical one. Indeed, its essential rightness would seem to be ratified by a piece of work done on the deck by the late Aleister Crowley which involved a further transposition on the Tree of the two cards 'The Emperor' and 'The Star'.

As I have said, *Tzaddi* is the letter traditionally associated with the 28th Path and the Tarot card 'The Star'. Whilst in Egypt in 1904, however, Crowley — who was then engaged in work upon *Liber Regis: The Book of the Law* — cast doubt upon this attribution, which he thereafter held to be quite wrong. Some modern authorities — Gareth Knight and Dolores Ashcroft-Nowicki among them — have come to agree with him, while others adhere to the original system, as indeed I have in this book.

Liber Regis purports to be (and, in view of its abstruseness, probably is) the result of a protracted Inner Plane Communication for which Crowley was the medium. In the course of this work, Crowley asked whether various Tarot/Tree attributions were correct, to which the communicator replied 'All these old letters of my book are aright; but *Tzaddi* is not the Star. This also is secret; my prophet shall reveal it to the wise'.

This — as Crowley himself remarked — was exceedingly annoying; and it was to remain a niggling irritation for many years, until the problem was finally resolved by placing the signs of the zodiac upon the glyph of the Moebius Ribbon, as in Figure 18.

This arrangement counterchanges two pairs of the signs (Leo and Libra, Aries and Aquarius), but it does not, of course, change the astrological attributions of the Tarot cards, and thus provides a very

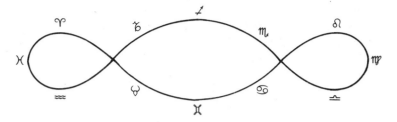

Figure 18: The Moebius Ribbon.

reliable authority for the transposition of the four cards represented by those signs — 'Strength' and 'Justice', 'The Emperor' and 'The Star'.

Only one little fly marred the smooth perfection of this new and pleasing ointment, and that was the obvious Aries symbolism that adorned the face of the card 'The Emperor'. Investigation, however, solved this problem too, for the rams' heads that figure so prominently in the design of modern cards were found to be conspicuously absent from their ancient counterparts. (I say that 'investigation . . . solved this . . . problem' — and it would indeed be very nice if this were so — but effectively the problem remains *un*solved, simply because there is ample room for doubt that it ever existed in the first place.)

Anyone who has worked the paths of the Tree of Life using the Tarot cards as 'keys' knows perfectly well that a case can be made for the placement of any single card upon any given path. Many cards enshrine similar principles and still more enshrine identical principles upon a higher or lower arc. The card 'The Star' is as applicable to the 15th Path as to the 26th; 'Justice' works as well upon the 19th Path as it does upon the 22nd — some would say better. The answer, the solution, the 'right thing', is always, in the end, a matter of personal preference; logic — the desire for every piece to fit within a philosophical jigsaw that must of necessity be a purely artificial intellectual tool — ought not (and indeed must not) be allowed to interfere with personal preference. The individuals who constructed the system with which we are working in this book were highly educated individuals — indeed it is true to say that they enjoyed a much higher standard of education than most of us enjoy today, and in addition had the benefit of a form of education that lends itself particularly well to this kind of work. The fact remains, however, that those men were human, and therefore prone to err. It may be that their desire to construct a perfectly logical system misled them — or did not. It may be also that their logic is not as seamless as it would at first appear to be — or perhaps it is.

These things must be borne in mind and, more importantly, the paths themselves must be worked over and over again before any conclusion is reached either for or against the theories they have espoused.

The word 'Justice' means at once the exercise of authority in the maintenance of right or law and the reward of virtue, and the punishment of vice. *Lamed*, which is the Hebrew letter associated with the 22nd Path, incorporates both of these meanings.

The noun *Lamed* means 'ox-goad', which is obviously the instrument that is used both to drive an ox forward and to guide it in the way it is supposed to go. In Hebrew, 'ox' is *Aleph*, the letter associated with the 11th Path, and *Aleph* represents the cosmic life breath. The inference is therefore that it is the energies of the 21st Path that urge the cosmic energy forward, set it in motion, and guide and direct the course of its manifestation.

This does not mean, of course, that the Hebrew letter *Lamed*, or any of the other symbology associated with the 22nd Path, represents a force that is *outside* of, or set apart from, the cosmic life force, for there can be no energy outside that force that is everything, animates everything, pervades everything. It simply indicates that the cosmic energy is self-directing and self-limiting, and that it maintains the balance of its operations by restricting its sphere of action. In other words, *Lamed* represents that aspect of the cosmic energy that ensures that the life force as a whole operates within a predetermined area and in a predetermined pattern rather than anarchically. It is, in effect, a disciplinary force that by exercising its authority, maintains law — and hence, of course, the Yetziratic Text, which calls this Path 'The Faithful Intelligence' because it represents a form of intelligence or consciousness which remains faithful to a predetermined pattern.

The figure on the face of the card is the 'Daughter of the Lord of Truth', and is representative of an all-seeing Divine justice and the balanced action of its immutable law. It therefore lacks the blindfold that always forms an integral part of any figure representing either human justice or impartial action only; for the blindfold simply signifies impartiality, which is a concept that is related to, but is not of, those represented by the 22nd Path.

The property attributed to the 22nd Path is 'work' or 'action', words which are the basic meaning of the Sanskrit word 'Karma'.

Karma is a concept that is often misunderstood in the West, which has seized avidly upon this word, but disassociated it from its inseparable twin *Vipaka*. Vipaka means 'reaction' or 'effect'. It is the complementary opposite of Karma, which means 'action' and 'cause'. The word 'Karma' therefore signifies a rectifying or balancing force.

It is not punishment. It is not fate. It is not destiny. It is simply an auditing and accounting force that records debits and credits, and takes steps to balance the books.

Justice of whatever nature is always a matter of balance and rectification, and these concepts are represented on the face of the card both by the scales and the sword.

The meaning of the scales is obvious. They are a device in which one thing may be weighed against another and adjusted until an even balance is achieved. The sword is the Sword of Geburah, which cuts away that which is diseased or no longer needed and which makes wars in order to enforce peace. Thus one edge of the sword destroys, while the other creates; for a cutting away of negative qualities ensures a rapid return to health and a proper and balanced condition. Thus, the sword is a regulator, a balancer, a setter to rights. It is a disciplinary force that maintains that condition of health and stability that is lawful.

The direction allotted the 22nd Path on the Cube of Space echoes the dual qualities associated with the sword, for it is *north west*, a position that conjoins the 22nd Path and its card 'Justice' with those paths represented by 'The Tower' and 'The Wheel' and thus introduces the idea of cyclic adjustment.

All the ideas put forward by the symbols discussed above are emphasized by the astrological attribution assigned to this path, which is Libra, a sign that symbolizes justice, order and harmony. It is ruled by Venus — a planet whose symbol encompasses every Sephirah on the Tree — and is the sign in which Saturn is exalted, or at its most effective for good. Libra rules the kidneys, the function of which is to clear waste from the body in a timely fashion, and thus keep the organism in a balanced, harmonious, healthy condition.

Someone, somewhere, in the now thankfully very distant past, remarked of his methods of dealing with the small schoolboys in his charge that 'pain is a good teacher'. This is not a pleasant precept, and it is certainly not one that one would advocate for use in modern schools, but it is nevertheless a true one, and it is, furthermore, one that is enshrined in the letter *Lamed*, for *Lamed* the verb means 'to teach' or 'to instruct'.

Obviously, inherent within the concept of justice — a balancing force — there also lurks the concept of punishment, which is the sting in the tail of justice and its means of rectification and adjustment.

It must be remembered in this regard firstly and most importantly that one man's punishment is another man's justice. It is only the transgressor that need fear either sword or scales.

Secondly, we do not inevitably and as a matter of course learn from our mistakes, just as we do not inevitably and as a matter of course listen to the voice of conscience. It is only the repercussions of our mistakes — the 'punishments' meted out for errors large or small — that truly 'instruct us'.

On a more personal level, therefore, the 22nd Path is that upon which the traveller must face the consequences for his own past actions. Those 'mistakes' appear in the form of 'The Dweller on the Threshold', a figure that is a composite of actions that are 'unlawful' according to cosmic law — which does not, of course, always accord with human law.

Naturally, in facing such a figure, the traveller sees his own faults and flaws only too clearly reflected, and must expect as well 'adjustments' to be made in his inner and outer environments. The experience is a painful but salutary one. The secret of coming through it well is to accept and absorb the *lesson* of the experience, and to see it as being not a punishment but an instructive and necessary process that will eventually result in inner and outer harmony and balance.

WHEEL OF FORTUNE

a) Face No. **10**.
b) The Lord of the Forces of Life.
c) The Mercy and Magnificence of Victory; Jupiter acting through Jupiter direct upon Venus.
d) Key No. **21**.
e)

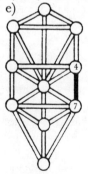

f) 4

Jupiter.
g) ꓘ

Kaph — The Palm of the Hand.

h) Opposing Human Conditions —
   Wealth and Poverty.
i) Violet; Blue; Rich Purple; Bright
   Blue, rayed Yellow.

The 21st Path is the *Intelligence of Conciliation*, and is so called because
it receives the divine influence which flows into it from its benediction
upon all and each existence.

The 21st Path links *Chesed* with *Netsach*, and is thus the second of
the two Paths that link the personality with the Higher Self through
the medium of the Pillars of Function. Its associated Tarot card 'The
Wheel of Fortune' depicts a wooden wheel, on the rim of which appears
eight stout wooden pegs. At the apex of the wheel sits a crowned and
throned King robed in crimson and ermine. He grips the rim of the
wheel with both hands as one would grip the edge of a table. To the
right of the picture another figure hangs upside down and clings
precariously to one of the wooden pegs. On the left of the picture
an identically dressed figure is caught in the act of climbing sturdily
up towards the seated King, using the pegs on the wheel as a ladder.
In the centre of the wheel, on its inner golden rim, a blindfolded woman
in a long white robe grips the handle that turns the wheel. Beyond
the wooden rim and its clinging figures, other, less distinct, wheels
can be seen stretching into the distance.

The wheel is a multi-purpose and very ancient symbol. It represents
evolution and involution, destiny, fate, and the eternal cycle of life itself
— birth, death, and rebirth. Primarily, however, its symbolizes a
particular kind of *motion* — one that is rotary, cyclic, sequential, and
perpetual.

Because of the association of the symbol of the wheel with the
concepts of life, death, and periodicity, the same symbol is naturally
connected also with the idea of reincarnation, and this particular factor
is referred to over and over again — either obliquely or directly —
by the symbols and attributions associated with the card 'The Wheel
of Fortune' and the 21st Path.

One of the most obvious of these references is that provided by
the position allotted the path on the Cube of Space, which is *west* —
a position that refers to the imminent closing of one cycle and the
commencement of another simply because it is in the west that the
sun sets, and by so doing heralds at once the approach of the end
of one day, and the beginning of the next.

Acceptance of the concept of reincarnation must obviously be based
upon mystical experience, for it is a belief that centres upon personal

gnosis rather than upon hard fact; but even when personal gnosis is present, it must be understood — as it often is not — that the nature of our personal 'days' and, indeed, those of the environment in which we live, is not dependent upon a blind and sometimes malevolent fate but is wholly within our own control.

When we speak of 'fate' or 'destiny', or of 'birth' and 'death', it seems natural to refer to these things as 'matters of chance', and to think of them as being areas over which we can exert no control at all. That this is, in reality, quite untrue, however, is unequivocally illustrated by the symbolism associated with 'The Wheel of Fortune' — the Lord of the Forces of Life — which without exception serves to emphasize the fact that that which would seem to be chance is really the expression of immutable law; that every effect is the inevitable consequence of a cause, and above all that everything has a rhythm and a cycle.

Of all the symbols associated with the 21st Path, the Hebrew letter most clearly sets forth all these ideas. It is *Kaph*, a double letter.

The opposing human conditions associated with this letter are wealth and poverty, conditions which — on a mundane level in any event — are factors wholly within the control of the individual, and are consequently indicative of the strength and efficiency of a man's grasp of circumstance.

On quite another level, of course, it is a man's grasp of the rules of life that ensures his inner wealth or poverty — but it must not be forgotten, in this context, that the inner condition reflects upon the outer, and vice versa. Certainly it is an extremely rare individual who, having gained control of his inner environment, lives in a state of squalor, poverty, or disorganization on the outer.

The Hebrew letter thus introduces the concept of control over the nature of the personal environment and the conditions of life — a concept that is emphasized by the meaning of the letter, which is 'a curve', or 'the closed hand of a man'.

Basically, what is meant by 'the closed hand of a man' is the hand of man as it appears in the act of grasping. To grasp something is to hold it, to understand it, or to master it. To have something within one's grasp is to own it or control it.

The nature of this understanding — this mastery or control — is indicated by the Yetziratic Text, which calls the 21st Path 'the Intelligence of Conciliation'.

'Conciliation' means adjustment of differences, and implies that an agreement has been reached, or that a state of accord exists between two separate parties or two opposing forces. Two important points arise from this interpretation.

The first and most obvious is that where two parties reach an agreement or act in accord, there can be no question of coercion on one side or the other, and no question either that one party is solely at the mercy of the other and has no voice. Thus it becomes obvious that man is solely responsible for his own actions, actions which in turn determine his own fate absolutely.

The wheel is the Wheel of Life, and therefore it is the Wheel of Karma also. The Wheel of Life turns according to a cyclic pattern and thus presents different sets of circumstances according to a pattern of creation that is itself determined by the *Aleph*, and policed by the *Lamed* energies of the All.

The actions taken by the life units existing within the All are within their own control, and are either within the pattern and thus within the law also, or not, as the case may be. It is this factor and this factor alone that will determine how the *Lamed* energies symbolized by the previous card 'Justice' will interact with the *Kaph* energies symbolized by this one to produce the 'fate' of an individual.

The second of the two points raised by the Yetziratic Text is that initiated by the idea of the interaction of 'opposing forces'. The cosmos is built upon the interaction of three forces — and, indeed, the design of the Prediction Deck's 'Wheel of Fortune' follows the earliest versions of the card and shows all three of these building blocks of manifestation in balance — but it is the energy created by the duality of two of them, the positive and the negative, pushing against each other that is the activating principle of the equation, and the source of its perpetual motion.

It is this interchange of opposites, in other words, that turns the Wheel of Life, and in so doing engenders the activity of manifestation that is regulated by the *Lamed* energies. This is why the card 'The Wheel of Fortune' depicts a secondary golden wheel within the primary wooden one to which the three figures cling. These two wheels are turning in different directions — they are mediating the energies of rotating opposites.

The motion of such a wheel is perpetual, simply because it feeds on its own energy, and the lesson here is that it is the consistent reconciliation of apparently opposing forces within the self that enables us to harmonize all the elements of our existence, inner and outer, in the long or the short term.

Jupiter is the astrological attribution of this path, and the Yetsiratic title, by its reference to 'Jupiter acting through Jupiter direct upon Venus', emphasizes the importance of this particular attribution, and in the process throws much light on the nature of the 21st Path.

In astrology, Jupiter is called 'the Lord of Fortune' or 'the Greater Benefic' and governs the circulation of the blood and circular motion generally; while Venus is 'the Lesser Benefic' and is best known as a goddess of love. The inference therefore is, of course — and however it looks to us as individuals struggling through life's ups and downs and with 'Karma' that must be 'worked out' — that the gift of life of whatever nature is always an expression of love, and the forces of cyclic life are ultimately beneficial.

This is the key lesson of this card and this path, upon which it becomes obvious that the law of life is love, and that responsibility for the self and its future rests with the self, so that there are no 'accidents', nothing that is 'unfair'; nobody that is 'unlucky'.

THE HERMIT

a) Face No. **9**.
b) The Magus of the Voice of Light; the Prophet of the Gods.
c) The Mercy of Beauty, the Magnificence of Sovereignty; Jupiter acting through Virgo upon Sol.
d) Key No. **20**.
e)
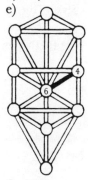

f)

Virgo.
g) [⤴]
Yod — The Hand.
h) Sense/Property — Touch.
i) Yellowish Green; Slate Grey; Green Grey; Plum.

The 20th Path is the *Intelligence of Will*, and is so called because it is the means of preparation of all and each created being, and by this intelligence the existence of the Primordial Wisdom becomes known.

The 19th Path connects *Tiphareth* and *Chesed*, and so forms part of the structure of the Ethical Triangle and the Higher Self. However, as this path is also a direct link between the first sphere of the body of Microposopos and the influx of forces from Macroposopos, it also forms a link between the Higher Self and the spiritual self, and represents the beginnings of manifestation, or that point at which manifestation becomes inevitable.

The card associated with the 19th Path is 'The Hermit', which depicts a figure in a long monastic robe who stands alone in the snow on the top of a rocky mountain plateau. The figure is bearded, and leans on a stout staff. In his right hand he carries a lantern, which illuminates his breast and face. Behind him, two transparent bowls meet and touch in a pattern reminiscent of an hour-glass in the grey and cloudy sky.

The 19th Path is the first of three important initiatory paths of the Tree, and its symbolism is correspondingly complex. Its Hebrew letter, *Yod*, is the most revealing of all the symbolism involved, and sets forth the nature of the path most clearly. We shall therefore be depending more heavily than is usual upon an interpretation of the Hebrew letter in order to understand the path.

Yod is a phallic letter that is intimately related to the Sephirah *Kether*. It is the first letter of the Tetragrammaton, or Divine Name, and represents primal Fire, the Supreme Will, that which initiates manifestation. In Qabalistic literature it is said to be '. . . above all' and therefore symbolizes the All, the Creator.

Thus we can immediately surmise that the energies to be met with on the 20th Path are fiery, masculine, and positive ones that are stimulating and energizing.

Yod itself means 'hand' — but this is not the closed hand associated with the previous card, 'The Wheel of Fortune', which symbolized a certain kind of limitation or restriction, but the open hand that is the sign of absolute power. The image of the hand in this context symbolizes both the spiritual self — which is a 'hand' of the Creator in that it manipulates and directs the Higher Self and all its vehicles — but also and very literally the 'hand' of the Creator in Creation, the linking factor between the Greater and Lesser Countenances.

The same text mentioned above says of Yod: '. . . and with Him is none other associated'. This concept of isolation is very important, for the 19th Path — like the path associated with 'The Hanged Man' — is another of the paths of union with the creative source.

'The Hermit' represents a state of union that is achieved through the medium of the spiritual self. It is symbolized on the face of the card itself by the figure and the environment in which the figure is depicted, and by the very name of the card — 'The Hermit'.

A hermit is one who lives in self-imposed isolation in order to achieve personal enlightenment. In others words (again like 'The Hanged Man'), he is 'cut off' from external distraction and is so able to turn his attention inwards and focus it upon his own internal landscape.

Enlightenment is achieved through union with the creative source — through touching it. Hence the sense associated with this path is 'touch'. In some texts, however, the sense is replaced with a property, and the property is physical love, which corresponds to the function of coition.

This function would seem to sit oddly on a path that deals with spiritual enlightenment through isolation, but it must remembered that it is not the *act* of physical love that is being referred to here, but only its *characteristics* or its effects upon the self.

Physical love is an intense and ecstatic experience that pulls the self into a union with another person that extends far beyond the physical. It is also a 'little death', in that normal self-consciousness contracts and loses itself in the expanded consciousness of union with another — which is one of the reasons why, of course, sex and death are so closely associated.

Much the same intensely blissful effects are experienced when union is achieved with the creative source through the medium of the spiritual self, and it is this experience also that is referred to in the Yetsiratic Text, which calls this path 'The Intelligence of Will'.

The word from which the translation 'Will' is derived means 'delight' or 'pleasure'. However, it also means 'intent', 'purpose' and 'determination', and these words refer not to the experience of union itself but to the effects of that union upon consciousness. Mystical experience is bliss, but it also involves permanent changes in consciousness, and the state of union that brings all this about is perhaps not quite what might be expected.

The astrological attribution of the 20th Path is Virgo, a sign ruled by Mercury, which is also exalted in that sign. Thus the emphasis is upon *self*-consciousness, and thus also the state of union referred to involves not the 'drowning' or 'suspending' of that aspect of consciousness as does the state of union dealt with by the card 'The Hanged Man' but its *exaltation*. The 20th Path, in fact, refers to a condition in which the highest manifestation of self-consciousness is experienced.

The effect of this union is the discovery of personal purpose, for it involves intimate self-conscious contact with the Divine Will of which the personal will is a part. The 20th Path is therefore that upon which it becomes obvious firstly that free will in individuals exists, and secondly that free will in individuals is only an expression of the free will of the All.

The same knowledge is, of course, made available by, say, experience of the 20th and 23rd Paths, but it must be remembered that the 20th and 23rd Paths deal with different aspects of consciousness, and further that different aspects of consciousness react differently to similar stimuli.

It is — as I have said many times before in this chapter — a rule that the subconsciousness is capable of transforming the structure of the body and shaping it to a more optimum pattern. However, it is also a rule that subconsciousness responds to the initiative of self-consciousness — and hence, of course, the importance of this path as an initiatory one.

An individual achieving the state of union represented by this card is changed for ever by the experience. He becomes, indeed, consciously aware of and active in fulfilling his real purpose in the great plan of things. He becomes an energizing, fertilizing force that is self-contained, self-controlled, and self-sustaining, an agent of the Supreme Will, a living 'hand' of the Creator.

The effects of these changes are symbolized on the face of the card by the lamp carried by the figure, which infers that the figure itself is a light-bearer and a way-shower. Naturally, the 'light' is in reality an internal one — it is the light of the indwelling and fully expressed spiritual self — and its effect on its surroundings is due to the impact of its positivity upon its environment, for everything that is is both conscious and subject to the Principle of Polarity.

North below, or the lower boundary of northern face, is the position allotted this path on the Cube of Space, and it is this position that most clearly reveals the method whereby the state of union represented by this path is achieved — or at least the preliminaries necessary to achieving it. *North below* links the lower ends of the vertical lines described by north east (a direction that is symbolized by the card 'The Emperor') and north west ('Justice'), and can itself be divided into the two separate components — north ('The Tower') and below ('The High Priestess'). Thus it can be seen that inner harmony, self-discipline, the potentiating and constructive use of the imagination and the consistent generation of new ideas are all essential ingredients for success on this path.

It is interesting to note, in view of the position of this card on the Tree of Life, that the Prediction Deck's version of 'The Hermit' shows a transparent figure in the background of the card that is reminiscent of an hour-glass. This is in some ways a return to tradition, for some older versions of the card depict the central figure as holding an hour-glass or an hour-glass-shaped lamp.

Saturn is not traditionally associated with the card 'The Hermit' or with the 20th Path, but still the concept of time undoubtedly is, since the card marks the junction between the Greater and Lesser Countenances and the commencement of manifestation; and thus inevitably marks a change in the nature of time also — albeit it does not, of course, mark the actual commencement of time.

It is worth bearing in mind, too, that an hour-glass by its very shape is a particularly good symbol of the occult precept 'as above, so below', a precept particularly apposite to this path.

STRENGTH

a) Face No. **11**.
b) The Child of the Flaming Sword; the Leader of the Lion.
c) Mercy Tempering Severity, the Glory of Strength; Jupiter acting through Leo upon Mars.
d) Key No. **19**.
e)

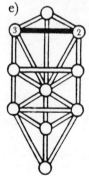

f)

Leo.

g) [ʊ]

Teth — A Snake.

h) Property — Taste.

i) Greenish Yellow; Deep Purple; Grey;
    Reddish Amber.

The 19th Path is the *Intelligence* of all the *Activities and Spiritual Beings*, and is so called because of the affluence diffused by it from the most high blessing and most exalted sublime glory.

The 19th Path is the reciprocal path that links *Chesed* with *Geburah* and is thus one of the three paths that make up the structure of the Ethical Triangle and the individuality or Higher Self. Like all of those paths, the 19th Path leads to the edge of the Abyss, the last and highest of the Three Veils of the Tree, and it is interesting in this regard to note that the symbol of the Lion is sometimes associated with Saturn which, as you will recall, is also associated with time and the material.

The 19th Path is the second of the trio of important initiatory paths that commenced with the previous card 'The Hermit'. Its associated card, 'Strength', depicts a man in a loose white garment, who struggles in the desert sand to subdue a snarling lion. A club lies dropped or discarded at the figure's feet; his right hand rests upon the lion's head, his left is buried in its mane.

The Hebrew letter associated with the 19th Path is *Teth*, and it contains within itself the entire meaning of this path, for Teth means 'snake' or 'serpent'.

The serpent is a composite symbol — a single glyph that represents a chain of associated concepts. Thus serpents symbolize secrecy, wisdom, and the serpent power — the Kundalini force that is at once the universal life principle and the primary source of illusion — as well as reincarnation, regeneration and immortality (because snakes shed their skins and thereby 'make themselves new').

The reference to the serpent force hidden in the Hebrew letter associated with the card 'Strength' is symbolized on the face of the card itself by the lion, for the lion and the serpent are to some extent interchangeable symbols. The lion is the symbol of physical strength, animal potency, and courage, and symbology admits of three different kinds of lion, all of which represent different levels of these qualities by the colour of their coats. A green lion, for example, represents the raw energy of nature that is not subjected to the will, while a red lion represents the same force under the control of the will. The last of the three, the old lion, represents the purified consciousness, and the complete integration of all the components of the self.

All three of these lions can be met with on the Tree of Life, but from the positioning of the card 'Strength' on that glyph, it can be surmised that it is the *red* lion that is intended to be represented by the 19th Path. Indeed, in some decks, the lion actually is coloured red on the face of the card 'Strength' itself.

The symbolic link that exists between the lion on the card and the serpent represented by the Hebrew letter is emphasized by the astrological attribution of the 19th Path, which is Leo, for Leo rules the back, the heart, and — most importantly — the spinal column, which forms the channel along which the Kundalini force is directed. In addition, Leo's glyph (♌) to some extent resembles a serpent.

There are two ways of portraying the concepts represented by the card 'Strength', and the one used by the author of the Prediction Deck is the older of the two. Thus the card in this deck shows a man (representing *solar* consciousness) *struggling* to subdue a lion, while other decks show a woman (representing *lunar* or *sub*consciousness) *gentling* a lion. The Prediction Deck's rendering of the card is possibly the most relevant to the nature of the 19th Path, which is indeed a path of solar power; but realistically, however the face of the card is drawn, the idea conveyed remains the same — it is the control of the *lower* animal nature by the *higher* will, which thus makes the vast strength of that aspect of nature truly its own.

Control of the Kundalini energy — which is the fundamental (and therefore the most powerful) force in nature — is the primary key to practical occultism, and it is the control of this power and the consequent overcoming of illusion that is the primary message of this card also. As usual, the symbols associated with the path reveal not only the *nature* of the force it represents, but the *method* whereby that force is used, and what it is used for.

The *nature* of the force is revealed by the sense and function attributed to the 19th Path — taste and digestion.

Both taste and digestion are related to the concept of eating or feeding, and consequently to the disintegration of one form and its reconstruction into another through a process of absorption. In symbology, the serpent that is the primary symbol of the path is frequently shown biting its own tail — feeding on itself in other words. Thus it can be surmised that the serpent power is a dual force — something that is at once active and passive. The interaction of its own phases is self-sustaining and productive of endless transformation through the absorption and conversion of its own energy.

The direction allotted the path on the Cube of Space — *north above* — serves to emphasize this concept of the self-sustaining interaction of active and passive energy, for it takes in the upper boundary of the nothern face, where it meets the top of the Cube. This line connects north-east and north-west and thus links three separate forces that are symbolized in the Tarot by the cards 'The Tower', 'The Emperor' and 'Justice', all of which represent either the building up or the disintegration of form.

It is vital that this process of disintegration and rebuilding be brought under conscious, or solar, direction. The Kundalini force is not an intellectual but a brute force. Under conscious control such force can be used to open up the higher levels of consciousness that exist on the other side of the barrier that is represented by the Abyss: uncontrolled it can chain consciousness at its lowest possible level (hence the reference above to 'illusion').

You will recall that the same apparently contradictory ideas were met with on the 26th Path, which forms the link between the personality and the higher self and which is represented by the card 'The Devil'. That path symbolizes a force that is similarly both destructive and constructive and, indeed, Case links the cards 'Strength' and 'The Devil' together, and states that the paths represented by these two cards act upon each directly, the change in consciousness symbolized by one path causing similar sympathetic changes upon the other.

The point made by the Sense attributed to this path and by the position allotted the path on the Cube of Space is further emphasized by the Yetsiratic Text, which by its reference to 'all the activities and Spiritual Beings' states quite unequivocally that the fiery force symbolized by the path is indeed the source of *all* force, and that all cosmic and personal activities are simply aspects or transmutations of the one activity or energy.

This text further infers, of course, that all activities are spiritual — an idea symbolized on the card by the white robe worn by the figure, for white is the symbol of purity. On a personal level, this means that all human activity, and all the levels of which a human being is made up, are similarly based upon a single spiritual principle.

The *method* whereby this single force or principle may be consciously directed is revealed by the sense attributed to the path — taste — which in this context refers to the discriminating selection and assimilation of food both physical and mental.

Solar consciousness experiences and interprets experience and instructs the subconscious, which is in turn in control of what Case calls the 'sub-human manifestation of the cosmic energy', symbolized on the card by the lion.

The 'animal' nature is, as we have seen by interpretation of the symbols associated with this card, by far the strongest of the elements that make up the self. Thus it is possible for solar consciousness, by its control or lack of control over this force, to set a pattern that is constructive or destructive. If the interpretation of experience is faulty or negative, or in particular if it is fearful, the result is destructive, for thought will become a vehicle for a negative pattern. However, if solar consciousness is controlled and — most importantly — rightly fed, the result is a positive one.

I have said in the above paragraph that solar consciousness instructs subconsciousness, and this is true; but the opposite is also true, for subconsciousness instructs consciousness during meditation — an exercise which, you will recall, utilizes sexual energy. Thus it can be seen that what the card is intended to convey is a synergic interchange between the various aspects of consciousness (which thus 'rightly feed' each other) that, once begun, is self-perpetuating and which causes physical and mental changes of a kind referred to over and over again throughout this chapter.

THE CHARIOT

a) Face No. **7**.
b) The Child of the Power of the Waters; the Lord of the Triumph of Light.
c) The Understanding of Severity and Awe; Saturn acting through Cancer upon Mars.
d) Key No. **18**.
e)

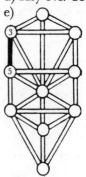

f) ♋

Cancer.

g) ח

Cheth — A fence or enclosure.

h) Sense/Property — Speech.
i) Amber; Maroon; Rich Bright Russet;
    Dark Greenish Brown.

The 18th Path is called the *House of Influence* (by the greatness of whose abundance the influx of good things upon created beings is increased) and from the midst of the investigation the arcana and hidden senses are drawn forth, which dwell in its shade and which cling to it from the cause of all causes.

The 18th Path links *Geburah* with *Binah*, and is the last of the series of the three important initiatory paths represented by 'The Hermit', 'Strength', and 'The Chariot', the latter being the card associated with this path. Thus the 18th Path is another path of union between the higher and the spiritual selves. Its associated card 'The Chariot' depicts a high-wheeled, canopied chariot pulled by two horses, one black and one white. The vehicle races along the edge of the rocky precipice of a high mountain pass, and is driven by a single occupant, who stands balanced and at ease, holding the reins taut in his right hand and a sceptre in his left.

One of the best descriptions of the inner meaning of the card 'The Chariot' is to be found in *The Book of Tokens*, where Case writes of the card:

I am the hedge of protection
Enclosing the field of existence.
In this field thou dwellest
And I am thy defense
Against the darkness which is without

Yet is this hedge of safety
Also a wall of limitation
And the darkness against which it defendeth thee
Is the radiant darkness of the limitless light
Too brilliant for thine eyes.

Many of the symbols associated with the card 'The Chariot' and the 18th Path refer either directly or indirectly to the idea of a defensive enclosure so eloquently described by these verses. The Hebrew letter associated with the path, for instance (which is *Cheth*), actually means 'a field enclosed by a fence' and thus suggests an enclosure or cultivated area which is also a place of safety. Cancer, meanwhile, the astrological attribution of the path, is symbolized by a crab — a crustacean that has a protective shell — and governs the breast, the chest, and the stomach, all of which are 'fences' in their own way.

The property associated with the path both emphasizes and expands on the ideas enshrined within the Hebrew letter and the astrological attribution, for it is *Speech*.

Speech is language, and language both defines and disseminates ideas. Words are descriptive building blocks that allow us to differentiate between one thing or one state and another in thought: they are fences enclosing exact meaning within precise limits. They are also protective devices.

The correct use of words both spoken and unspoken determines the degree and nature of the power of protection they offer. The impetus to plan, to act, to invent or create does not originate within the self. It is a *response* to an external agent that is experienced through the subconscious mind which channels all experience into the enclosed field of the self. All thought, and consequently all speech, is therefore subconscious in origin — a reaction to external factors. It is also, and most importantly, the moulding agent of all response, and can only fulfil its purpose if a vocabulary exists that will allow it to do so efficiently.

Because this is so, a very great deal depends not only upon the receptivity of the subconscious mind to the directive forces of the cosmos, and the nature and extent of the link that is formed between the subconscious mind and normal consciousness, but upon the organization and training of normal consciousness itself.

Paul Foster Case very rightly states that the control of every force in nature, both personal and cosmic, is within the range of subconscious direction. More importantly, he goes on to say that the human mind is capable, once it has achieved dominion over itself, of extending its dominion over nature also, and both the astrological attribution and the Yetsiratic Text attributed to this path are expressive of the supreme power of the subconscious, and the necessity of its receptivity to a specific dimension of external influence; for the former is a psychic and receptive sign that is ruled by the moon, while the latter calls the 18th Path the 'House of Influence' and

refers to the '*hidden senses . . . which dwell in its shade,* and which cling
to it from the cause of all causes'.

Thus the primary inference behind the symbolism of 'The Chariot'
is that it is upon the 18th Path that one may discover the secrets of
the power and use of the 'hidden senses' which receive their energies
from 'the cause of all causes' by achieving integration and control over
the field that is the self, and by the right use of and control of language,
which increases receptivity simply because it is capable of interpreting
the results of it.

Personal integration of the self results (as I have said with reference
to other paths) in an understanding that the self is an instrument of
the supreme will. Complete receptivity therefore results in the most
powerful manifestations of that will, which is at once the will of the
individual and the will of the All.

Language is, of course, a solar or conscious faculty, and the emphasis
upon it may therefore seem misplaced upon this path, which is
primarily a lunar one representing subconscious mental activity —
as its position on the Cube of Space, *east below* shows, for this line
connects the eastern and bottom faces attributed to *Daleth* and Venus,
Gimel and the moon. However, it must be understood that The Chariot,
although guided by the moon, is closely related to the sun.

Arthur Edward Waite wrote that 'The Chariot' represented a
completion which was a 'conquest on all planes', because the chariot
carries the influence of the higher to the lower, thus linking the
'darkness' referred to in Case's verses with the 'light' of Tiphareth.
The chariot can therefore be seen as the Chariot of Helios, the sun,
which — in early cosmogonies — was rightly portrayed as being
subordinate to the moon.

THE LOVERS

a) Face No. **6**.
b) The Children of the Voice Divine; the
   Oracles of the Mighty Gods.
c) The Understanding of Sovereignty
   and Beauty; Saturn acting through
   Gemini upon Sol.
d) Key No. **17**.

e)

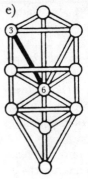

f)

Gemini.

g)

Zain — A sword or weapon.

h) Sense/Property — Smell.

i) Orange; Pale Mauve; Yellow (New Leather); Reddish Grey inclined to Mauve.

The 17th Path is the *Disposing Intelligence*, which provides faith to the Righteous, and they are clothed with the Holy Spirit by it, and it is called the Foundation of Excellence in the state of higher things.

The 17th Path links *Binah* with *Tiphareth*, and thus joins the point of the emergence of form with the central point of manifestation. Its associated card 'The Lovers' depicts a man and a woman standing together in a pleasant green landscape under a warm blue summer sky. The man is gazing into the woman's eyes, while her head is tilted to look up at the Cupid who hovers over the heads of the couple, and aims an arrow at the heart of the man.

The title of this card, 'The Lovers', has obvious reference to marriage, the state of a union of opposite but complementary beings which produces life. The picture on the face of the card shows a man, a woman and an angel representing consciousness, subconsciousness and super-consciousness respectively. The positioning of these figures in relationship to each other reveals the mode of function of that which they symbolize, for the man (consciousness) looks to the woman (subconsciousness) to form a link between him and the angel (superconsciousness).

So far, so simple. Unfortunately — and as might be expected from a path so high on the Tree as this one — all is not quite as simple as it would appear to be from a cursory glance at these primary symbols of the 17th Path.

In some ways these symbols — although they have validity when interpreted as above — can be misleading, for although the card does represent a union of opposites, the union to which it refers is always that of the complementary opposites that exist within the self.

As stated in a previous chapter, true duality appears only in the world of Yetsirah, the duality essential to manifestation being before that point *inherent*, but not *expressed*. That duality expresses itself within manifest man *not* as a duality of nature so far as good or evil is concerned (for although man has a capacity to react to good or evil, neither is truly a quality of the self), but in the duality of being that is the sexual differentiation between male and female. Every man has a feminine self within him, and every woman a masculine one. These parts of the self are twins — mirror images that together form the whole that is the true nature of man.

Thus, the pleasant landscape that is shown on the face of the card is the 'Garden of Eden', that state of being from which the soul is 'expelled' to go down into manifestation, and to which it returns once the cycle of manifestation is complete; and the three figures shown on the card are representative of the leave-taking that takes place when the soul goes into manifestation, and the reunion that takes place when it returns therefrom.

The symbology of the 18th Path naturally emphasizes these concepts. The Hebrew letter is *Zain*. It means 'a sword or weapon cutting to divide' and consequently refers to the ideas of separation and discrimination, which is the ability to distinguish or perceive the difference between one thing and another. In addition, because the weapon that cuts to divide is a sword rather than some other instrument, there is inferred also the qualities of acuteness and clear division and definition.

These latter ideas are emphasized by the Yetsiratic Text, which calls the 17th Path 'the Disposing Intelligence', and by its use of the word 'disposing' infers arrangement, division, and apportionment; but the astrological attribution concentrates on the concept of the apparent division of a whole, for this is Gemini, the sign of the twins.

The twins referred to here are the sun and the moon, the solar and lunar parts of the self, and because they are pictured on the card in a landscape representative of the 'Garden of Eden', the inference is that the twins can be reunited again only through death. So far as the incarnate living person (trudging his way laboriously along the paths of the Tree) is concerned, this is obviously not the death of the body but the death of the idea of separateness within the self, and the dissolving of the veil that exists between the opposite but complementary parts of the self. So far as the soul returning from manifestation is concerned, however, the death referred to is not the death of the body either, for this has already taken place, but that 'death' which occultists call 'the second death'.

The second death is the death of the personality that was the vehicle of a single incarnation, which is absorbed — together with all its life lessons — into the individuality of which it was in any event intended to be a 'twin'. This reference to the 'second death' is hinted at in the astrological attribution to the 17th Path, for Gemini is ruled by Mercury, who is sometimes personified as Anubis, the jackal-headed mortuary god who is called 'The Opener of the Ways'.

The sense attributed to the 17th Path is perhaps the most difficult of all its symbols to come to terms with, because it is smell.

Smell is the oldest of the physical senses, the most subtle and the most acute of them all. It has always been associated with keen perception because it is a *discriminatory* sense — something which differentiates between one thing and another — and so with wisdom also, for wisdom is based upon discrimination.

The position allotted this path on the Cube of Space deals less with the actual results that can be hoped for from this path than the methods whereby those results can be ensured. *East above* is the line that joins the eastern side of the Cube of Space with its top face, thereby linking above (Mercury) to east (Venus) *and* the vertical north-eastern line ('The Emperor') to the vertical south-eastern one ('The Hierophant'). Thus it can be seen that the union symbolized by the 17th Path and its associated card 'The Lovers' is achieved by the conjunction of the creative imagination — a function of the feminine and lunar subconscious — with its complementary opposite and 'twin', the organizing and discriminatory talents of the solar and masculine self-conscious mind.

THE HIEROPHANT

a) Face No. **5**.
b) The Magus of the Eternal Gods.
c) The Wisdom and Fountain of Mercy;
   The sphere of the Zodiac acting
   through Taurus upon Jupiter.
d) Key No. **16**.

e)

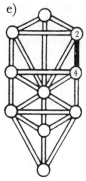

f)

Taurus.

g)

Vau — A nail or hook.

h) Sense/Property — Hearing.

i) Red Orange; Deep Indigo; Deep Warm Olive; Rich Brown.

The 16th Path is the *Triumphal* or *Eternal Intelligence*, so called because it is the pleasure of the Glory beyond which is no other Glory like to it, and it is called also the paradise prepared for the righteous.

The 16th Path links *Chesed* with *Chokmah*, the Supernal Father with the sphere representing the masculine impetus to manifestation. Its associated card 'The Hierophant' depicts an elderly figure, robed in scarlet, white and gold, crowned with a triple tiara representative of the Supernals. The figure carries a golden staff tipped with the Papal Cross — the triple barred cross of Western peoples — in his left hand. His right hand is raised in a gesture of blessing. At his feet, two monks kneel in an attentive attitude, heads inclined as though listening.

The 16th Path links Macroposopos to Microposopos on the Pillar of Mercy. It is therefore a path of union — a linking agent that joins two separate but related things together — and many of its associated symbols naturally reflect this fact.

The Hebrew letter associated with the path in particular emphasizes the concept of union, for it is *Vau*, which means 'nail' or 'hook'. Both of these mundane objects fasten things together by forming a link between them, and both, too, are a means of support in that it is possible to hang objects from them. The Hebrew letter therefore introduces the concepts of assistance and sustenance as well as union.

However, it is the titles of the card that best express the fundamental nature of this path, for they not only represent the idea of union, but indicate the form of that union and its extent as well.

The alternative title for this card is 'The Pope'. This particular title refers to the concept of union directly, for the word 'pontiff' is taken from a Latin word which means 'a bridge'. However, the same word has come to mean 'chief priest', and it is interesting to note that its derivative 'pontifical' (the primary meaning of which is 'of or befitting a pontiff') means 'assuming infallibility'.

This latter meaning obviously infers that the quality of infallibility falls like a mantle upon the holder of the office of pontiff immediately he assumes that office, *and simply because he has assumed it*.

This is an extremely important point, because it makes it quite clear that the 'infallibility', or power, of the pontiff is not his own, but is 'borrowed' from a source outside himself; and thus it becomes clear that a pontiff is a *mediator* — one who forms a living bridge between the higher and the lower, the outer and the inner — and that his words (which are of necessity the primary expression of his 'infallibility') are not his own, but are channelled through him from a higher source.

Because a mediator is a bridge between the manifest and subtle worlds, his most important faculty is that of hearing — and hence the faculty of hearing is attributed to this path. The 'hearing' referred to is not, however, 'hearing' as we usually think of that term.

Physical hearing unites man to his fellows and to his manifest environment, but it is inner hearing that links man to the Creator and his inner environment. A mediator, or pontiff, is one who is capable of 'listening' to the inner, discerning the 'voice' of the Divine Will, and reflecting it outwards from himself undistorted by personal desire or intellectual pride or dishonesty. This latter point is extremely important because the faculty of hearing — whether physical or psychic — is highly selective. Effectively, we hear what we want to hear on any level. When Christ said 'He that hath ears to hear, let him hear', he was referring to this human capacity for selective hearing, and not to the possible physical incapacity of some few of his audience.

The more usual title of this card, 'The Hierophant', emphasizes a rather different aspect of the function of a 'chief priest', for the word 'hierophant' means 'revealer of sacred things'. As the word 'sacred' itself means 'consecrated', 'holy', and 'belonging to, commissioned by, or devoted to a deity', a Hierophant is consequently a teacher committed to the exposition of those subjects both by example and by word of mouth.

All of these qualities are reflected in the astrological attribution associated with the 16th Path, for this is Taurus.

Taurus is ruled by Venus and is the sign in which the Moon is exalted, or at its most potent. The sign is consequently representative of latent power and imagination that stems directly from the subconscious — which is the channel of mediation. In addition, the sign of Taurus is symbolized by a bull, which also symbolizes the Hebrew letter *Aleph*. Thus the 16th Path can be seen to be intimately related to the 11th Path, which is represented in the Tarot deck by the card 'The Fool'. Case says that 'The Voice of the Hierophant gives verbal form to the vision of "The Fool"'; but effectively — and because of the positioning of this path on the Tree — it essentially gives *manifest form* to that vision.

The position allotted the 16th Path on the Cube of Space reiterates the message of the astrological attribution, for it is *south east*, which line connects the lower south east corner of the Cube with the upper south east corner and conjoins the southern and eastern faces of the Cube. Consequently, this particular position blends solar and Venusian qualities, self-consciousness with subconsciousness.

Thus it can be seen that the 16th Path is primarily concerned with the unity of the self at that level which promotes the development of the faculty of precise 'hearing' on the inner levels, and with the results that might be expected from a mastery of that faculty.

It is particularly important with reference to this path to appreciate that the faculty of 'hearing' referred to here is capable of development in every person, being neither the prerogative of the few nor in the gift of any established religion, however powerful. Every man is inherently a hierophant and a pontiff; but he who would teach must first learn, and what he must learn is method and not facts, for once the method is mastered, the facts become freely available to all.

THE EMPEROR

a) Face No. 4.
b) The Son of the Morning, the Chief among the Mighty.
c) The Wisdom of Sovereignty and Beauty, and the Originator of them; the Sphere of the Zodiac acting through Aries upon Sol.
d) Key No. 15.

e)

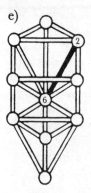

f)

Aries.

g)

Heh — A window.

h) Sense/Property — Sight.

i) Scarlet; Red; Brilliant Flame; Glowing Red.

The 15th Path is the *Constituting Intelligence*, so called because it constitutes the substance of creation in pure darkness, and men have spoken of the contemplations; it is that darkness spoken of in Scripture, Job 38:9, 'and thick darkness a swaddling band for it'.

The 15th Path links *Tiphareth* with *Chokmah*, thus constructing a bridge between Macroposopos and Microposopos by linking the Supernal Father directly with the Son. Its associated card, 'The Emperor', depicts a seated figure, robed in white and wearing a crown surmounted by a golden eagle that sits at rest, its wings folded. The figure carries a staff in his right hand, and the shield leaning against his throne bears an heraldic eagle representative of imperial power.

The path that forms a direct link between the Supernal Father and the central point of balance within the body of Adam Kadmon is a solar, and therefore a self-conscious, one. Self-consciousness is an analytical, reasoning and rational form of mentation, the hallmarks of which are acute observation and the application of logic. Self-consciousness is, in fact — at this level of the Tree, in any event — pure intellect, or that which sheds light on the darkness of ignorance, and creates sense by imposing order upon chaos. All of the symbology associated with this path is therefore related to the central idea of light, and the factors that are dependent upon the light for their existence or proper operation.

The Hebrew letter associated with the 15th Path, for instance, is *Heh*, which means 'window'. A window is something which admits light into a closed environment, thus making that environment appreciable. At the same time, however, a window greatly extends the vision — and thereby the possibilities of control and supervision — of the occupant of such an environment, by permitting *outlook*.

Such outlook as this is at once concentrated and regulated. The view from any window is to a certain degree both parameterized and focused by the limits of the window itself, which frames the outlook and sharpens it by contrast to the darker areas created by the walls that surround it. Thus it becomes clear that the 'window' provided by the 15th path permits of 'vision' that is orderly and defined, for the 'sight' it allows is not diffuse but concentrated and brought to bear upon a single area. It is channelled and limited in much the same way as the vision of a blinkered horse is channelled and limited.

Logically, sight is the sense allotted to this path, for it is sight that permits the appreciation of light, and which — by concentrating the attention — allows inspection, investigation, or the exercise of vigilance.

The word 'emperor' itself means 'sovereign having absolute power' and is derived from a Latin word which means 'to prepare or make', 'to order', or 'to command'. These ideas of government, guidance, organization, invention and leadership are all emphasized by the astrological sign attributed to the 15th Path, by its positioning on the Cube of Space, and in particular by its Yetziratic Text.

The astrological sign allotted to the 15th Path is Aries, a sign that is ruled by Mars — a planet symbolizing energy, strength, courage and swift action — and in which the sun is exalted. The position allotted the path on the Cube of Space is *north east*, the vertical line which forms the edge of the Cube and thus joins the eastern and northern faces and the north east upper corner with the north east lower corner. The northern position is represented by the Tarot card 'The Tower' (Mars) and the Eastern one by 'The Empress' (Venus). Thus this particular card links the faculties of imagination and generation with a force representative of destruction and limitation.

These latter ideas can be difficult to reconcile, but it must be remembered that the concept they seek to portray is action within certain defined limits.

The Yetsiratic Text calls this path 'The Constituting Intelligence'. To constitute something is to make or to originate or to invent it. Thus the Yetsiratic Text introduces the idea of fatherhood — the production or origination of life. These ideas obviously relate to Chokmah, the Supernal Father, the spring of limitless life. At the same time, however, the Constituting Intelligence is obviously also a defining principle, in that a constitution is a charter that limits action by the imposition of law. In fact the Constituting Intelligence is the consciousness that orders and regulates life and defines the laws under which life will operate — the laws that are policed by *Lamed*. These latter ideas are explicitly emphasized by the reference to Job in the Yetsiratic Text, for the whole of the chapter referred to in that text deals with the ordering of the cosmos and the limits set upon it by its Creator.

It is particularly important to understand, however, that while the 'vision' symbolized by this path is not a 360 degree vision, it is nevertheless a two-way vision, for the path itself is a 'window' that admits light from both sides.

The 15th Path is the path of the vision of God, face to face. It is therefore the 'window' through which the creative light of Chokmah is reflected into Tiphareth, and through which Chokmah receives the interactive influence of Tiphareth and sees itself. The 'mirror vision' of the 15th Path is thus a defining principle, and what it defines is the nature and extent of the self. 'The Emperor' is therefore at once both the Great Architect of the cosmos, and the ruling reasoning being within the self, which is, in the last analysis 'emperor' within the limits of its own kingdom, the formulator and father of its own fate.

THE EMPRESS

a) Face No. 3.
b) The Daughter of the Mighty Ones.
c) The Wisdom of Understanding; the Union of the powers of Origination and Production, the sphere of the Zodiac acting through Venus upon Saturn.
d) Key No. 14.

e)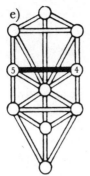

f)

Venus.

g)

Daleth — A door.

h) Opposing Human Conditions
— Grace and Sin.

i) Emerald Green; Sky Blue; Early
Spring Green; Bright rose or cerise,
rayed pale green.

The 14th Path is the *Illuminating Intelligence* and is so called because
it is that Brilliant One which is the founder of the concealed and
fundamental ideas of holiness and of their stages of preparation.

The 14th path connects *Binah* and *Chokmah*, and is a reciprocal path
symbolic of unity and the interaction of the complementary forces
that are usually referred to as 'the Father' and 'the Mother'. Thus
the esoteric title of the Tarot card associated with the path, 'The
Empress', is called 'the Daughter of the Mighty Ones'. The card itself
depicts a woman seated on a stone throne. Clouds form a veil between
the figure and the horizon, indicating that this path is a demarcation
line in consciousness — something that exists between the known,
where the Empress's rules apply, and the unknown, where they do
not. Like the Emperor, the Empress is crowned, and like him she
sits behind a shield bearing an heraldic eagle. The Empress, however,
holds a sceptre rather than a staff, and is seen full face on, rather than
in profile.

The word 'empress' means 'she who sets in order' and is usually
applied on a mundane level to the 'first woman' in the land or to a
feminine ruling power. The card 'The Empress' is therefore symbolic
of the Great Mother, creator and destroyer of life, reconciler of

opposites. Consequently all the symbols encountered in connection with this path and its associated Tarot card are symbols of birth and death and the cyclic nature of life, for birth and death, growth and destruction, are complementary opposites, each of which is necessary to the other.

The card 'The Empress' is obviously symbolic of a restrictive principle, for the Great Mother, in building life forms, also establishes the parameters of life itself. However, and as is obvious from the astrological attribution of this path, which is Venus, the laws and restrictions so established are based upon love, the guiding principle of all life.

The Hebrew letter allocated to this path is *Daleth*, which means 'door'. A door is something that allows or denies ingress or egress. The Hebrew letter therefore enshrines not only the idea of birth in that the womb is the door of life, but also the concept of defence, since a door is something that protects, separates, and divides. It will be noted that this same idea of defence, which infers safety and preservation due to the existence of a barrier of some kind, occurs in many of the symbols of those paths that directly abut the Supernal Triangle. The 'door' of this path, the 'window' of the previous one, and the 'hedge' of the 18th Path are all protective devices, and all defend against or mitigate the effects of 'the darkness that is without' that is in reality 'the radiant darkness of the limitless light'.

The ideas expressed by the Hebrew letter are emphasized by the opposing human conditions allocated to this path, Wisdom and Folly, for these two opposing states are conditions created by the action of our own internal 'door'.

'The Empress' is subconsciousness in action, an energy that responds to any stimulus either by bringing something forth or by destroying it, and subconsciousness — as we have said earlier in this chapter — is the 'door' through which external stimuli are admitted into the arena of the self. Subconsciousness acts creatively upon information fed to it by the conscious mind, bringing forth ideas or repressing them dependent upon the accuracy of the original material. The result is naturally wisdom or folly.

The direction allocated the 14th Path on the Cube of Space also concentrates on the idea of a door, but it additionally serves to introduce the fresh ideas implicit in the Yetsiratic Text, for it is *east*, and east is the place of the birth of light, the 'doorway' through which the sun enters the world each day.

The Yetsiratic Text itself reverts to those ideas expressed by the Hebrew letter and the opposing human conditions, but expresses them rather more fully, for although the Great Mother is inextricably linked with the earth and with manifestation, governing as she does all that is natural to the formation of life on earth, she is also the channel through which the light that is transmitted from Chokmah flows into manifestation. 'The Illuminating Intelligence' therefore at once refers to that light and to the activity of the subconscious mind, which enlightens by its action upon the material supplied it by consciousness.

Like all the paths on the upper reaches of the Tree, the 14th Path is very difficult of interpretation. Primarily, this is because (unlike those concepts symbolized by the lower paths, which are clearly differentiated one from the other) the concepts it seeks to portray by way of its symbolism are very subtle — separated from other concepts that are the legitimate property of other paths only by the finest shades of meaning.

Thus, this path and this card, which symbolize the action of the subconscious mind as a receptive force that generates life and ideas by way of a process of deductive reasoning whereby a single impetus is given a multiplicity of facets, must be studied in relation to the 13th Path, a path which deals primarily with the function of memory, another activity of the subconscious mind. Further, both these latter paths can only be appreciated in the light of the 12th Path, which symbolizes that form of consciousness that must instruct subconsciousness correctly if it is to produce wisdom and not folly.

THE HIGH PRIESTESS

a) Face No. **2**.

b) The Priestess of the Silver Star.

c) The Crown of Beauty, the beginning of Sovereignty and Beauty, the Primum Mobile acting through the Moon on the Sun.

d) Key No. **13**.

e)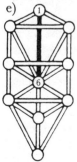

The position of the Sephirah D'aath on the Tree of Life:

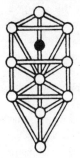

f)

The Moon.

g)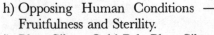

Gimel — A camel.

h) Opposing Human Conditions — Fruitfulness and Sterility.

i) Blue; Silver; Cold Pale Blue; Silver, rayed Sky Blue.

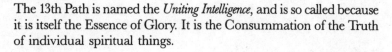

The 13th Path is named the *Uniting Intelligence,* and is so called because it is itself the Essence of Glory. It is the Consummation of the Truth of individual spiritual things.

The 13th Path links *Tiphareth* with *Kether,* and is the long straight path that runs directly up the centre of the Tree, bridging the last of the three veils and passing through the centre of *D'aath,* the 'invisible' Sephirah. Its associated card, 'The High Priestess' depicts a woman seated on a stone throne that is set between two pillars. The back of her throne supports a veil which, together with the clouds that drift behind it, partially obscure the landscape and horizon behind the figure, although some planets can be seen lazily turning through the sky at the top of the picture. The central figure wears a triple crown like that of the Hierophant, and holds a large book open on her lap. The symbol called a lemanscate (which represents infinity) appears laid in the tiles at the figure's feet.

Qabalistic literature states quite categorically that there are ten Sephiroth, and only ten, and by this token D'aath — the eleventh sphere — simply does not exist. However, strong emphasis upon any statement often serves to refute rather than to prove it, and this might be said to be the case in this instance.

It must be remembered that Qabalistic literature forms part of an extremely ancient tradition that has occupied the attention of some of the best minds in Europe and the Near East for many, many centuries. Most importantly, it must be borne in mind that all evolution is the evolution of consciousness, and that an evolution of consciousness necessarily involves an alteration of perception.

Consequently, it can be immediately inferred that in their enumeration of the Sephiroth of the Tree, Qabalists of the past counted only those spheres which they could themselves perceive, or which authoritative sources had perceived and recorded for them. D'aath is now perceptible as a sphere — however dimly — rather than as a state not wholly fulfilling all the conditions of a sphere, and this fact is therefore indicative of evolution in action rather than the faulty perception either of ancient Qabalists or their modern counterparts.

The title of the Sephirah D'aath means 'knowledge', and the sphere itself straddles the demarcation line between Microposopos and Macroposopos that is created by the Abyss, third and last of the three veils. A definite distinction exists between the energies of the Supernal Sephiroth that stand on one side of that veil and the Inferior Sephiroth that stand on the other. D'aath thus acts as the transformer between the potential and the actual in relation to the Tree as we presently perceive it — and hence of course the reference to the 'Uniting Intelligence' in the Yetsiratic Text. The 13th Path is a 'reconciler' in that it unites the Supernals with the Inferiors while preserving their polarity.

Our perception of D'aath remains hazy in the extreme — probably because it exists on rather a different level than its ten sister spheres, being really neither in this dimension nor precisely in some other, but forming as it were a gateway to various dimensions. Indeed, our only precise knowledge of this Sephirah is that experience of it is necessary to cross the Abyss.

On a personal level, D'aath represents the highest point on the Tree accessible to the Higher Self. The material body — vehicle of a single incarnation — is based in Assiah. The personality and the conscious mind — both of which are also created specifically for each incarnation — are formed of the Sephiroth Netsach, Hod and Yesod, and are based in Yetsirah. The Higher Self and the unconscious — the 'permanent' fixtures of every individual for the duration of a complete cosmic cycle — are formed of the spheres Chesed, Geburah, and Tiphareth. The Higher Self is thus based in the upper reaches of Yetsirah, and although this aspect of the self receives its influence from Chokmah, still it touches its spiritual beginnings directly only in D'aath and by way of the 13th Path; for Briah cuts the 'invisible' Sephirah neatly across its centre horizontally, while the 13th Path divides it vertically.

The demarcation line that exists between the Supernals and the Inferiors is discernible as an impediment to vision or free passage in the symbolism of the cards and paths that abut the Supernal Triangle, and is usually referred to as 'the Abyss'. The most commonplace symbol of this last veil is a desert, which — in mundane terms — is something that lacks not only water but specific points of reference.

A desert is, of course, a landscape, but it lacks the fixed points, or 'features', normally associated with landscapes. In fact, like the ocean, a desert is constantly in movement. Its sand creates wave-like dunes in response to the wind that are as impermanent as the waves of the ocean.

This symbol of the Abyss as a desert, and the images the word 'desert' evokes in the mind, are extremely important to an understanding of the 13th Path and the experiences associated with that path. Water, as we have said, is a symbol of consciousness. Deserts lack water, and yet evoke images of oceans full of that commodity. These seemingly dichotomous images make up an excellent symbolic picture of the 13th Path and of the Abyss.

The Hebrew letter allocated to this Path is a particularly appropriate one, for it is *Gimel* which means 'Camel' — an animal frequently referred to as the 'ship of the desert'. A camel is primarily a beast of burden and a mode of transport, and camels have a long history of carrying goods — usually valuable — across the trackless and waterless wastes of the world. The Hebrew letter is therefore primarily expressing the ideas of travel and commerce. However, the most important things about a camel, so far as this path is concerned, is firstly that it is an animal, and secondly that it is an animal particularly well equipped for survival in the desert, in that it stores water within its own body, and is therefore its own source of essential moisture.

These latter facts constitute vital pointers as to the inner qualities essential to safe passage along the 13th Path. The Abyss is a desert — a featureless, waterless waste. In other words, it is a bleak landscape that offers little or no outward stimulus, no points of reference, and no resources for survival save for those that are carried by the traveller. It therefore becomes obvious that in order to cross the 'desert' of the Abyss, all stimulus and resource, and every point of reference, needs to come from within the self. In addition, it is quite clear that the energy necessary to make the crossing is provided by that part of the self that is usually symbolized by an animal.

The Hebrew letter expands upon these ideas by introducing the concepts of communication, co-operation, association, combination and partnership, for camels rarely travel through the desert alone, but journey instead in 'strings'. These 'strings' or 'camel trains' usually consist of upwards of twenty camels who between them carry the goods and human representatives of more than one merchant. In addition to such tangibles as spice and human beings, of course, they will also carry news and letters, and — of necessity — the ways and social *mores* of countries different to their country of destination. Indeed, it is interesting to note that the individuals who control and guide camel trains are frequently desert dwellers who are 'foreign' to the country from whence they set out, and equally 'foreign' in their country of destination. This is particularly good D'aath symbolism, considering the extra dimensional nature of that sphere.

The opposing human conditions attributed to this path concentrate on the simple concepts of co-operation and communication, and go some way to explaining the emphasis placed upon these factors by the Hebrew letter. These conditions are peace and strife, states which are the result of either good or poor communication between people, since good communication usually results in understanding and peace while poor ones create misunderstanding and consequently strife.

The peace and/or strife that exist within the inner and outer environments of man are dictated by the level and quality of the communications that exist between his subconscious and conscious minds for, as we have said, subconsciousness will repeat and perpetuate any errors that result from the faulty perceptions of the conscious mind.

Thus both the Hebrew letter and the opposing human conditions allotted to this path illustrate the true nature and well-spring of the inner resource required to pass through the 'desert' of the Abyss — the co-operation of the various aspects of the self, which must achieve full communication and partnership before the journey along this final 'dark night' path is attempted.

To a certain degree, the name of the card also refers to the concept of co-operation, albeit obliquely. The usual title of the card is 'The High Priestess': it alternative titles are 'The Female Pope' or 'The Papess'. All three titles mean 'chief female priest' and thus infer the primary receptive aspect of the life force. Consequently, it can be seen that 'The High Priestess' is an aspect of 'The Empress' — the 'first woman' — and that her function is a co-operative one that precedes that of the actual construction of form.

In this regard, it is useful to note firstly that the card 'The High

Priestess' is ruled by the Moon, controller of the tides of consciousness and so regulator and channel of all thought patterns, and secondly that when the Tree is folded in a certain way, the Sephirah D'aath falls directly over the sphere of Yesod. Both this latter sphere and the Moon are associated with etheric activity, and indeed 'The High Priestess' represents the etheric conditions that of necessity stand between the masculine impetus of the father and the feminine form-making activities of the mother. 'The High Priestess' is therefore the primary source of all the vibratory patterns of the cosmos.

The astrological attribution, by its association with Yesod and the etheric applies to the idea of co-operation mentioned above only in that it introduces the important concept of memory. 'The High Priestess' on the face of the Tarot card holds in her hands a large book. This book represents the Akashic Records — the memory of the cosmos that is in reality imprinted upon the Astral Aether.

Again, this particular attribution emphasizes the connection of D'aath with Yesod and the 'likeness' in function of these two spheres. Yesod is the 'Treasure House of Images', that dangerous and delightful 'picture palace' where all that was and is on earth is preserved forever in the Astral Light like a fly in amber. D'aath is the Treasure House of Memory, where all that is and was and will be is faithfully recorded in the Astral Aether. Some personal memory is in any event carried over from one incarnation to another by the subconscious mind, but only the man who has mastered himself can turn the pages of the High Priestess's book — where, of course, the record is complete in every detail from beginning to end. Time in D'aath is not linear: the role that the cosmos and all its inhabitants must play out over aeons of time in manifestation exists there in the 'eternal now'. It was complete and finished at the instant it appeared.

In both Treasure Houses there exist the possibilities of duplicity, illusion and deception; but it must be remembered that all these things are born within the self. The higher the sphere, the greater — and more subtle — the illusion, and the greater also the danger of falling victim to that illusion. Discrimination is one of the virtues of Malkuth, and it must be mastered before the individual can wander safely through the Treasure House of Images. All the virtues and lessons of the Inferiors must be absorbed before the traveller tackles the Treasure House of Memory, and the hidden paths that radiate out from the sphere of D'aath and make of it another Tiphareth.

Most of the other symbols of the 13th Path and the card 'The High Priestess' reiterate and expand upon the ideas introduced by the Hebrew letter, rather than producing completely new ones. The esoteric title of the card, for instance — the Priestess of the Silver Star — refers directly to Sirius and therefore to Anubis, the mortuary god of the Egyptians who was portrayed as a jackal. Jackals are particularly good pathfinders, and excel in discovering water where no water might be thought to exist. The god Anubis, Opener of the Ways, guides the dead to the other-dimensional world of the after-life, and the living through the equally other-dimensional worlds of altered consciousness.

The direction allotted the path on the Cube of Space, *below*, refers to the subconscious mind, which is secondary and subordinate (and therefore below) the conscious mind, upon which it is dependent and which should control it.

THE MAGICIAN

a) Face No. **1**.
b) The Magus of Power.
c) The Crown of Understanding; the beginning of material production, the Primum Mobile acting through Philosophic Mercury on Saturn.
d) Key No. **12**.
e)

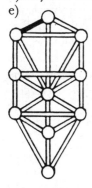

f)

Mercury.

g)

Beth — A house.
h) Opposing Human Conditions — Wisdom and Folly.

i) Yellow; Purple; Grey; Indigo rayed
   Violet.

The 12th Path is the *Intelligence of Transparency* because it is that species of Magnificence called *Chazchazit*, which is named after the place whence issued the vision of those seeing in apparitions.

The 12th Path links *Binah* with *Kether*, the First Manifest with the feminine form-making principle of the Supernal Triad. Its associated Tarot card, 'The Magician' depicts a man shrouded in a voluminous red robe brocaded with geometric figures in gold thread. His hat is worn over the hood of the robe, and its brim forms the traditional figure-of-eight shape symbolic of infinity. The figure sits facing a table upon which lie three of the symbols of the four elements. The fourth of these symbols — the Stave or Wand — he holds in his left hand. He stares into a crystal which he holds in his right hand. The stone obscures much of his face. Behind the figure, curtains, maps and papers screen the room from the outside world, giving the impression of a closed environment, an area purposefully set aside. A large book rests in a prominent position on the desk, a key already inserted in its lock.

The astrological attribution of the 12th Path is Mercury, god of communication, science and magic, whose Caduceus Wand has now become the symbol of the healing arts. The Egyptians called Mercury 'Thoth', and attributed to him the authorship of 42 books of science, and the invention of writing. Thus it can be seen that the 12th Path is associated with the intellect, with knowledge and — most importantly — with words, which are sound and vibration, language and speech.

Words are a vehicle for ideas, and writing is merely a clever system whereby idea-carrying words may be disseminated over a much wider area and in defiance of time and space. Because they are a medium for ideas, however, words, as we have said before, are essentially creative. Indeed they are purposive, intelligence-laden sounds/vibrations. Thus words can be either creative or destructive — but even when they are used destructively they remain at root a creative force.

Words carry the potential for misunderstanding and deceit, just as the conscious mind, by its incorrect observation, carries the potential for misunderstanding and deceit, but it must be remembered that these faults lie not in the words or in the conscious mind themselves, but in the use of these things. Incorrect usage will always produce incorrect results.

It will be noted from the passage above that the words 'vehicle', 'carry' and 'medium' have all been used to describe the function of words; and the nature of these three words has much to say of the nature of the card 'The Magician' and the 11th Path also.

'The Magician' is a vehicle, a medium, a carrier, a transmitter. He is not a source. Just as words transmit ideas, so 'The Magician' faithfully transmits the idea of creation. He encloses that idea — clothes it in 'words' — and sends it outwards; he pronounces the idea, formalizes it, directs it, but he is not it. 'The Magician' can pronounce the name of God, but he is not the Almighty. The 11th Path is therefore the channel through which the life energy of the Fool is organized and passed down. It is the first step towards the evolution of matter — a vibration that acts like a stone thrown into a pool of still water. It is a purposeful channel for a wilful power.

The Hebrew letter attributed to the 12th Path emphasizes the idea of creative enclosure introduced above, for it is *Beth*, which means 'a house', and a house is a form built in a specific way to enclose a specific area. The Yetsiratic Text, on the other hand, concentrates on the idea of the 11th Path as a channel for a force coming from above, for it calls this path 'The Intelligence of Transparency' and thus infers a mode of consciousness that allows force to flow through it, without offering it any let or hindrance.

This is an important clue as to the nature not only of this path but of all those other paths that have a self-conscious (or conscious) function. As I have said now many times, consciousness directs and determines subconscious reactions. These reactions are creative or destructive — which is why, incidentally, life and death are the opposing human conditions attributed to the path. The functions of consciousness are observation and tabulation, *not* deduction, which is the prerogative of the subconscious. If consciousness is allowed to usurp in part the function of subconsciousness by indulging in deductive reasoning on its own account, then it ceases to be an 'Intelligence of Transparency', and the result is the 'wrong feeding' of the subconscious, which produces errors that are not only self-perpetuating but cumulative.

The design of the Tarot card 'The Magician' seeks to portray this observing/tabulating function of the conscious mind by filling it with objects that measure or arrange or parameterize. The table, for instance, represents the Mage's field of attention and arena of action. Upon this table he must arrange his instruments in their proper order if they are to function correctly. These instruments are, of course, representative not only of aspects of the self but of essential aspects of the manifest world. The Wand (Stave) is the Magician's will and the quality of light, the Cup represents knowledge and water, the Sword air and courage or daring, and the Coins food and peace or silence.

The direction allotted the 11th Path on the Cube of Space, *above*, emphasizes the directive quality of consciousness but only by inference. The word 'above' means 'over' and 'superior'. It also means 'overseer' — and an overseer is essentially an onlooker, not a doer.

This latter fact, of course, must be looked at from both ends, as it were. In other words, because 'The Magician' — or the mode of consciousness represented by 'The Magician' — is essentially only a channel for a higher power, it can be seen that consciousness directs subconsciousness only by using the energies of superconsciousness. Thus consciousness is, in effect, a focusing device as well as a transformer that allows two other forces to interact. Acts of attention or concentration allow such a focusing to take place — and true concentration, as Paul Foster Case so rightly says, is 'perfect transparency'.

THE FOOL

a) Face No. **0**.
b) The Spirit of the Aether.
c) The Crown of Wisdom, the *Primum Mobile* acting through the Air on the Zodiac.
d) Key No. **11**.
e)

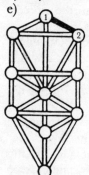

. THE FOOL .

f)

Air.

g)

Aleph — An Ox.
h) Primal Force — Air.

i) Bright pale Yellow; Sky Blue; Blue
   Emerald Green; Emerald, flecked
   Gold.

The 11th Path is the *Scintillating Intelligence*, because it is the essence
of that curtain which is placed close to the order of the disposition,
and this is a special dignity given to it that it may be able to stand
before the Face of the Cause of Causes.

The 11th Path links *Kether* with *Chokmah*, the energy source of the
All with the masculine impetus towards manifestation. The rendering
of its associated card 'The Fool' in the Prediction Tarot constitutes
a considerable departure from the usual design, although some original
features remain. It depicts a figure who stands in a stone archway
against a backdrop of circling planets. The figure is robed in a
voluminous red coat that is closely buttoned and belted and so long
as to obscure its feet. A hat is pulled well down over its eyes, so that
these — the most revealing feature of any face — cannot be seen.
The figure's expression is bemused, and its nose very red. The effect
is that of intoxication. The figure holds a white rose in its right hand,
placing this flower behind its ear. The figure leans on a whip curved
like a shepherd's crook and beribboned in blue. A simple straight staff
rests under its left arm. The staff has a leather bag such as that once
used to carry possessions tied to the end of it. At the figure's feet, a
small white dog stares, panting, directly out of the picture.
    The 11th Path is one of such simplicity as to be incomprehensible
to any save a child or an idiot. Its associated Tarot card 'The Fool'
has had many titles ('The Lord of Misrule' is a particularly enlightening
medieval one) but — until now, in any event — it has only ever had
one primary symbol: that of the jester.
    In the Middle Ages, jesters held an extraordinarily important
position in the world and were not, as is often thought to be the case,
simply entertainers — although this was, of course, a vital part of their
function. In the first instance, they were highly talented but anarchic
figures who — being immune from any punishment or retribution
for the things they either said or did (albeit they were often the butt
of cruel jokes and tricks) — did exactly as they liked, obeying no rules
save those set down by their own conscience, and holding no fixed
place in the strictly hierarchical society of the day. Additionally, they
were often used as spies, or as mediums for the judicious and timely
dissemination of information.
    It is very difficult for us now to understand the logic behind the

concept of using such a glaringly obvious individual as a jester for a spy, but it was nevertheless a good concept, and one that worked very well indeed, for it was based upon the nature of the accepted duties and prerogatives of every jester.

A jester's primary forté was mime, rather than the spoken word, and his humour — whether silent or not — was always politically based and, under its slapstick veneer, extremely clever. A jester's task was to hide sharp truth under a cloak of foolery and to make it palatable by rendering it humorous. Consequently, a good jester was an excellent mimic and well informed as to current affairs, as well as being a tumbler, a juggler and (sometimes) a musician and a linguist. He was expected to use his eyes and ears to feed his talent and provide his material, and was allowed to do so with impunity — often gaining access to people and places barred against other, and perhaps more important, men.

Much of what a jester heard or saw was never repeated at all, but some of it was — and to the best possible advantage. Many a shattering political bombshell — gleaned from gossip with servants and masters alike, or simply overheard in or out of the counsel chamber — has been dropped to devastating effect under the guise of a joke by a wily and clever jester who knew exactly what to say and when and how to say it. Many a European prince has had good cause to be grateful to his jester — cleverer, more observant, and more experienced than himself in the potentially deadly political arena of the Middle Ages — for his life.

Jesters wore, for their robes of office, rags, the white garments of the penitent, or the traditional cap and bells and parti-coloured hose and cotte of the accredited Court Jester. Butts and scapegoats, wits, confidantes, and solitary mockers of princes, tumbled by everyone and touched by none, jesters — the ultimate outsiders — both renounced the world and formed its policies, and in the process found their way into the courts of the mighty, the market places of the common man, and even into the body of the established Church. Many a jester danced and fooled his way through Holy Innocents Day in monasteries and cathedrals, and thus injected the oldest rite of the ancient Mysteries into the new religion of Christianity.

All that is left now to remind us of the power and the activities of these extraordinary men is Christmas Day (which is associated with the jester in his role of the Lord of Misrule) and April Fool's Day, but many of their attributes and beliefs are echoed in the symbolism of the 11th Path and its associated card 'The Fool' — silence, and laughter, for instance, protection and freedom, and most importantly the concept of a self, whole, unaligned, self-governing, joyful, responsible, and complete unto itself.

The Hebrew letter associated with this path is *Aleph*, which is the first letter of the Hebrew alphabet and which means 'bull' or 'ox'.

In ancient times, oxen provided all-important motive power as well as food. They pulled the plough, turned the wheel that ground the grain, and pulled the cart to market, or the household and its goods to a fresh location. Thus it represented improvement of natural conditions to the ancients, and indeed it remains to this day a symbol of wealth in many parts of the world.

In addition, and because of its great strength, the ox is a symbol of creative power and life energy. It is this last idea, when allied with the idea of motive power mentioned previously, that best portrays the important concept intended to be conveyed by the Hebrew letter Aleph; for this alliance of ideas reveals the ox to be a source of energy that is self-motivating — as symbolic of the self-regulating motive power of the cosmos, in fact.

This concept of life energy is itself emphasized by the attribution of the element of Air to this path — but it is important from the outset to realize that the element of Air referred to in this context is symbolic of the vital principle of *breath*, and that it is an active principle rather than a passive one.

The Hebrew word for breath is *Ruach*, but this word infers much more than just breath *per se*. Essentially, indeed, it means the activating energy that animates every living creature — the force that makes the vibratory sounds of 'The Magician' (and ergo the vibratory patterns of 'The High Priestess' and the forms created by 'The Empress') possible. The Aleph, 'The Fool', initiates the Beth, 'The Magician', and by so doing activates all.

The Yetsiratic Text calls the 11th Path 'the Fiery or Scintillating Intelligence'. It is very often difficult to reconcile the images brought to mind by the words 'fiery' and 'scintillating' with those evoked by the words 'air' and 'ox', but it must be remembered that just as it is impossible to either light a fire or keep it alight in the absence of air, so is it impossible to keep the fire of life alive in the body without breath. The 'Fiery and Scintillating Intelligence', in fact, is that which breathes life into everything, and which supports life once it is manifest.

Obviously, since everything that is is conscious, the Fiery and Scintillating Intelligence, placed as it is between Kether and Chokmah, is pure consciousness — a mode of thought that contains and directs all manifestation from within itself. In this context, it is worth remembering that the Sephirah Kether is the root of all the elements, and recognizing that three of those elements have already been referred to directly by the symbolism dealt with to date: Air (Primal Force), Fire (Yetsiratic Text) and Earth (the Ox). Thus is can be appreciated that the 11th Path is all things, and contains all things, and carries all things into manifestation, because it is the *will*, or motive power, behind all things.

The number allotted to the Tarot card 'The Fool' (and it should be recognized that this number is retained by every Tarot/Tree system notwithstanding the fact that the positioning of the card on the Tree frequently differs from system to system) is zero, and this is perhaps one of the most revealing symbols of all those associated with this card.

Zero is a complex mathematical symbol that equates with the pregnant nothingness referred to earlier in this book with reference to the Unmanifest. It is the nothing from whence all things come. It is a state of equilibrium that is neither plus nor minus, male nor female. It is a vacuum — a fertile nothingness from which things may be taken away or to which things may be added. It is the Universal Egg of spirit — a pure potency that is undefined.

It is these latter qualities, and the innate nature of the life breath, that have been reflected in previous designs of the Tarot, and which have led to the acknowledgement that 'The Fool' is an androgenous figure, neither plus nor minus, male nor female, but having the potential of all these things.

'The Fool' represents a very simple concept that appears complicated only because we make it so. In the Supernal Triangle the 11th Path functions as superconsciousness, an initiating principle that produces those aspects of consciousness that we have termed subconsciousness and consciousness, and which themselves unite to produce superconsciousness. The 11th Path is thus the father and the son, a self-generative and self-perpetuating principle that forms the blueprint for all creation.

Chapter 9.

Through A Glass, Darkly

The secret of reading Tarot successfully is a very simple one. It is: *Learn to use your deck correctly.*

The accent here is on the word '*learn*' — and quite rightly so, because the degree of proficiency achieved by the Tarot reader depends to a very great extent not upon pure psychism, as it is often thought to do, but upon a sound knowledge of the physical construction of the deck and a good understanding of the different functions and attributes of each separate section of it.

The deck is divided and sub-divided many times — and these divisions are purposeful rather than coincidental. They are intended to establish *parameters* — little fences that divide one subject from another, subjective from objective, people from things, one meaning from another.

Thus, *suit divisions* reveal the *subject* of a reading, and divide *subjective* from *objective*; Spot and Court cards divide *things* from *people* respectively, and *dignity* differentiates one *meaning* from another.

Most of the difficulties that readers experience are caused by a simple failure to appreciate the existence and purpose of these vital parameterizing principles.

Let's assume, for instance, that the Hierophant falls as the final card in a spread. What does this card mean?

A moment's thought will tell you that this question is unanswerable until one knows: **(i)** what the spread is about; and **(ii)** the dignity of the card 'the Hierophant', because the possible meaning of any card is wholly determined firstly by what has gone before it and secondly by its dignity.

We have said above that *suit* indicates *subject*. Thus, the highest number of cards of any given suit — Staves, Cups, Swords, Coins, or the Major Arcana — present in a spread indicates the *subject* of the spread, or the area of life to which the problem relates. This preponderance of a particular suit in a spread is called a *Majority*.

A Majority is therefore the very first thing you should look for in a spread — and when you have found it, you can immediately go on to look for its sister subject indicator, the Secondary Majority.

Secondary Majorities are formed — logically — of that suit which has the second highest number of cards present in the spread; and the *relationship* between the Primary and Secondary Majorities determines **(a)** whether the subject of the spread is *subjective* or *objective*, and **(b)** whether the suits involved are inherently *resonant* or *dissonant* to each other.

There are two subjective suits, and two objective ones. Staves and Coins are *objective*. Cups and Swords are *subjective*. Objective suits refer to those things that are *factual*, *tangible*, and *real*. Subjective suits refer to those things that are *intangible* and *subtle*.

For example, if any given spread contained a Majority of Cups, it would obviously concern the emotional life of the Querent, which is subjective in nature.

If this subjective Primary Majority of Cups were supported by a Secondary Majority of an objective suit — either Staves or Coins — then the latter cards would safely 'ground' the reading, making it factual and placing it on a firm footing in the material world.

If, on the other hand, the subjective Primary Majority of Cups were to be supported by a Secondary Majority of Swords — a suit that is also subjective in nature — then the situation as revealed by the spread would also be wholly subjective, having no basis in the material world we call 'reality' at all.

The *resonance* or *dissonance* of one suit to another mentioned in point **(b)** above is determined by the elemental attribution of the suits involved, and is based upon the interaction of the qualities of those elements as shown in Figure 10 on page 94 of Chapter 6. From that diagram it is possible to draw up the following list for easy reference:

> Staves are **dissonant** to Cups, and vice versa.
> Swords are **dissonant** to Coins, and vice versa.
> Staves are **resonant** to Swords and Coins.
> Swords are **resonant** to Cups and Staves.

This means, of course, that a Stave card surrounded by Swords or Coins would be *strengthened*, while the same Stave card surrounded by Cups would be *weakened*. If a Stave card is surrounded by both Cups and Swords, however, the dissonance of these two *latter* suits must be accounted for before the central Stave card can be interpreted at all.

Imagine now that Cups form the Majority and Staves the Secondary

Majority in our original example. From this information, it is immediately possible to determine that the reading is about a *real* personal relationship — and possible, too, to turn one's attention to the *dignity* of the all-important last card, 'The Hierophant'.

As a teacher of innumerable Tarot classes, I have noted a surprisingly marked reluctance in Tarot readers — even professional readers — to utilize the rules of dignity correctly or at all. Some readers — beginners in particular — will go to almost any lengths to avoid the very appearance of an ill-dignified card, up to and including sleight of hand. Others simply refuse to allow ill-dignified cards to figure in either deck or spread at all — and consequently consistently work with what is really a 'fixed' (and therefore wholly inaccurate) deck in which the dignity of all the cards is artificially preserved. A few — and it is a very few — know and use the rules of resonance and dissonance mentioned above which make working with an all-dignified deck possible, albeit difficult.

An aversion to ill-dignified cards is, of course, quite understandable. Reversals do, after all, tend to represent the less attractive aspects of the cards, and it is unpleasant and embarrassing to have to confront a Querent with the sort of information that such cards usually convey. Nevertheless, it is a complete waste of time to try to get over this difficulty by the simple expedient of dispensing with the rules of dignity; because while it is, of course, quite possible to avoid the physical fact of reversal — by fair means or foul — it is absolutely impossible to avoid the *reality behind the appearance* of such a reversal.

It is a fact that the Tarot will consistently rectify itself so as to produce a true and accurate account of the facts. Whether it achieves this end by the most logical method open to it, or by some other and more tortuous route — by way of card position and juxtaposition, for instance — is up to the reader; but achieve it in one way or another it most certainly will.

Even if the rules of dignity are properly applied, of course, they cannot of themselves supply the answers to all a reader's questions, for dignity is *indicative* rather than *specific*. For example: the Hierophant can mean:

i)   Good counsel.
ii) Advice and teaching.
iii) A seeker after knowledge and wisdom.
iv) A preference for the orthodox.   } dignified
v)   A need to conform.
vi) Strict adherence to religion.
vii) Marriage sometimes.

viii) Slander.
ix)   Propaganda.
x)   Bad advice.   } ill-dignified
xi)   Misrepresentation in advertisement or
       sale of goods.
xii)   Unconventional behaviour.

If we therefore return to my original statement in paragraph 6 on page 221 and amend it to read '. . . that the Hierophant falls *dignified* as the final card in a spread', then the rules of dignity *indicate* that it is possible to strike out *half* the variables of the entire meaning list, but they do not *specify* which of the remaining meanings is the correct one. It is only on the basis of all the other facts relevant to our example that such a decision can be made.

Neither, of course, can the mere dignity of a single card determine that the outcome of a given reading will be 'good' or 'bad'. Dignity in the Tarot indicates *meaning* pure and simple, and that *meaning*, when referred to events, is neither 'bad' nor 'good': it simply *is*, a single factor in a complexity of factors.

For instance, we have decided that the dignified Hierophant in our example is preceded by a Majority of Cups that is grounded by a subsidiary Majority of Staves. Thus we have determined that the reading concerns the Querent's *real* emotional life and (as no further Major Arcana cards appear to complicate our example) the only likely choice of meaning for our Hierophant is, therefore, the last of the listed dignified meanings — 'Marriage sometimes'. However, it must be remembered that the Majority and the subsidiary Majority consist of suits that are *dissonant* to each other, for this fact *modifies* the 'good' slant that is given to the reading by its optimistic last card.

This latter is an extremely important point, for it makes it unmistakably clear that dignity alone cannot be said to ensure a result that is wholly gratifying to the Querent — and likewise that reversals in and of themselves are not always portents of impending doom. In other words, the fact that our Hierophant is dignified does not indicate that the situation portrayed is an unqualified success for the Querent, just as a reversal of the same card would not have indicated unqualified failure. Moreover, if the Querent had asked a question in this situation, the answer could not have been an unqualified 'yes' or 'no' either.

A spread is a loose association of randomly chosen cards, *none of which are operating as a single pure force*. The forces represented by the individual cards *enhance*, *mitigate*, *attract*, *repel*, and *modify* each other to a greater or lesser degree depending upon their dignity and position in the spread. A dignified card actually means therefore that a *favourable* answer can be expected, or that everything will work out right *in the end*. It does not mean that the result is *good all round, now*.

It is therefore very bad Tarot practice to rest a reading upon the favourable dignity of a single card, because the meaning of any single card exists only *in relationship* to the other cards in the spread; and it is bad Tarot practice also to begin by *analysing* individual cards in a spread as though they were each standing in a void, alone and palely loitering, rather than to begin by making a *synthesis* of all the available cards.

The rules of dignity and the fact of suit division facilitate *synthesis*, which in turn leads to accurate *analysis*. This logical and systematic method of reading is the only method that will invariably produce the correctly applicable meaning of each individual card in a reading, and thus a true exposition of the facts pertaining to the reading as a whole.

The natural but disastrous human tendency to want to 'make things right' for the Querent that causes readers to shy away from a correct use of the rules of dignity obviously spreads over into areas other than those involving reversals. Indeed, it rears its ugly head wherever it may.

I have noticed, for instance, that once the spread is laid out, a large proportion of readers take one look at it and decide that they are very unhappy with what chance had chosen to set before them, and that they had better take steps to change it forthwith — and this is particularly so where no definite question has been asked, and an apparently unfortunate card ends the reading, or the all-important last card turns out to be that awful bugbear, a Court card.

As is explained (indeed, illustrated) above, an ill-dignified card at the end of a reading does *not* necessarily indicate an unfortunate result; but I have nevertheless seen readers — even professional readers — in these circumstances turning over the next card in the deck, and the next, and the next, and the next after that if need be, until they come to a manifestly 'good' and dignified card upon which to bring the reading to an end.

Important as it is that the Querent should leave a reading feeling confident and refreshed, this sort of behaviour is a little bit 'over the top'. Worse still, it smacks of desperation and (since the average Querent is neither totally blind and insensitive nor yet a complete fool) the tense atmosphere thus produced soon infects everyone involved.

Note, please, that I am not saying that this 'freehand' method does not work, or that there is no place for it in the reader's repertoire. It does, and there is. But there is really no need for a well-informed reader to stoop to such a practice unless circumstances particularly demand it — which, usually, they don't. It is in any event worth considering what a reader addicted to this practice would do if faced with the Ten of Swords as the last card in a spread such as Le Grand Jeu, which uses every symbol in the deck and where there are therefore *no* excess cards to which he could appeal . . .

When an apparently unfortunate card appears at the end of a reading, the correct thing to do (as always) is to turn to first principles — which in this case means to the rules governing the *principle of progression*.

The universe is immutable. It runs according to the laws of cause and effect. Thus, if you examine the meanings of the Small cards in any one suit, you will see that there is a logical progression from Ace to Ten. In other words, when read through in numerical order, the meanings of the cards in each suit *appear to be telling a story*.

This state of affairs is no more of a happy coincidence than are the parameterizing devices that litter the deck. It occurs because — as you have seen — the Small cards are allied to the ten Sephiroth of the Tree of Life, which themselves form a logical progression which tells the story of creation.

The order in which the suits are assembled internally (i.e. according to the order of the Sephiroth) is therefore an aid to prediction, and if one thoroughly understands the principle of progression, which is based upon that order, one can make further predictions from the last card in the spread without any recourse at all to the remainder of the deck.

In effect, the rules of progression provide the reader with the equivalent of an invisible last card, and enables him to ascertain the possible progress of any reading in either of two ways.

Firstly, the final card in a spread will give way to the next card *of that suit* in numerical order, i.e. the five to the six, and so on.

Secondly, the final card in a spread will give way to the card of the next highest value but *of the predominant suit in a reading*, or that suit which provides its *Primary Majority*. Thus, if the Primary Majority in a spread is Cups, and the last card of it is the Seven of Coins, then the future would be indicated by the Eight of Cups.

Following established Qabalistic principles, which state that the Malkuth of one level is the Kether of another, *Tens* give way to *Aces* so far as the rules of progression are concerned. Thus the Ten of Staves would be followed by the Ace of Cups, and so on.

If the last card in a reading happens to be a Court card, this does not present any obstacle to interpretation either — particularly if the *event-oriented* meanings of the Court cards (which can be found annexed to Chapter 10) are used in preference to their *people representative* meanings.

A Court card occupying the final position in a spread could thus mean one of two things, i.e. *either* that the person indicated by the card holds the Querent's happiness in their hands for better or worse (according to dignity), *or* that the card refers to an event. The correct one of these two alternative choices will — obviously — always be made clear by the nature of the spread, the presence and type of its Majorities (if any), and the general appearance of the cards in it.

The 'final card problem' tends not to arise when one of the Major Arcana cards holds this place in a spread, because Major Arcana cards are generally much more specific in their indications; but the same basic principle of progression can be applied to these cards also if necessary.

Of course, these 'invisible' cards are not really part of the spread, and cannot therefore be considered to be *actual* symbols, but only *embryonic* ones. Such cards belong even more to the realm of probability than does the rest of the spread — which in any case it must be remembered indicates only what *might* occur rather than what *will* or *must* occur.

In addition, events foretold by invisible cards following the rules of progression will be outside the time scale of the spread you are using — and it is impossible to determine *how far outside* unless the card itself turns out to be a timing card, or unless the spread is large enough to determine timing by way of the device referred to on page 234-5 of Chapter 10.

There is no rule of thumb method to say which of the two systems of progression given above should be used in any particular circumstance; but frequently (and particularly in the case of experienced readers) one card (the correct one) of the two possibilities will simply project itself into the mind — sometimes against all logic and reason — for despite the emphasis placed upon rules and principles in this chapter and throughout this book, the Tarot cannot be mastered simply by way of a good memory and a slavish adherence to system. The greater part of the work that goes into making a Tarot master goes on inside the psyche of the reader himself, who improves his intuitional faculties by improving his fundamental self according to established spiritual principles. The rules of the deck exist to make this work *easier*, but they do not and cannot make it *unnecessary*.

Chapter 10.

All Done With Mirrors

Spreads are windows into the shadowy twilight world of prediction and probability. The length and breadth of vision they provide; the direction upon which they focus, and the amount of light they admit, all depend upon the ability of the reader to understand and control them. It is therefore very important that every reader learns to construct and use spreads intelligently, because his ability — or lack of it — in this single area can make or break him.

Broadly speaking, there are two main types of Tarot spread — *positional* spreads and *sequential* ones.

Positional spreads allot titles to the various card positions of which their pattern is made up, so that each position becomes meaningful in and of itself. Thus positional spreads restrict (and sometimes even determine) the meaning of the individual cards occupying the positions within their pattern by forcing those cards to operate within an extra and very narrow parameter.

Usually, the pattern of a positional spread admits of five or six titled positions, and uses no more than three cards per position, if that. Thus, the purely predictive potential of these patterns is not particularly good; but their capacity for real precision is very good indeed.

Take, for example, the positional spread pattern shown in Figure 19. As you can see, this particular pattern is essentially astrological in format. It is constructed of thirteen positions in all, twelve of which are placed in a circular pattern on its perimeter, while the remaining one is positioned in the centre.

These thirteen positions can be utilized in two ways. They can represent the twelve astrological houses — in which case the central position will be occupied by a deliberately chosen Primary Significator, as per Figure 19 — or they can represent the twelve months of the year, when the central position will be occupied by a 'Keynote' card, as per Figure 20.

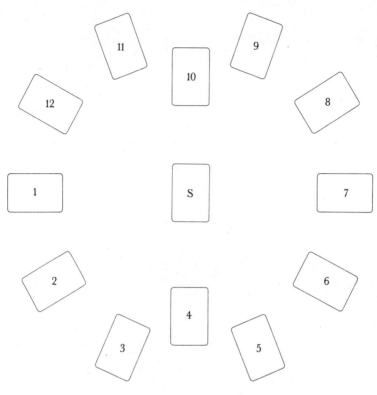

Position Key

1 — Aries — Represents the Querent, his disposition and his current problems.
2 — Taurus — Represents the Querent's financial situation.
3 — Gemini — Represents travels and communication.
4 — Cancer — Represents the Querent's home life, his siblings and his parents.
5 — Leo — Represents the Querent's pleasures.
6 — Virgo — Represents the Querent's health.
7 — Libra — Represents partnerships and marriages.
8 — Scorpio — Represents inheritances and deaths.
9 — Sagittarius — Represents philosophy, religion, education and dreams.
10 — Capricorn — Represents the Querent's career.
11 — Aquarius — Represents the Querent's friends.
12 — Pisces — Represents the Querent's burdens, restrictions, and secret fears.

Figure 19: Astrological Spread Type 1.

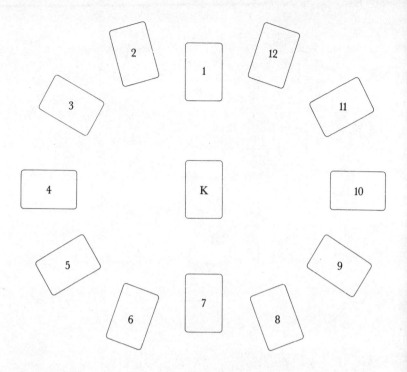

Card position 1 always represents the present month for the purposes of this spread.

The 'Keynote card' sets the 'tone' for the year, but readers should remember that this particular card is subject to being coloured by the attitude of the Querent, and read it accordingly.

Figure 20: Astrological Spread Type 2

As you will see from the 'Position Key' annexed to Figure 19, this particular version of the spread has a markedly subjective and psychological cast. Thus, it is also almost totally non-predictive in nature — and will remain so even if the reader uses as many as four cards per position and utilizes the principle of progression to progress (or regress) its individual cards; because the effect of such progression would be to produce images representative only of past or future psychological conditions. Indeed, the 'event-oriented' aspects of this pattern (as revealed, of course, by suit attribution) are all primarily causal — confined in the main, in other words, to the past and to those events which actually created the purely subjective conditions revealed by the spread. In addition, the spread pattern gives no indication as to time at all by card position, and — due to the underlying nature of the pattern — such timing cards as are turned up randomly by the spread will indicate time *only for the position in which they appear*, and not for the spread as a whole.

When, on the other hand, the positions of the same spread pattern are used to indicate the months of the year, then the spread instantly becomes predictive, objective, 'event-oriented', and very precise as to time; but its predictive capabilities are necessarily limited by the number of cards allotted to each card position and the inherent ability of the reader to relate the events of one position to the events of the next — and this will remain the case whether the reader utilizes the principle of progression or not.

Thus it becomes clear that positional spreads will supply quite precise information as to time or activity, and can be used to secure either a subjective or an objective picture. However, it should be borne in mind that these patterns rarely offer optimum predictive opportunities to the less-experienced reader, and also that they rarely offer really satisfactory 'time-oriented positions' and 'event-oriented positions' together in a single spread either; such a combination is extremely difficult to construct and use successfully.

Sequential spreads utilize serial patterns, in which the lines or blocks of cards tell a consecutive story. In order to do this successfully, these patterns usually organize the blocks or lines of which they are constructed into large positional-type areas entitled 'Past', 'Present' and 'Future', which enable the reader to place the events of the Querent's 'story' into a suitable time scale.

The 'Romany Spread' (see Figure 21) is a very good example of a sequential spread, with a serial, or 'line of cards' timing device. From the diagram, it can be seen that such patterns are capable of offering objective/'event-oriented' *and/or* subjective information and — because of the space they allot to 'Past' events — some indication of causation also. However, it will also be seen that they are inherently extremely imprecise in their construction simply because they do not 'cubby-hole' events by type, as positional spreads do.

Sequential spread patterns like this one always look as though they should be much easier to use than positional patterns, simply because they appear to offer the reader much more room to manoeuvre. In

Figure 21: The Romany Spread — A Common Sequential Pattern.

fact, however, this is not true, for sequential patterns are much more demanding and difficult than positional ones.

In the first place, of course, the use of sequential spreads demands that the reader understand the divisions of the deck, because without this knowledge he could not formulate an opinion as to what the 'story' revealed by the spread is about or whether that 'story' is in fact subjective or objective.

Secondly, when it comes to sequential spread patterns the reader must be capable literally of giving each and every card its full weight, because if he is not so capable, the reading will be far too vague to be of any constructive use to the Querent.

In addition, and because a specifically chosen Primary Significator is rarely used in these spread patterns, the reader must be continually on the watch for randomly appearing Primary and/or Secondary Significators — and be aware also that the appearance of such a Significator may, by appearing in his causative, 'Past' positional grouping, *either* rob him of the contents of most of that position and all of the following one, thus presenting him with an excess and quite burdensome number of wholly predictive cards, *or* cause the otherwise moderately accurate timing parameters to 'lie' simply because the Querent himself is 'living' in the past and thus has his consciousness centred there — *or* both.

From the examples given above, it will be obvious that spreads, like computers, do not produce gratuitous information and will not function outside the definite parameters set by their original design. It is therefore in every reader's own best interests to take the time and trouble to think about the problems that reading entails, and equip himself accordingly with a portfolio of spreads that will cover any and every eventuality.

A good place to start designing such a portfolio is — logically — the questions that are asked by the average Querent. This will yield a list that looks something like this:

What shall I . . .?
Who shall I . . .?
When shall I . . .?
Will I/he/she/it . . .?
Why . . .?
Is . . .
If I . . .?

1. 'What shall I . . .?'

This is a question that obviously demands the use of a positional spread with placements that represent two or more alternatives. In addition, the reader might, in the interests of precision, consider the use of a split, rather than a full, deck.

The decision to split the deck depends, of course, on the nature of the question. 'What shall I do about my marital difficulties?', for instance, might well demand the use of a full deck; but 'What shall I do about my employer, who is giving me hell at the office?' certainly would not — Staves, Coins and the Major Arcana being the optimum split for the purpose of this latter example, since it excludes the dangerously subjective suits of Cups and Swords and throws the onus of all subjectivity on the Major Arcana, which is a more stable 'suit' for this purpose.

2. 'Who shall I . . .?'

This is a dangerous question, for it infers a choice between two people or two groups. In attempting to answer such a question, the reader is therefore treading on very shaky ground indeed, and should firmly resist the idea of using any spread pattern that contains a determinative final position at all.

A positional spread with inbuilt alternatives is, of course, almost certainly the best pattern type for the purpose, and would definitely come up with the required answer; but effectively any reader faced with this problem would be best advised tactfully to alter his Querent's phraseology altogether before he begins the reading, and plump for a custom-designed and predictive 'If I . . .?' positional spread which will enable him to pass this hot potato of an issue neatly back into the Querent's hands — where, of course, it belongs.

3. 'When shall I . . .?'

This question is a snare for the unfortunate reader's feet, for not only is it riddled with assumptions on the part of the Querent (which may or may not prove to be accurate or desirable), it is also demanding of an extremely complex spread pattern if it is to be answered satisfactorily.

The Querent is asking a bald question. He will not, however, be thrilled if proffered an equally bald reply, like 'Yes' or 'No'. Furthermore, by asking 'When shall I . . .?' he is assuming firstly that he will indeed do something at some future date; and secondly, that he will continue to want to do this particular thing regardless of the passage of time. 'When shall I?' is therefore obviously a question that requires:

(i)   precise positions to indicate whether or not the Querent is going to do something in the first place;

(ii) sufficient sequential material for the reader to determine the 'whys' (or 'why nots') of this latter fact;

(iii) sufficient predictive capacity to allow the reader to inform the Querent what will happen between the time of the reading and such time as he will (or will not) do what he presently thinks he is going to, and what will happen thereafter;

(iv) an extremely precise timing device.

Such a spread pattern is an impossible animal — a reader's nightmare — and, human nature being what it is, it is also the animal he is most likely to need.

The only pattern I have managed to come up with so far that even remotely covers all the points outlined above adequately is the 'Yes, No, and If So, When? Spread' that is reproduced in Appendix II to this Chapter from the Tarot Workbook — and this is by no means the spread pattern to end all spread patterns, being exceedingly inelegant in design.

The predictive capacity and sequential material of this particular pattern are both to be found in the stacks of twelve cards that do (or do not, of course, as the case may be) precede each Ace; while the Aces themselves answer the actual question by way of dignity.

The spread itself is easy and quick. The only difficulty the reader is likely to have with it is therefore the Querent's reaction to the appearance of three reversed Aces — which will in effect be saying: 'No, no, no; not now, not next week, and not ever' — or indeed any result that does not accord with what he wants to hear . . .

There are, of course, other timing devices that can built into suitable sequential or even positional patterns. The one devised by Jean Goode, for instance, and detailed in Sasha Fenton's *Fortune-Telling by Tarot Cards*, is very clever indeed, and works very well. The trick with it is to go backwards through the spread from the last card until you fall on a Small card. The timing can then be worked out as follows:

Years are indicated by **Coins**.
Months are indicated by **Swords**.
Weeks are indicated by **Staves**.
Days are indicated by **Cups**, but only when they fall next to a **Coin** card.

This method looks complicated on first reading, but in practice it is really very simple. Most importantly, its success ratio is quite high in an area of Tarot reading in which very few thing work accurately — or at all.

4. 'Will I . . .?'

This question demands a position spread with a definite 'Yes/No' position that will, of course, indicate the correct answer by way of dignity. Surrounding placements should include positions indicating 'fors' and 'againsts' and — most importantly — consequence.

Again, these latter placements *must* be included, because if the reader comes up with a bald 'Yes' or 'No' — even if this answer is accompanied and enlarged by a complete interpretation of the card providing this answer — the Querent will inevitably ask 'Why?', or 'Why not?', which will (if these answers are not built into the 'Will I . . .?' spread in the first place) inevitably call for yet another round of shuffling, cutting, laying out, etc., all of which takes time that the reader (or his patiently waiting next client) may not have.

Thus this very small spread which allots a dual purpose to each of its three placements, makes a very good 'Will I . . .?' spread, as shown in Figure 22. The reader should start this pattern at card position 1, and read the answer to the question by way of the dignity of that card (dignified meaning 'Yes', and ill-dignified meaning 'No'). He should then immediately follow with 'because . . .' — which he will gain from an interpretation of the card occupying position 2 — and

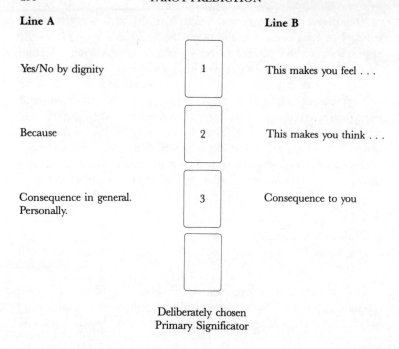

Line A

Yes/No by dignity

Because

Consequence in general.
Personally.

Line B

This makes you feel . . .

This makes you think . . .

Consequence to you

Deliberately chosen
Primary Significator

Figure 22: The 'Will I . . .?' Spread.

then go on to interpret the card occupying position 3 as fully as he can in order to forecast consequence.

Having completed that section of the pattern, the reader can begin again at the top of the spread and examine the Querent's subjective response to the situation (card positions 1 and 2) and the consequences of that response (card position 3). These latter subjective interpretations of the cards must, of course, be made having reference to the nature of the deliberately chosen Primary Significator occupying the fourth and last position.

A further dimension can be added to this pattern by way of the rules governing the principle of progression, working that principle both backwards (regression) and forwards (progression) in time. The 'invisible card' preceding card 1 would then add an extra dimension — not to that card, but to card 2, 'Because', while the 'invisible card' preceding card 2 would expand upon card 3. The rules governing resonance and dissonance should, of course, be applied throughout at every stage of the reading.

In this way, the causes lying behind the appearance of the three
'invisible' cards (which, because they are in the past, are not probable
but actual), and the eventual effects of those causes (which are, of course,
only probabilities) can all be gained for very little effort. Indeed, these
'invisible factors' effectively expand this tiny spread to quite respectable
dimensions.

5. 'Why?'

'Why' can be a bugbear simply because the answer can prove
unpleasant for the Querent — and so, at second-hand, for the reader
himself, who must provide the tissues, the tea, the sympathy and a
more cheerful direction for the sufferer's mind. It naturally demands
a sequential spread with the usual positional elements of 'Past', 'Present'
and 'Future'; but it should be borne in mind — because the Querent
is actually asking for causes — that this particular question is one that
responds very well to the application of the principle of progression
in its 'regressive' mode, and thought should therefore be given to this
aspect of the matter when constructing such a spread.

Causation alone can always — and very easily — be established
from an adjustment of an ordinary positional spread, always assuming
that the positions themselves are made sufficiently meaningful; but
the real secret of success with a 'Why?' spread is to make the spread
reveal circumstances fully in the first instance — thus making a
sequential spread with a large central 'the situation is this' section
by far the most viable of all options.

The next section of such a pattern should then obviously be designed
to reveal the causes behind the manifest effects of those circumstances;
and the last one a future leading on and away from the present.

In this way, the reader again covers all possible eventualities, and
saves himself the time and work involved in laying out further spreads
in order to answer further questions.

Quite apart from all the points mentioned above (and despite the
fact that I have not mentioned *size* of pattern at all when dealing
with any of those points) one of the most important things that any
reader can learn about spreads and their construction is that bigger
is not better — all evidence to the contrary notwithstanding.

The idea that bigger is better usually takes root in the readers' mind
when he is a beginner, convinced that 'just one more card' (or two,
or three) or 'just one more position' (or a dozen) would make everything
clear for him, and — very naturally — it grows like the green bay
tree when his initial experience apparently proves him right.

The improved success ratio achieved by beginners using large spread patterns is very simply explained: such spread patterns offer him many more options, and thus a far greater margin for error, than do small ones.

The beginner does not truly understand his deck or its functions. Furthermore, he has not done enough work on the cards for the meanings to be second nature — indeed, he is still at the stage where he forgets the odd one here and there and is forced to spend time 'looking things up'. Consequently he dreams of large spreads which will provide him with a multitude of options, fifty per cent of which at least will inevitably prove familiar to him and thus allow him to say something relevant to the Querent — which the Querent will, in the way of all Querents everywhere, fall upon with wonder and delight.

It does not occur to the beginner, at this stage, to realize that he is looking for a soft option or an easy way out. Nor does he remember, in the first flush of his 'success', that he has 'skipped' cards left and right during his journey through the reading — or that he will only increase his chances of committing this awful sin if he consistently overburdens himself with the complex options and alternatives provided by large spreads. He does not consider either the time it takes him to lay out such a spread, or the space he needs in order to lay it out comfortably. In fact, as he pores over his latest forty-card creation, safely laid out in all its splendour on a dining table designed to seat eight people, the beginner enamoured of the 'really big spread' is just a man in a round tower pierced by arrow slits who has convinced

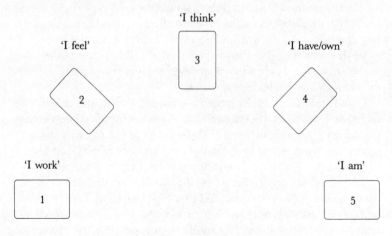

Figure 23: A Small Multi-purpose Spread Pattern.

himself that he faces a picture window offering 360 degree vision.

A well-equipped reader is therefore a reader who — having examined his own potential and ability honestly — takes care to utilize both it and the physical construction of the deck to the best advantage in order to produce a complete portfolio of neat, compact, self-designed, purpose-built spreads that are both short and to the point.

Building very small spreads is easier than it looks. Take, for example, the simple five card pattern illustrated by Figure 23, which can, if the rules of the deck are utilized to the best advantage, become an invaluable and user-friendly tool.

This spread is fundamentally positional, and any number of titles can be applied to its pattern to achieve a specific result. For example, by allotting the titles 'I Work', 'I feel', 'I think', 'I have/own', and 'I am', the spread can be made to cover every area of the Querent's life.

In addition, the pattern can be approached in one of two ways; the first of these will narrow the parameters of the individual positions still further, simply by utilizing the parameterizing functions built into the deck as rigidly as possible.

In order to achieve this end, the reader must split the deck into its five component parts: Staves, Cups, Swords, Coins and Trumps. He should then 'fan' these sections one by one, asking the Querent to choose one card at random from each fan; these randomly chosen cards should then be placed in the positions allotted to them by the pattern.

This process naturally ensures that the positions of the spread are filled with cards 'like' those positions in nature (i.e. the Stave card goes to the Career position, and so on) so that each card in the spread is eminently fitted for its particular position by suit.

When the spread pattern is used in this way, each individual card in it becomes a picture of self and circumstance at an instant in time — and that instant is *now*. Indeed, if the spread pattern is used in this way it will reveal *only* what is happening, or thought, or felt, *now*; and although each card can be contrasted with every other — i.e. the 'I feel' placement allied to the 'I work' placement to enlarge upon the work situation — it must be remembered that the result can never be *predictive*, but only *factual in the now*. Thus this is a good method with which to begin a series of spreads, but it is not suitable for single spread reading situations, nor to answer a question or end a reading.

When, on the other hand, the same spread pattern and position titles are used with a randomly shuffled deck, its positions being filled with cards taken 'off the top' so that the 'I work' spot may be filled with a Cup or any other card, then it automatically becomes predictive as it stands — and this predictive potential can be further enhanced by use of the rules of the principle of progression/regression in either of its variations. In addition, and because any spread that contains three or more cards becomes subject to the rules of Majority, the size of the spread enables the reader to judge of the most important aspect of the Querent's life at the time by this means.

Obviously, this same pattern can be used over and over again for different purposes simply by changing the titles of its positions to fit circumstances and the needs of the Querent. Thus, an entire reading series — commencing with, say, a general sequential spread to 'set the tone' as it were — can be undertaken by way of this single pattern, each 'mini-reading' of which would be designed to expand further upon the information gained in the original general spread.

Spreads need not, of course, even be as large as this five card pattern to be successful — as, indeed, I have illustrated above — but in reality patterns consisting of less than five cards demand an extraordinary amount of knowledge and effort on the part of the reader. Five, in fact, is the bottom line number for readers who are not in complete control of their deck and all its functions; for when it comes to reading with fewer cards than that, the process requires not only that the reader understands his deck completely, but also that he has total command of a large symbol language, the ramifications of which will lead him faultlessly and safely along a single symbol string to the truth that lies at the end of it.

This method of reading — which offers quite precise information of a kind not usually associated with Tarot cards — is based upon an intricate system of correspondences devised in the distant past. The foundations of that system are firmly rooted in first principles, and thus — despite its very great age — it is a system that is valid today and will remain so in perpetuity. It is also a system that is fundamentally Aquarian in nature — 'like' all those things and attributes we associated with Aquarianness — and although it has been neglected, and almost forgotten, during the Piscean Age, it is naturally coming into its own again now.

The Tarot itself is a small but vital part of the whole system — a single, but central piece in a very large jigsaw, a tiny key to an enormous door. Its images derive from the same source, and remain true to the same purpose; and through them we can *see* that source and purpose, which is also, of course, our own.

The Tarot images link us with the past which is always with us because it is an essential part of us, and so with the future, which grows inexorably out of the past. They are images of yesterday —

immeasurably ancient — and images of today — immeasurably relevant and functional. Through them we can trace the mental footsteps of our kind through time, and through them — our images for tomorrow — we can discern a true way into the shifting sands of the future.

Appendix I

Meanings at a Glance

THE MINOR ARCANA

STAVES

Season — Spring. *Direction* — South.

Ace

Dignified:
New beginnings, innovative ideas, inspiration and initiative. Virility and inception. Strength, vigour and energy applied to a thing. Natural, as opposed to invoked, force.

Ill-dignified:
False starts. Projects conceived but not initiated. Impotence. Failure through lack of initiative.

Two

Dignified:
Earned success, authority, prosperity and profit. Property deals and property ownership. Contracts of employment and partnership agreements successfully and profitably concluded. Job related benefits and 'perks'. Dominion over things. Influence over others.

Ill-dignified:
Revenge. Pride and overweaning ambition. Greed. Partnerships dissolved. Business transactions delayed or concluded at a loss or break-even. Property 'chains' delay the conclusion of a transaction. Unforgiving or obstinate behaviour impede progress in a matter.

Three

Dignified:
Successful trade or commerce. Establishment of a new business or new branch of an existing business. Mergers. Fruitful collaboration between companies or individuals. Success and profit through the practical assistance of another. Opportunities generally. Realization of hope. Completion of labour.

Ill-dignified:
Obstinacy. Proud and arrogant behaviour. Conceit. Refusal of assistance and consequent failure. Failed or abortive ventures. Conflicts of personality or interest.

Four

Dignified:
Security and securities. The successful completion of projects and arrangements. Growth and expansion. Property transactions successfully concluded. Rest after labour. Prosperity and celebration. Clever or subtle reasoning. Conclusions correct, and drawn from previous knowledge.

Ill-dignified:
Obstacles or problems caused by over-anxiety or hurried action. Completion delayed but imminent. A quiet period before great activity. Insincerity. Conclusions based on erroneous information, but strongly held.

Five

Dignified:
Strife, trouble, tests, competition, opposition. Jostling over power or position. Disputes over rights, ownership or policy. Difficult negotiations. Acrimonious discussion and opposing viewpoints. Desire to have a thing at no matter what cost. Desire to succeed against all odds.

Ill-dignified:
Legal disputes and litigation. Compulsive and unnecessary competition with others; opposing viewpoints within the self and consequent inability to come to a decision. Lusting after things that are out of reach.

Six

Dignified:
Victory and triumph after strife or prolonged effort. Agreements reached, problems overcome, litigation won or settled. Promotion or success due to hard work. Good news.

Ill-dignified:
Disappointment and fear due to the undeserved advancement of another over the self. Trouble caused or extra work to be done due to someone else's laziness or inefficiency. Rewards delayed by red tape. Delayed or bad news. Insolent behaviour. Excessive pride in self or self's achievements or possessions.

Seven

Dignified:
Obstacles or powerful opposition to be faced, and problems to be overcome if loss is to be avoided. Quarrelling, wrangling, threats and pretence. Success determined by courage and steadfastness in the face of adversity.

Ill-dignified:
Indecision and fear result in lost opportunities. A refusal to face opposition or problems squarely. Moral cowardice. Fear of responsibility. Fear of success.

Eight

Dignified:
Swift action: an end to obstacles and delay. News communications, telephone calls and letters present new opportunities to broaden horizons and expand on existing business or social affairs. Business related travel or visits. A love of outdoor sports or pastimes. Success at sport.

Ill-dignified:
Impetuous action. Too much force applied to a thing too suddenly. Foolhardy speech or communication results in lost opportunities. Bad news or dismissal from employment. Embezzlement or theft. Plans or journeys cancelled or delayed due to events beyond the Querent's control. Industrial action sometimes. Accidents or mishaps whilst engaged in sport or outdoor pursuits.

Nine

Dignified:
Victory preceded by opposition, apprehension and fear. An unassailable position in life. Safe and assured tenure of employment or property. Pensions and insurance. Stability, productivity and good health. Recovery from illness. Curiosity. Many questions asked by or of the Querent.

Ill-dignified:
Weakness or intractability of character. Inability to compromise leads to defence of untenable positions. Loss of a secure position, status or tenure due to own actions. Impractical and unproductive schemes. Possible illness. A desire to keep up appearances. A hiding of the truth.

Ten

Dignified:
Great success and increased responsibility therewith. Excessive time spent dealing with matters of business. Great good fortune with its attendant demands on time. Generosity and self-sacrifice.

Ill-dignified:
Excessive overtime or responsibility. The unnecessary burdening of oneself with tasks best delegated to others. Over-conscientiousness.

Selfish spoiling of the pleasures of others. Deceit, slander and obstinacy. Ill-will, levity and envy.

CUPS

Season — Summer. *Direction* — West.

Ace

Dignified:
New project or hobbies of a creative or artistic nature. Love, fertility and abundance. Birth sometimes. New friendships and an enhanced social life.

Ill-dignified:
Loss of faith, unhappiness and dissatisfaction. Friendships or relationships on the wane. Barrenness. Emotional distress. Creative faculties blocked or distorted. Creative abilities neglected or set aside.

Two

Dignified:
New romances or partnerships. Harmony and co-operation. Differences resolved, quarrels made up. New ideas generated by co-operation or collaboration. Pleasure in commitment. Warm friendships and laughter. Pleasant meetings.

Ill-dignified:
Quarrels and misunderstandings. Separations, divorce, love not returned, or inequitable regard. Failure of partnerships due to unforeseen circumstances. Folly, dissipation and waste.

Three

Dignified:
Celebration, parties, house-warmings. Weddings. A birth or the inception of a new project. Renewed health and vitality. Success and great happiness. Good luck, unexpected prizes and winnings. New clothes.

Ill-dignified:
Self-indulgence. Sensuality and selfishness. Over-indulgence in food, tobacco, alcohol or sex. Selfish exploitation of others. Greed. Excessive expenditure on pleasure, clothes, or social events.

Four

Dignified:
Pleasure at an end. Boredom and dissatisfaction. New interests, new and stimulating ideas and opportunities are within the Querent's reach if he would only bring himself to notice their existence. A time for re-evaluating what is important in life. Present happiness may not continue. Anxiety as to future happiness.

Ill-dignified:
Satiety and excess. Novelty and excitement sought for its own sake and bringing little or fleeting pleasure. A need for work and meaningful physical and mental employment.

Five

Dignified:
Worry, disappointment and sadness. Broken engagements, emotional letdowns. Regret of hasty action. Thoughts and dreams of what might have been. Legacies of an emotional or monetary nature. Unkindness from friends.

Ill-dignified:
The end of a period of unhappiness which will nevertheless leave emotional scars. New friendships, expectations and opportunities, the enjoyment of which is flawed by the memory of past events. Anxiety caused by unexpected and rapid change. Trouble from unexpected sources. Kindness from others repulsed or not repaid.

Six

Dignified:
Pleasant memories show the way to present success and the fulfilment of wishes. Past work has brought present reward, past associations present relationships. Family gatherings, meetings with old friends and contacts.

Ill-dignified:
Fruitless nostalgia. The key to future success depends upon the Querent cutting himself free of the past and its associations or relationships. Shows the need for a complete change of scene. Pride in past accomplishment proves a barrier to fresh achievement. A childish clinging to parents or a love of outworn habits and customs.

Seven

Dignified:
Choice — sometimes between the mystical and the material, or the real and the illustory. Confusion. A plethora of opportunities must all be carefully examined if a serious error of judgement is not to be made. Success dependent upon sound judgement.

Ill-dignified:
Illusion, deception, vanity and failure. Self-delusion, fantasy, drunkenness and fornication. Violence against women and domestic violence generally. Disappointment in self and life but the blame for misfortune cast elsewhere. Success gained but not followed up. Deception in love or friendship.

Eight

Dignified:
Indolence and laziness in success. Restlessness and compulsive movement. Security cast aside. Rejection of established lifestyle, social *mores* or modes of thought. Temporary success, but of short duration.

Ill-dignified:
Success abandoned. Decline of interest in anything. Depression. Recklessness. A search for an impossible idea, with all realistic alternatives abandoned. A turning to fantasy to escape an unacceptable reality.

Nine

Dignified:
Contentment and physical well-being. Material success and an assured future. Success on the stage or in the arts. Achievement of wishes or fame. Vanity. Conceit. Need for self-expression and self-display. Complete happiness.

Ill-dignified:
Complacency which may lead to failure by a narrow margin. Vanity and self-indulgence at the expense of duties leads to failure. Spendthrift tendencies lead to shortage of money or loss of credit.

Ten

Dignified:
Permanent and lasting success. True friendships, lasting happiness and security. Generosity and kindness. Happy family life. Matters arranged to the satisfaction of the Querent.

Ill-dignified:
Family quarrels. Loss of friendship or home. Sudden violent disruption of a happy and ordered environment, sometimes caused by children, adolescents or the very old.

SWORDS

Season — Autumn. *Direction* — East.

Ace

Dignified:
New beginnings. A rebirth. Victory and success. Triumph. A complete

change of mind, which affects all areas of the Querent's life. A complete recovery from illness. A 'new lease on life'. A change of environment stimulates a feeling of health and well-being. Power invoked for good.

Ill-dignified:
Destruction, violence, misuse of power. Disastrous communciation or hasty action on the part of the Querent spoils prospective business arrangements or relationships. Ill-health. Physical death sometimes and dependent upon other cards. Force invoked for evil.

Two

Dignified:
Relief. Differences resolved but tension in the relationship only gradually fading away. Truce. Peace restored. Justice. Pleasure after pain or anxiety. A weight lifted from the mind. Sorrow and sympathy for those in trouble. Tact and diplomacy.

Ill-dignified:
Release. Movement of affairs away from difficulty; but sometimes slowly, or in the wrong direction, or upon misguided advice. Lies. An inclination to take advantage of the good nature or tolerance of others. Tactlessness. Selfishness and lack of appreciation of the needs of others. Injury done to others through lack of forethought.

Three

Dignified:
Strife, conflict, heartbreak, tears, separations. Quarrels and disruption. Relationships brought to an end. The death of a pet or the loss or theft of an object of great sentimental value.

Ill-dignified:
Confusion, loss, rejection and sorrow. Promises or threats adhered to. Much pleasure felt in the venting of spite and the sowing of discord. Treachery and deceit.

Four

Dignified:
Hospitalization, convalescence, recovery from illness. A sabbatical, a retreat. Relief from sorrow, anxiety or the unwanted intrusion of

others. Solitude, quietness and rest. Change for the better.

Ill-dignified:
Enforced seclusion. Banishment from social affairs. 'Sent to Coventry'. Imprisonment in a set of circumstances, or actual institutionalization in a gaol, hospital, or psychiatric establishment.

Five

Dignified:
Failure, trouble, poverty, defeat, loss, cowardice. Malicious, spiteful talebearing. A separation of friends through the lies of a third party. Negative thinking and negative attitudes. Fruitless envy of the good fortune of others.

Ill-dignified:
Contest finished and decided against the person. Weakness, indecision and paranoia. Avarice and a grieving over the gains or happiness of others. Slander or libel, and evil-speaking generally. A busybody and separator of friends.

Six

Dignified:
Success after trouble and anxiety. Passage away from pain or difficulty. Release from poverty or unhappiness. Long journeys and travel generally. Obstacles overcome. A brief sojourn away from home restores family harmony.

Ill-dignified:
Retreat from difficulty brings temporary relief. Retreat from financial difficulty achieved by change of residence. One obstacle has barely been overcome before another takes its place. Struggle.

Seven

Dignified:
Short journeys, change of job or residence or both. Restlessness. Instability of purpose or lack of ambition ensures that no real progress is made. Confidences unintentionally betrayed.

Ill-dignified:
Indecision, laziness, and failure of nerve. Reluctance to complete what has been well begun. Empty boasts or promises. Hollow compliments. Misleading displays of power, influence, affluence or affection. Love of display. Spying on another.

Eight

Dignified:
Restriction and enforced isolation. Censure and jealousy from family, friends, or workmates. A situation which cannot be escaped. Too much attention paid to detail, leaving larger and more important issues unaddressed. A fondness for giving or receiving gifts and money. Generosity and cleverness.

Ill-dignified:
Freedom, release and relaxation obtained by distancing the problem rather than solving it. Hard and uncongenial work. Selfishness. A lack of feeling for others. Malice. Pettiness. Domineering behaviour.

Nine

Dignified:
Bad dreams and premonitions of disaster. Deception, depression and suffering. Miscarriage or abortion. Violence, scandal and loss. Unpleasant and untruthful rumours surround the Querent, who is worried and upset about a situation he is unable to come to grips with or pin down. Death of a loved one sometimes.

Ill-dignified:
Malice. Misery and despair. Isolation either actual or imagined. Depression caused by the acts or words of others. Suicide sometimes.

Ten

Dignified:
Sudden misfortune. Accident. Mugging. A personal injury. Theft. A 'stab in the back' from an unexpected source. Malicious words or actions. Causing deliberate hurt to another, or ruining another's plans or pleasure.

Ill-dignified:
Desolation, disruption and ruin. Violent and extreme enforced change.
Death sometimes. Unprofitable speech. A repeating of things heard
in confidence or overheard.

COINS

Season — Winter. *Direction* — North.

Ace

Dignified:
A change for the better financially. Beginnings of a period of financial
gain and material comfort. An increase in power or wealth. A rise
or promotion.

Ill-dignified:
Greed, parsimony, lack of faith in anything beyond the material. An
unwillingness to spend to improve material conditions, but no lack
of ability to do so.

Two

Dignified:
Constant fluctuation in fortune, due to nature and conditions of
employment. An unwillingness or inability to work consistently. An
unwillingness or inability to remain long in employment or place of
residence. Visits to friends or relatives. Pleasant change. Instability
of purpose. A warning to budget carefully, and avoid purchasing on
credit.

Ill-dignified:
Reckless spending. Fecklessness. Insufficient effort. Inability to complete a project or keep a job due to concentration on the pleasures of the moment or mental condition — now elated, now depressed. Debt. Welcome outstayed.

Three

Dignified:
Business opportunities. Success and promotion through effort and hard work. Gain in commercial transactions. Increase in material things. Cleverness in business. Extension or improvement of property or premises. The realization of money from the timely sale of stock or property. Commencement of a matter to be established later.

Ill-dignified:
Preoccupation with gain. Hoarding and miserliness. Opportunities passed up for fear of loss. Narrow and prejudiced ideas and behaviour.

Four

Dignified:
Material stability, success, rank, and social acceptance. Increase of power through wealth and influence, but nothing new commenced. Presents.

Ill-dignified:
Greed, suspicion, and lack of enterprise due to fear of loss. Covetousness and envy. Prejudice and suspicion. Inability to delegate authority and love of own authority. Discontent. Lack of enterprise or originality.

Five

Dignified:
Loss of money position or profession. Financial difficulty caused by over-extending on a business project. Building, farming, manual work and hard labour. Poverty and struggle. Redundancy or seasonal labour at an end.

Ill-dignified:
Unemployment long continued. Known skills outdated and unusable. Hardship and financial distress. Money regained after hard labour sometimes.

Six

Dignified:
Benevolence. Philanthropy. Patronage. Charities, gifts, and awards. Power, influence, rule over people. Good fortune and success.

Ill-dignified:
Prodigality. Gambling. Loss through theft or carelessness. The necessary division of property or money due to divorce, death, or other settlement arrangements.

Seven

Dignified:
Disappointment. Loss resulting from a project previously thought promising. Hard work for little reward. Unprofitable employment and speculation. Profitable employment neglected through lack of interest. Promises of success unfulfilled.

Ill-dignified:
Financial difficulties. Bankruptcy, debt and loss. Hopes deceived and crushed. An unavailing search for employment. Interviews for employment gained, but come to nothing. Hopes of refinancing or remortgaging dashed. Loans applied for but refused.

Eight

Dignified:
Prudence and industry. Diversification. The acquiring of new skills or further education. Skill in material affairs. Gain of money in small sums. Carefulness in respect of money. Savings. Conservative investments, stocks and bonds. Diplomacy.

Ill-dignified:
Penny wise, pound foolish. Greed, miserliness and hoarding. Sharp or dishonest dealings. Misuse of skill to improper ends. Petty theft.

Nine

Dignified:
'Golden handshakes' and redundancy settlements. Money from unexpected sources. Inheritances, settlements, winnings and monetary

gifts. Great material increase. Large sums gained from the disposal of property or goods. Unearned income of any kind.

Ill-dignified:
Tainted or stolen money. Theft, embezzlement or fraud.

Ten

Dignified:
Retirement, prosperity and wealth. Relaxation and ease of living. Material security founded upon the work of others, or upon own past endeavours. Pensions, and insurances.

Ill-dignified:
Completion of material gain and fortune, but nothing beyond. Old age. Early retirement. Redundancy or other unemployment at an age where further positions are unlikely to materialize. The restrictive effects of great wealth or those of living on a reduced income. Problems with wills or trusts. Disagreements about money within the family. Enforced idleness.

THE COURT CARDS

There are two separate sets of meanings given for all of the Court cards. The first set of meanings refer to *people*, the second set to *events*. Meanings referring to events are marked with an asterisk (*).

Those meanings which refer to people are divided as to dignity. Those referring to events are not so divided, and it should be borne in mind that all these alternative meanings are very strongly dependent upon both the dignity of the card as it appears in the spread, and upon the cards that surround the card in the spread.

STAVES

King

Dignified:
An honest and conscientious person, loyal and generous, loving traditional ways and family life. A just and enterprising man of authority.

Ill-dignified:
An autocratic and intolerant person, prejudiced, ruthless and lacking in feeling for others.

* Mediation and arbitration. Successful business dealings. Philanthopic and charitable organizations. The military and military men or military pursuits. Politics, politicians, and parliamentary affairs.

Queen

Dignified:
A generous woman, practical and kind, capable of independent thought and action, but home-loving.

Ill-dignified:
A jealous and domineering woman, obstinate and tending to imagine wrongs. A woman who allows her loved ones no independence or resorts to emotional blackmail. One apt to turn against another without cause.

* Successful ventures. The countryside, country activities and country living. Voluntary organizations. Social security and welfare organizations. Charitable works, and fund-raising functions.

Knight

Dignified:
An unpredictable or impetuous person, swift to act, and enjoying action and outdoor pursuits.

Ill-dignified:
A narrow-minded and contentious person. A bigot. A procrastinator and lover of discord for its own sake.

* Hasty decisions and actions. Rapid change of residence and sudden departures. Guerrillas and guerrilla warfare. Militant religious factions

or groups. Militant political factions, organizations and publications. Terrorists and terrorism. Paramilitary groups and organizations. Anarchy, anarchists and anarchical groups.

Page

Dignified:
A resourceful and ambitious individual of great vigour and enthusiasm, quick to respond emotionally either with love or anger.

Ill-dignified:
A domineering theatrical and superficial person who wants to achieve much by the shortest possible route, and so can be untrustworthy and deceitful.

* Change of career or news of career, for better or worse. Exciting, stimulating or infuriating news. Youth clubs and uniformed youth organizations. Summer camps and adventure holidays. Outward-bound courses or youth exchange programmes.

CUPS

King

Dignified/Ill-dignified:
An intelligent, imaginative, subtle man, artistic and amiable. An individual calm on the surface, but passionate within. A character powerful for good or evil, but more attracted by evil if this is allied with power or wisdom. A man of business or law and a skilled negotiator. A kind man, considerate and responsible, but very ambitious. An individual often easily influenced if approached correctly.

Ill-dignified:
A dishonest and unscrupulous man, given to double dealing. A violent and treacherous man.

Note: Character as described by this card is more than usually dependent upon dignity and upon the nature of those cards which surround it.

* The cultural establishment. Art galleries, opera houses and symphony orchestras. Publishing houses. The established Church and servants of the Church. Powerful esoteric organizations. Medicine, medical men and the health service.

Queen

Dignified:
An imaginative, affectionate and gifted woman, but lacking in common sense and inclined to hysteria. Highly intuitive and sometimes psychic, but dreamy and easily influenced by other people, events, or 'atmosphere'. Kindly and feeling, but not given to taking trouble for another.

Ill-dignified:
An unreliable woman, not to be depended upon or trusted, as her opinions change swiftly and without logical or just reason. A perverse woman.

* Women's magazines and romantic publications and publishers. Greeting card and fancy goods manufacture. Emotional satisfaction and happiness. Regret caused by indiscretion. Spiritualism, paganism, the 'Old Religion'.

Knight

Dignified:
An amiable and intelligent person, but a dreamer and easily led or discouraged. A graceful, poetic, indolent individual, but enthusiastic if roused.

Ill-dignified:
An idle person, and a congenital liar. A weak, vacillating individual.

* 'Alternative' cultural activities and organizations. 'Fads', fashion houses and the fashion industry. Cults and cult activities. Television and the media. Invitations, opportunities, trust, goodwill and pleasant

journeys. Trickery, deception and fraud. Confidence tricks and confidence tricksters. Pornography and pornographic publications. Drugs and the drug 'industry'.

Page

Dignified:
A quiet, reflective and artistic person, gentle and kind, but dreamy at times. A lazy individual, but conscientious about important matters or subjects that appeal.

Ill-dignified:
A selfish and idle person, given to lies and harmful gossip. An individual much given to looking after or pampering the self.

* Change of feeling about a thing or person for better or worse. News of a birth, marriage or engagement. The uncovering of a deception. False pregnancy. Fantasy and comic books or publications. Science fiction. Fairy stories. Cartoons and cartoonists.

SWORDS

King

Dignified:
A rational man with a logical and inventive turn of mind, but sometimes overcautious and old fashioned. A man of law and an upholder of authority.

Ill-dignified:
A mistrustful and suspicious man, obstinate, calculating, and of

impersonal temperament. A malicious individual, unjust, tyrannical and cruel.

* Universities, professional associations and schools. All aspects of the law, and upholders and interpreters of the law. Integrity, good judgement, and balanced arbitration. Injustice, loss of money or prestige. Unfounded accusations and baseless scandal.

Queen

Dignified:
An intelligent and complex woman, observant, perceptive and quick-witted. An individual who is skillful at balancing opposing factions one against the other to further her own ends. A confident woman, graceful and fond of dancing.

Ill-dignified:
An unreliable woman, deceitful and sly under a smiling and pleasant exterior. A narrow-minded and intolerant woman. A gossip.

* Success in intellectual pursuits. Academic achievement and successful examination results. Minor awards for writing or speaking. An invitation or opportunity to speak in public or to act as a spokesperson. Salesmanship and oratory. Matrimonial unhappiness, loneliness, abandonment and widowhood. Failed examinations and functional illiteracy.

Knight

Dignified:
An active, clever individual, inventive, subtle and skilful, but inclined to be domineering. One who is over-careful in small things.

Ill-dignified:
A secretive and sly individual, deceitful, belligerent and quarrelsome.

* Events moving swiftly in and out of the Querent's life for good or ill. Communications and the machinery of communication. Large corporate entities in the communications industry, or inventions in that field. Advertising agencies, subliminal advertising, psychology and propaganada. Quarrels, treachery, betrayal, malicious gossip, slander or libel. Detectives or enquiry agents/agencies.

Page

Dignified:
A graceful, dextrous and diligent person, wise in material things. A subtle individual. A diplomat or arbitrator.

Ill-dignified:
A devious individual, frivolous and cunning, vindictive, spiteful and two-faced.

* Change of mind for or against a thing or person. A message presaging a fortunate or desired change, usually arriving unexpectedly. A message presaging an unwelcome or unforeseen change. Ill-health. Unforeseen events cause sudden change in established plans. Holidays delayed or cancelled. Loss suffered due to pick-pockets or confidence tricks. Anonymous letters and whispering campaigns.

COINS

King

Dignified:
A steady, methodical and reliable man, loyal, trustworthy and patient, but slow to think and act. An individual clever in all material matters.

Ill-dignified:
A materialistic person, dull, timid, avaricious and grasping. An obstinate, heavy-handed person, given to jealousy and domestic tyranny.

* Increase of wealth or status. Establishment in a profession or secure position in a corporate structure. The attainment of a degree in accountancy, law, or similar field. Large corporate entities or governmental departments generally. Failure of a business enterprise. Professional failure. Removal from a register of qualified practitioners. Expected benefits fail to materialize.

Queen

Dignified:
A shrewd, sensible and down-to-earth woman, but wanting money and material possessions for her comfort. An individual who loves splendour and personal display.

Ill-dignified:
A changeable woman, moody, narrow in outlook and suspicious of what she does not understand. A grasping and careful person, yet a spendthrift in matters that concern herself.

* The urge to make money and acquire the outward trappings of success. A talent in need of development or awaiting use. Money ill-spent, or spent on luxuries rather than necessities. Ostentatious display that conceals poverty and want. Gambling and gambling establishments.

Knight

Dignified:
A practical person of conventional virtues or views. Patient, hardworking, and clever with material things, but rather slow and inclined to lack awareness of the feelings of others.

Ill-dignified:
An avaricious and grasping person, rather timid and much given to jealousy or envy.

* Financial backers. Large commercial organizations such as banks and commodity or brokerage houses. Money markets and monetary funds. Financial acumen and ability. Successful investments. Liquidation, Receiverships and Trustees in Bankruptcy. Credit agencies and finance companies. Monetary affairs at a standstill or at breakeven.

Page

Dignified:
A thrifty, practical and conscientious person. kindly, diligent, steady, reliable and good-natured, but careful with money, goods and personal possessions, and disinclined to share. Slow to anger, but furious when roused.

Ill-dignified:
A materialistic, wasteful and prodigal person, mean and over-meticulous in small things. Narrow-minded and dull. A careless and destructive person.

* Change in material situation for better or worse. Increase of matter. Increase of good or evil. Good news, pleasant events, and the success of hopes. Bad news regarding financial matters. The sudden and unexpected loss of money or property.

COMBINATIONS

Look out for combinations of cards of the same face number appearing in a single spread, for these combinations have meaning that can be applied to the matter at hand.

Aces

4: Great power or force.
3: Riches and success.
2: Change of place (residence or work).

Twos

4: Conferences and conversation.
3: Reorganization.

Threes

4: Resolution and determination.
3: Deceit.

Fours

4: Rest and peace.
3: Industry and industriousness.

Fives

4: Quarrels and fights.
3: Order and regularity.

Sixes

4: Peace.
3: Gain and success.

Sevens

4: Disappointment.
3: Contracts.

Eights

4: Much news.
3: Much travelling.

Nines

4: Added responsibilities.
3: Correspondence.

Tens

4: Anxiety and responsibility.
3: Correspondence.

Pages

4: Schools and colleges, education, new plans and new ideas.
3: Children in groups.
2: Play, fun and sporting events.

Knights

4: Armed forces or dominant clique. Swiftness and rapidity of action.
3: Groups of people. Parties or celebrations.
2: Old friends from the past.

Queens

4: Local or city government.
3: Groups of women. Clubs. Powerful friends.
2: Gossip or slander.

Kings

4: *State or world government. Meetings of the great.*
3: *Fraternal organizations or lodges. Groups of men. Fashion.*
2: *Business opportunities.*

THE MAJOR ARCANA

The World

Dignified:
The matter at hand or the subject of the question. Completion, success, fulfilment. The end of a personal cycle, project or series of events. Synthesis — a uniting of all the elements of the life into a workable whole. New environments, travel, change of place.

Ill-dignified:
An indication that events have not yet reached a conclusion, but are nearing completion. An indication that a project or set of circumstances is not yet concluded despite appearances to the contrary. Final decision. Judgement or sentence. Determination of a matter.

Judgement

Dignified:
Awakening. Renewal. Joy in accomplishment and pleasure in achievement. Renewed health and vitality. Sometimes indicates the presence of decisions which must be made and which will change the life for the better. Retirement, or the end of a phase or cycle in the working life.

Ill-dignified:
Loss, separations, endings and guilt. Fear of change. Fear of death sometimes. Possible ill-health. Refusal to make decisions which must be made, so causing delays in events.

The Sun

Dignified:
Liberation, gain, riches, material happiness. Good health, confidence, success and celebrations. An abundance of energy. Acclaim, approval and rewards. Academic achievement, particularly scientific

achievement. Inventors and new inventions. Matters relating to children and the success or well-being of children.

Ill-dignified:
Failure. Broken engagements and contracts. Troubled marriages and partnerships. Misjudgement. Fantasies of success. Hypersensitivity and hyperactivity. Allergies sometimes, particularly in children. Autism learning difficulties, and behavioural abnormalities.

The Moon

Dignified:
Voluntary change. Imagination, intuition, dreams. Psychism and psychic work sometimes. Work in the entertainment industry or with the media — acting, fiction writing, and advertising. Faith healing and all forms of healing that react upon the subconscious mind or stimulate the limbic system, such as aromatherapy. Psychoanalysis and psychoanalysts. Psychology and psychologists.

Ill-dignified:
Deception, illusion, hidden enemies and insincerity. An inability to cope well with reality and a consequent escape into daydreams. An inability to distinguish truth from illusion or tell the truth.

The Star

Dignified:
Insight, hope, inspiration. Help from unexpected sources. A widening of horizons, mental and physical. Influence for good over others. Confidence, vigour, renewed energy. All altruistic or humanist pursuits such as animal or civil rights, sexual or racial equality. Sexual felicity in a relationship.

Ill-dignified:
Stubbornness. Inability to see another's point of view. Rigidity of mind and outlook. Inability to adapt to changing circumstances or accept the opportunities that changing circumstances bring. Self doubt and lack of trust in others. Sexual insecurity. Difficulties with sexual identity. Dreaminess. Hopes deceived.

The Tower

Dignified:

Change, conflict and disruption. The overthrow of an existing way of life. Change of job or residence — sometimes simultaneously. Actions which have unexpected and widespread repercussions. Change bringing freedom from restrictive influences.

Ill-dignified:

Chaos and destruction. Loss of security. Unexpected and drastic changes in circumstance. Circumstances rob the individual of freedom of expression. Imprisonment sometimes, but more usually the imprisonment of the individual in a set of circumstances that he cannot, for the moment, alter.

The Devil

Dignified:

Desire for physical or material things. An indication of the propensity to collect and hoard material objects or money. Material wealth used as a tool of power. Extraordinary effort expended to ensure material success. The Querent's knowledge of his own needs and desires.

Ill-dignified:

Abuse of power and position. Bondage to a person or thing that is undesirable or unhealthy. Emotional blackmail. Sexual aberrations. Comprehension of the use and value of money, possessions, secular power and personal charisma has centred attention on these things to the exclusion of everything else. 'I want' has become 'I must have', and this feeling includes people as well as things.

Temperance

Dignified:

Good management and economy. Co-ordination and co-operation. Innovation through combination. The ability to adapt to circumstance. Modification. A placid and well-balanced temperament and outlook. Arbitration and the reconciliation of opposing forces. Successful negotiation.

Ill-dignified:

Poor judgement. A tendency to try to combine disparate activities or people, or to indulge in too many activities in too short a time. Volatility and restlessness. An unwillingness to conform or to co-operate with others. An aggressive and selfish pursuit of own interests. Quarrels and disagreements.

Death

Dignified:
Transformation and change as a result of circumstance. Physical death sometimes, but more usually a complete and absolute change of circumstances, way of life, or behaviour pattern. Loss of a friend, relationship, or valued position.

Ill-dignified:
Refusal to face, or fear of, change. Inertia. Stagnation. Forcible removal of something that should have been released voluntarily.

The Hanged Man

Dignified:
Surrender to the inevitable. Unwillingness to adapt to changing circumstance. Flexibility of mind. Present sacrifice for future benefit. Suspension of judgement or movement in affairs — decisions delayed while the Querent awaits the outcome of events. The sacrifice of one thing to obtain another. Spiritual wisdom and initiation. Ordination.

Ill-dignified:
Preoccupation with the material and the concerns of the self. Material losses or reverses. A tendency to let opportunities go by for fear of losing lesser things already possessed. Preference for the status quo despite drawbacks. Victimization. Physical, moral or emotional pressure applied for unacceptable or wrong reasons.

Strength

Dignified:
Health, strength and courage. Power. Strength of position in present circumstances. The synergic interaction of mental and emotional forces. Control of passion. Defeat of base impulse. Directed will. Presence of mind. Self-control.

Ill-dignified:
Weakness, defeat and concession. Self-indulgence and surrender to
unworthy impulse. A conflict of interest sometimes. Success delayed
through own weakness sometimes.

The Wheel

Dignified:
Destiny. Good fortune. Change for the better in areas denoted by
surrounding cards. A turning point. The beginning of a new cycle.
Progress, advancement and improvement.

Ill-dignified:
As above, but in the longer term. Resistance to change which is
inevitable sometimes and dependent upon surrounding cards.

The Hermit

Dignified:
Reflection, prudence, planning, foresight and forethought.
Circumspection. A warning against precipitous action or thought.
An indication of a need to retire or dissociate oneself from activity
in order to think and evaluate circumstances. Occult or inner
knowledge. Counsel sought and taken, and wise counsellors. A need
to be alone or in a quiet place, to examine one's thoughts and feelings.

Ill-dignified:
Counsel or assistance refused. Reliance on one's own inadequate
resources. Groundless suspicion of the motives of others. Obstinate
continuance of bad habits or unproductive lifestyles. Fear of loneliness.
Fear of silence. A need to surround the self with noise or activity for
fear of being confronted with the void within. Fruitless activity. A lack
of inner resource.

Justice

Dignified:
Fair play. Legal matters. Contracts, settlements, litigation, divorce.
Redress. Judgment. Arbitration and agreement. Treaties. Marriage
sometimes, dependent upon surrounding cards and only when
marriage contracts or other legal or financial documents form an
integral part of the intended union.

Ill-dignified:
Separation not yet legalized or ratified by law. Legal complications.
Expensive and long drawn-out litigation. Inequality, injustice and bias.

The Chariot

Dignified:
Self-control. Self-confidence. Mastery of external factors. Will power.
Triumph over life's obstacles. Success as a result of effort, not fortune.
The careful building up of a successful life within the bounds set by
the conditions of life. Talents exploited to the full, and all avenues of
personal advancement conscientiously followed up.

Ill-dignified:
Imbalance and destruction. Waste of personal gifts and opportunities.
Always expecting too much or too little of life and of self. Envy of
those more successful than oneself and insistence that this is due to
fortune and not work. Loss of self-control under pressure of external
circumstances due to flaws in the character. The maintenance of
outworn traditions and ideas in the face of change. Deliberate
self-limitation.

The Lovers

Dignified:
Love. Affectionate partnerships. Attraction, harmony and beauty.
Choice to be made intuitively rather than intellectually. Inspiration.
Second sight. Abstract thought. Inner harmony. The union of inner
ideals and outer objectives. True partnerships where the individuals
involved resonate on every level of being.

Ill-dignified:
Contradiction. Duality. Conflict with self. Partnerships disrupted by
external factors or inner dissonance. Vacillation. Inconstancy of
purpose. Choices made against all inner feeling. Decisions made
without reference to all the factors involved or without reference to
those factors which are intangible.

The Hierophant

Dignified:
Intuition. Inspiration. Teaching. Marriage and alliance. Good counsel,

advice and teaching. A seeker after knowledge and wisdom. Friendships and acts of friendship. Tradition and stability. A preference for the orthodox and a need to conform. A desire to be 'socially acceptable'. Strict adherence to orthodox religion sometimes.

Ill-dignified:
Slander, propaganda and bad advice. Misrepresentation in the advertisement or sale of goods or the presentation of self in formal documents. Distortion of truth. Unconventionality. Eccentricity. Partnerships and alliances not ratified by law. Deliberate flouting of rules or social mores. Anarchy. Contempt for authority or law.

The Emperor

Dignified:
Stability. Reason. Ambition. The overseeing and control of personnel. Authority and temporal power. Leadership. Father figures and mentors. Governmental and corporate identities. Powerful individuals or entities. Applied science or mathematics. One who likes to work in a structured environment.

Ill-dignified:
A dislike of authority and rules, corporate, governmental or parental. An inability to deal with authority or discipline. An inability to command oneself or others. Loss or lack of ambition. Immaturity. Possible bondage to a parent or parental figure.

The Empress

Dignified:
Fertility, abundance and material wealth. Creativity in all things and dependent upon surrounding cards' security and growth. Fulfilment in any receptive area of life, i.e. love, art, the theatre, and so on. Creative activities/professions, and professions primarily to do with women like hairdressing or beauty care. Marriage and pregnancy sometimes and dependent upon other cards. a comfortable life. Safety and security in the home.

Ill-dignified:
Domestic upheaval. Sterility or infertility. Unwanted pregnancy or abortion. Poverty sometimes. Stifled or blocked creativity. Promiscuity, dissipation and sensuality.

High Priestess

Dignified:
Mysteries, secrets and hidden things. Hidden influences at work and in the home. Hidden influences from the psyche affect personal circumstances. Fluctuation in fortunes. The influence of women. Clairvoyance and intuition.

Ill-dignified:
Problems resulting from lack of foresight. Surface or facile knowledge. Self conceit sometimes. In men, an unwillingess to accept that part of themselves which is feminine, or a distorted idea of femininity and the feminine principle. In women, an inability to understand or come to terms with themselves or other women.

The Magician

Dignified:
Constructive power, initiative, skill and subtlety. Will, mastery and oratory. A willingness to take risks. An ability to perceive and utilize one's own skills and potential. Organizational and communicatory skills. Confidence, boldness and self reliance.

Ill-dignified:
Deviousness and unreliability. Salesmanship. Trickery. Lies. Timidity. Hesitation and shyness. Indecision. Self-depreciation. A poor self image. An inability to utilize time or talents properly. Difficulty of self-expression. Hesitation of speech. Poor co-ordination. Learning disabilities sometimes.

The Fool

Dignified:
The beginning of a new cycle and all new beginnings. Circumstances and occurrences that are unexpected and unplanned. Optimism. Originality. Happiness and force. Important decisions and choices to be made.

Ill-dignified:
Reckless or impulsive action or choices. Indiscretion. Folly, eccentricity, inconsidered and inconsiderate action. The frittering away or waste of creative energy. Sometimes indicates an individual who starts many

things but finishes nothing, and who consistently seeks a change of environment or job.

Appendix II

Spreads

PRACTICE SPREAD ONE

Establishing Cause and Effect

One of the swiftest and most reliable ways of establishing cause and effect is to utilize the structure of the Triads of the Tree of Life to build a positional spread.

As you will recall, there are three of these Triads: the Supernal, the Ethical, and the Astral, each one of which will be represented in the spread by three cards, which will be laid out according to the Path of the Lightning Flash. Alongside each of the sets of cards representing the Triads will rest a fourth card, which will at once represent the essence of the three preceding cards and act as a 'linking agent' between the separate Triads.

Each of the three Sephiroth that make up the individual Triads is representative of one of the three ways in which force can manifest — positive, negative, and equilibrized. Thus the three cards that represent the individual Sephiroth will also represent a positive, negative, or equilibrized force, and the spread will look something like Figure 24.

Each card in the spread will have to be interpreted not simply according to the Triad in which it appears, but according to its position within that Triad, and the fundamental nature of that position.

The cards of the first, or Supernal Triangle, will represent distant, or Karmic, causation — factors which the Querent has brought forward with him from previous incarnations and which have some effect, either directly or indirectly, upon the matter at hand.

Obviously, these cards are out of the Querent's control. They *are*, and are indicative of a state of affairs that *is* (at the present, in any event) something about which the Querent can effectively do nothing. Certainly these cards are not subject to rapid change, and further —

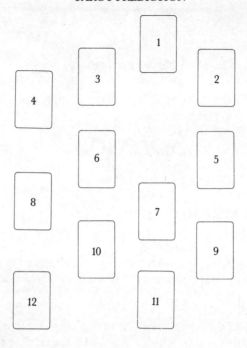

Figure 24: Practice Spread One.

and most importantly — they do not give any indication at all as to the actual past events that caused their appearance in the present spread, being only indicative of the results of those past life events, which results have a bearing upon events current in the present life.

It is therefore *not* possible to do a past life reading from these three cards, and nor is it advisable to attempt to do so, as the results will be incomplete and therefore misleading.

The three cards that go to make up the second, or Ethical, Triangle, will show two quite separate things. Firstly, they will show the effect of the events of the distant past upon the Querent's present personality — an effect that could be anything from a fear of water to a dislike of a certain kind of authority. The second will be the input of the other people involved in the matter of hand — which input might, of course, be active, passive, or equilibrized depending upon card position.

The interaction pattern of these two separate factors causes the reaction of the Querent, and will enable the reader to see why the Querent has reacted as he has to the stimulus of the matter at hand. This is useful in that, allied with the information gained from the cards making up the Supernal Triangle, it can frequently explain the presence of apparently abnormal reaction patterns that are 'foreign' to the Querent's fundamental character as it usually expresses itself.

The Astral Triangle represents both the possible course of future events, and those avenues of possible action that are open to the Querent. This will allow the reader to present various alternatives to the Querent, and thus (hopefully) enable him in turn to choose that which is least damaging.

The last card of all, of course (number 12 on Figure 24), is simply an illustration of how the matter at hand has crystallized in the Querent's life. It is the culmination of all that has gone before, and will show how he is feeling, or what he is thinking, or enduring, or doing — dependent, naturally, upon suit and dignity.

It will be obvious from the above description that this is not a spread that should be used for minor questions, and that in fact its primary purpose is to get at the root causes of *cyclic* problems, or problems which recur over and over again in different guises. Indeed, this is a spread — when allotted these particular positions, in any event — that is designed to deal with the question 'Why does this *keep* happening to me?', and is useful in that it both supplies the answer to this question and suggests possible ways of solving the problem, thus avoiding its recurrence. It is not, however, a spread that will reveal the nature of the problem *by position*, because it is only designed to reveal causation. It is therefore by nature a supplementary, rather than a primary, spread, or a spread which can be used to further investigate the information revealed by a previous and more general one.

PRACTICE SPREAD TWO

Establishing Time

Because of the difficulty in prognosticating the timing of any given event accurately, it is always as well to incorporate a number of timing spreads into your working repertoire. One such spread is the astrological spread that appears in Chapter 10. Another is this 'Yes or No, and If So, When?' spread.

This spread is designed to provide a clear answer as to time in response to a clearly formulated question — a question that demands firstly the reply 'yes' or 'no', secondly an indication as to when the subject of the question will or will not take place, and thirdly an indication as to why the answer given is positive or negative.

The spread is a very simple one to lay out. Once the question has been asked, you should begin count off, from the top of the deck, one card at a time. When you have counted off thirteen cards and

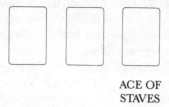

ACE OF
STAVES

Figure 25: Practice Spread Two — Example.

if no Ace has appeared, square the pile you have made, and commence another pile. If, however an Ace does appear before you reach card number 13, stop that pile there, and move on to the next one.

You should complete this second pile in the same way, stopping only when you reach either card number 13 or an Ace, and then go on to complete a third pile in exactly the same way.

This spread is as simple to read as it is to lay, as the example in Figure 25 will show.

Here, as you can see, we have two Aces — one in position 2 and one in position 3. One of them — the card in position 3 — is dignified, which means that the answer to the question is 'Yes' in the long term. Obviously, since the card shown is a Stave, 'the long term' means spring, but whether this year or next depends on the month when the spread is read, and the cards in the two piles that precede position 3.

The positioning of the card in position 1 reveals that the question is not yet decided, and from the nature of that card it might be surmised that the question is not decided because the Querent has not made up his mind.

The card in position 2 shows that by late summer the Querent will have made up his mind, but that the situation will not move until early spring (position 3). The reason for the lack of movement will be found in the cards under the Ace of Staves in position 3.

Should you obtain 3 Aces in this spread, all ill-dignified, then the answer to the question will be a categorical 'no' — at which point you may wish to read the contents of all three piles to find out why not.

In the same way, should you obtain no Aces at all (a result which always means that the matter is undecided), you may again wish to read the contents of all three piles to ascertain why this is so.

Whatever happens, however, you will receive a definite answer to a definite question — and a time frame to put it in.

PRACTICE SPREAD THREE

Establishing the Nature of the Self

The same kind of spread as that used in Practice Spread One can be used to try to understand the self, and to look at the basic structure of the self; but this is a very complex exercise, and one that is best approached very slowly — even if this means laying out the spread piecemeal over long periods of time, and keeping extensive notes of previous results. The spread should in any event be laid out Triad by Triad, because a complete Tree is simply too much information to even look at, least of all evaluate.

In order to examine the self, the spread must conform to the actual structure of the psyche as closely as possible, and the reader must understand the symbolic structure he is using — in this case, the mandala of the Tree — very well indeed. Thus, the first stages of the spread itself would look something like Figure 26.

In this arrangement, card number 1 represents 'the Unmanifest', or that which has gone before in another life and has been 'brought forward' into this one, while the ringed cards represent the Sephiroth, and the remainder the Netibuth.

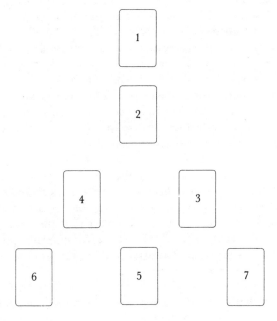

Figure 26: Practice Spread Three.

The best way to commence reading such a spread would be to lay the cards out face down according to the pattern shown on the diagram, all save card number 1 which should be face up. After this first card has been examined, the remainder can be turned over in sets of three, commencing with cards 2, 3 and 4, and then going on to read cards 4, 5, and 6 and so on. The conjoining card in each case (card number 4 in the example given above) must, of course, be read together with those cards that precede it and those that follow it, simply because it is the pivotal link between two separate concepts.

Obviously, particular attention must be given to any card that actually falls in a position with which it is associated, i.e. fives following in the position allotted to the sphere of Geburah in the spread, and so on.

In a spread like this one, the fundamental nature — i.e. positive, negative, or equilibrized — of the cards occupying both Sephiroth and Netibuth must be taken into account. Further, it must be remembered that — and particularly with reference to the cards representing 'the Unmanifest' and the Supernal Triangle — that what is symbolized is a debit and credit account, as well as a state of being.

The Triads in this spread will naturally represent the spiritual self, the individuality and the personality just as they do on the Tree of Life, and some effort must therefore be made to synthesize the information gained about all three sections.

Naturally, too, really badly aspected cards in Netibuth placements in any Triad should be contrasted with the Major Arcana cards traditionally associated with those paths. In this way, basic flaws can be identified and — with the help of the Major Arcana and some painful meditation work — mitigated or eradicated altogether.

Readers should be neither surprised nor alarmed to find something pretty dreadful staring them in the face from every angle when they come to the Astral Triangle. This happens because the Astral Triangle is representative of the personality and will therefore inevitably show signs of damage. So far as this is concerned, work should simply be commenced in the place of greatest trouble — and you should remember in this regard that the Triads are reflections of each other. Because this is so, three poorly aspected cards in related positions in all three Triads constitute a much more serious problem than does one real shocker isolated at an astral level.

Obviously, this spread represents much labour and quite a lot of pain, for it demands that time be spent, and that the reader go in for a lot of total honesty with himself. However, it is worthwhile, and — if adequate records are kept — will eventually produce obvious and gratifying results in the cards on the table, as well as within the self.

This is a spread that can be laid out for another person, but the reader should at once have a very good reason for doing this, and be completely in control of his deck as an entity *and* as it relates to the Tree, simply because such a situation would demand that the spread be laid in its entirety at one sitting. The results achieved would be exhausting, simply because the spread, when laid complete in this way, both reveals causation and forecasts events and situations as well as the structure of the Querent's self; but the effort expended would be enormous, and the spread is therefore not something to be undertaken often nor used as a normal working tool.

PRACTICE SPREAD FOUR

Establishing the Condition of a Business

This positional spread is basically a very simple one, the value of which lies in the precision and the order of its placements. The finished spread should look like this, the cards being laid according to the numbers shown on Figure 27.

In this spread, the cards must be read in 'blocks' of four that are interrelated by their nature, dealing as they do with factors that are interactive in any business. These 'blocks' break up as in Figure 28.

Obviously, this method means that many of the cards must be read twice or three times relative to various different subjects, and it must therefore be remembered that it is the relationship of one position to another that is important in this spread.

This will mean, of course, that both dignity and suit are vital components of the spread, as is the principle of resonance and

Finance	Sales	Administration
1	2	3
Cash Flow	Marketing	Personnel
4	5	6
Credit	Assets	Partners
7	8	9
Accounts	Premises	Plant/Machinery & Vehicles
10	11	12

Figure 27: Practice Spread Four.

dissonance, for it is these things that will establish the *nature* of the relationship concerned and serve as the keys to its complexities.

Any given card — that representing 'marketing' for instance — may be intensely positive in relationship to one 'block', and indeed to two cards of a second 'block', while remaining unequivocally negative to the remaining card of that second 'block'. Only dignity, suit, and resonance and/or dissonance will enable the reader to identify these 'black spots' in the spread, and assess the reasons for their existence and their possible potential for damage to the business as a whole.

PRACTICE SPREAD FIVE

Establishing the Nature and Potential of a Relationship
Like Practice Spread Four, this positional spread is a simple one that depends on the order and precision of its placements for its efficiency. Like Practice Spread Four, too, it is designed to be read in 'blocks', as in Figure 29.

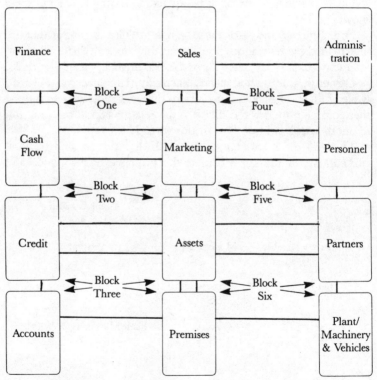

Figure 28: Breaking up the 'blocks'.

Again, this spread depends heavily on the proper use of dignity, suit and the rules of resonance and dissonance, and demands that the reader knows his deck very well and be capable of a proper synthesis of all the factors involved so that the elements of the relationship are seen in proper perspective. Unlike Practice Spread Four, however, this spread is not suitable as a primary spread, but should only be used as a supplementary to a more general spread.

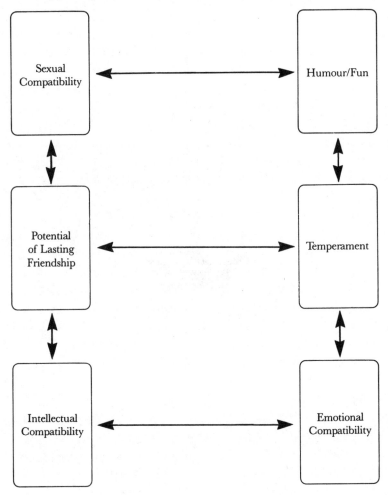

Figure 29: Practice Spread Five.

Index